ALAN CALLENDER
6 DETHING HSE
CONGREVE ST
WALWORTH
S.E. 17.

ALAN CALLENDER
6 DETHING HSE

Junior Colour Encyclopedia

Junior Colour Encyclopedia

compiled and edited by
Gerald E. Speck

WARD LOCK LIMITED·LONDON

©Ward Lock Limited 1972

ISBN 0 7063 1146 9

First published in Great Britain 1972 by
Ward Lock Limited, 116 Baker Street,
London, W1M 2BB

Text filmset by TEK International Limited.

Printed and bound by Editorial Fher
S A Bilbao.

AARD-VARK is an African animal about 4 feet long with a tapering tail half as long again. It is armed with powerful claws which it uses for tearing open termite hills and burrowing into the earth. It is rarely seen by man as it lives in burrows during daylight and only does its hunting for termites under the cover of darkness. The aard-vark has a long sticky tongue for licking up the termites on which it feeds. When attacked it defends itself with its chiselpointed claws.

ABACUS or 'counting frame' is a simple frame with ten wires running across it, each wire carrying ten beads. In various forms it has been used since early times, especially by the ancient Egyptians and Greeks. It is still widely used by people in the Far East to this day.

ABOMINABLE SNOWMAN is the popular name for the 'yeti', a creature said to exist in the frozen wastes of the Himalayas. Mountain dwellers of the region claim to have seen it and several mountaineers have photographed its supposed footprints, but so far no one has seen it close up.

ADDAX is an antelope native to the Sahara desert and sometimes known as a 'screwhorn' antelope because of the twists in its horns. Its coat is a dusty grey with dark markings on the face.

AFGHANISTAN is a kingdom north west of Pakistan. It is 256,960 square miles in area and has a population of just over 16,000,000. Large areas are covered with barren mountains. Afghanistan is mainly agricultural and exports dried fruits and lamb skins. The capital is Kabal which stands on a river of the same name.

AFRICA is three times larger than Europe (about 11,500,000 square miles) and the second largest continent on earth. Most countries in Africa are now independent republics. See map on the following page and entries under the name of the particular country.

The termite-eating aard-vark of Africa

Artist's impression of an abominable snowman or yeti climbing snow-covered mountain slopes

Tribal dance being performed by Africans

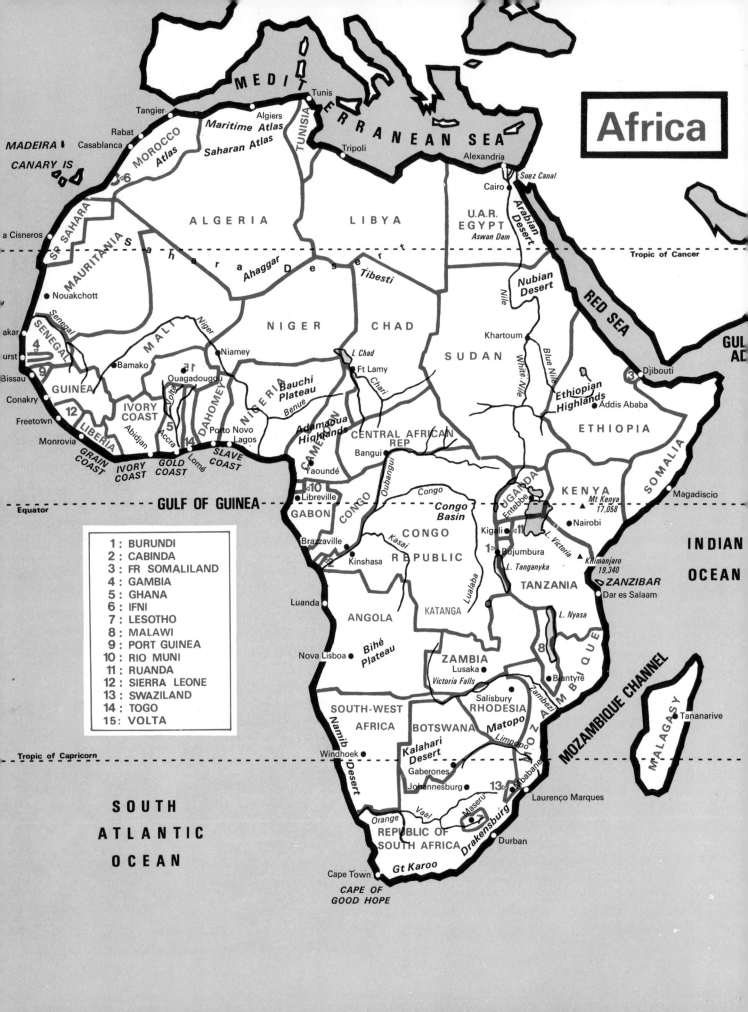

Africa

MEDITERRANEAN SEA

MADEIRA
CANARY IS

a Cisneros

akar
urst

Bissau

Conakry

Freetown

Monrovia

Tangier
Rabat
Casablanca

Tunis
Algiers

Tripoli

Alexandria
Suez Canal
Cairo

MOROCCO
Maritime Atlas
Saharan Atlas
Atlas

SR SAHARA

MAURITANIA

Nouakchott

SENEGAL
Senegal

Bamako

Niamey

Niger

MALI

Ouagadougou

IVORY
COAST
Volta
Abidjan
Accra

GUINEA

LIBERIA

GRAIN
COAST

IVORY
COAST
GOLD COAST

DAHOMEY
Porto Novo
Lagos
Lomé
SLAVE COAST

ALGERIA

Ahaggar

LIBYA

Sahara Desert

Tibesti

NIGER

CHAD

L Chad
Ft Lamy
Chari

NIGERIA
Bauchi
Plateau
Benue

Adamaoua
Highlands

CAMEROUN
Yaoundé

CENTRAL AFRICAN
REP

Bangui

Oubangui

Congo

U.A.R.
EGYPT
Aswan Dam

Tropic of Cancer

Nubian
Desert

Nile

Khartoum

White Nile
Blue Nile

SUDAN

ARABIAN DESERT

RED SEA

GUL
AD

Djibouti

Ethiopian
Highlands
Addis Ababa

ETHIOPIA

SOMALIA

Magadiscio

GULF OF GUINEA

Equator

Libreville

GABON

CONGO

Brazzaville

Luanda

ANGOLA

Nova Lisboa

Bihé
Plateau

Congo

Congo
Basin

CONGO
REPUBLIC

Kinshasa

Kasai

Lualaba

KATANGA

UGANDA
Entebbe

Kigali

Bujumbura

L. Tanganyka

TANZANIA

L. Nyasa

KENYA
Mt Kenya
17,058

L. Victoria
Nairobi

Kilimanjaro
19,340

ZANZIBAR

Dar es Salaam

INDIAN

OCEAN

1 : BURUNDI
2 : CABINDA
3 : FR SOMALILAND
4 : GAMBIA
5 : GHANA
6 : IFNI
7 : LESOTHO
8 : MALAWI
9 : PORT GUINEA
10 : RIO MUNI
11 : RUANDA
12 : SIERRA LEONE
13 : SWAZILAND
14 : TOGO
15 : VOLTA

ZAMBIA
Lusaka
Victoria Falls

SOUTH-WEST
AFRICA

Namib Desert

Windhoek

Kalahari
Desert

Gaberones

Johannesburg

Salisbury
RHODESIA

Matopo

BOTSWANA

Limpopo

Zambezi

Blantyre

MOZAMBIQUE CHANNEL

MALAGASY
Tananarive

MOZAMBIQUE

Swabane

Maseru

13

Laurenço Marques

Tropic of Capricorn

SOUTH

ATLANTIC

OCEAN

REPUBLIC OF
SOUTH AFRICA

Orange
Vaal

Gt Karoo

Cape Town

CAPE OF
GOOD HOPE

Drakensburg
Durban

Above, ox-pulled plough and an example of primative farming. *Below,* modern mechanized farming using a group of combine harvesters

Diagram showing the main parts of an aeroplane with both jet and piston engines

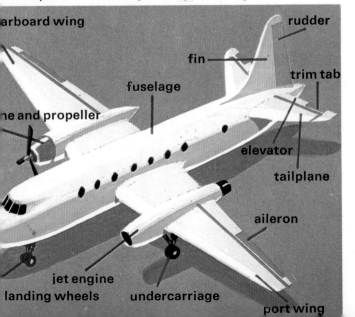

arboard wing

rudder

fin

trim tab

fuselage

ne and propeller

elevator

tailplane

aileron

jet engine

landing wheels

undercarriage

port wing

AGOUTI is a RODENT found in South and Central America. It is about the size of a rabbit and is tailless. Agoutis feed on fruits and leaves.

AGRICULTURE means 'cultivating a field' and the science of agriculture is concerned mainly with the care of the land, the growing of plants and the rearing of domestic animals. People must eat if they want to go on living, and agriculture is easily the biggest single item in world trade. About 12,000 years have passed since Man first learned to grow crops and domesticate animals, and over the long centuries many improved forms of crops and livestock and a lot of complicated farm machinery have been evolved. There are still countries, however, where farming methods are very primitive; but because the need to produce more and more food is daily becoming more important, the backward agricultural countries are being helped by the more advanced nations. The largest farms in the world are the collective farms in the U.S.S.R. The largest wheat fields in the world are in the U.S.A. and Canada, and the largest sheep and cattle stations are in Australia.

AEROPLANE is a heavier-than-air craft where the wings support the weight of the aeroplane and keep it stable, and the fin and rudder control the direction of flight. The propeller or jet engine thrust moves the machine forward, and thus makes air flow past the wings. Because of the special shape of the wings and the angle at which they meet the airstream, a powerful upward force is produced. It is made up of two parts: 1, the suction caused by the air flowing over the upper curved surface of the wing and 2, the pressure of the air against the inclined lower surface.

The tailplane and elevators enable the pilot to fly in just what manner he desires. Thus a pilot can climb by opening the throttle and raising the elevators, and dive by depressing the elevators. The ailerons on the trailing edge of the wings allow turning and banking. Slots are devices to increase lift, and flaps both increase lift and act as air-brakes to slow the machine down; they are particularly useful in landing.

The aeroplane has played an important part in modern history; this is too long to recount here; however, the following gives some of the important landmarks in aviation history:

1783 First manned balloon ascent made by Pilatre de Rozier and the Marquis d'Arlandes.

1802 First parachute descent made by Garnerin (in England) from a balloon over London.

1809 Sir George Cayley experimented with a glider in England.

1848 John Stringfellow built and flew the first powered model aeroplane. Power came from a small steam-engine.

1852 Giffard made a flight in an elongated balloon steered by a rudder and propelled by a steam-engine driving a propeller.

1896 Otto Lilienthal, known as 'the father of the aeroplane', killed in an accident after a series of gliding experiments in Germany.

1900 Zeppelin's first airship made its trial flight.

1903 Orville Wright made the world's first controlled, power-driven aeroplane flight at Kitty Hawk, North Carolina. See Plate 1, 1.

1905 First officially recorded flight was made by Wilbur Wright at Daytona, Ohio. He flew 11-12 miles in 18 minutes 9 seconds.

1906 Santos Dumont, in France, made the first officially recorded aeroplane in Europe.

1906 M. Louis Blériot, a Frenchman, flew the Channel from Les Baraques, near Calais, to a point near Dover Castle, a distance of 32 miles.

1910 Zeppelin completed his first passenger airship. E. T. Willows, in his airship 'Willows III', made the first airship flight from England to the Continent.

1911 First airmail in the United States. Experimental airmail service operated between Hendon and Windsor in United Kingdom.

1918 Handley Page V/1500 biplane flew over London carrying 40 passengers and sufficient fuel and oil for a six-hour flight.

1919 John Alcock and Arthur Whitton Brown (both later knighted) made the first direct Atlantic crossing by air, flying from Newfoundland to Ireland, a distance of 1,890 miles, in 16 hours 12 minutes.

1926 Commander R. E. Byrd, with Floyd Bennett as pilot, flew from King's Bay, Svalbard (Spitzbergen), to the North Pole and returned in 15 hours.

1927 Colonel Charles A. Lindbergh, United States, made first solo crossing of the Atlantic, flying from New York to Paris. Flight-Lieutenant S. N. Webster, A.F.C., won the International Schneider Trophy for Great Britain at a speed of 281.656 m.p.h.

1928 H. J. Hinkler flew from England to Australia, covering 12,250 miles in $15\frac{1}{2}$ days. Juan de la Cierva of Spain flew by autogiro from London to Paris.

1929 Airship *Graf Zeppelin* made a world tour. Squadron-Leader H. Orlebar, Great Britain, set a world speed record of 357.7 m.p.h. at Calshot, England.

1930 Amy Johnson, Great Britain, completed 9,900 mile flight from London to Australia in $19\frac{1}{2}$ days.

1931 Professor Auguste Piccard and Dr. Charles Kipfer ascended to record height of 51,775 feet at Augsburg, Germany, in a balloon.
Wiley Post, U.S. pilot, and Harold Gatty, Australian, as navigator, encircled the globe in 8 days 15 hours 51 minutes, a record-breaking 15,474-mile flight.

1931 Flight-Lieutenant G. H. Stainforth, Great Britain, made new seaplane speed record of 406.997 m.p.h. at Calshot, England.

1932 Miss Amelia Earhart flew from Newfoundland to Ireland in $13\frac{1}{2}$ hours, the first solo flight across the Atlantic by a woman.

1933 Wiley Post, flying solo, encircled the globe in 7 days 18 hours 50 minutes, covering 15,596 miles.

1935 Fred and Al Keys set a new refuelling endurance record over Meridian, Mississippi, by staying in the air 3 weeks 3 days 5 hours and 34 minutes.

1937 Three Russian airmen, M. Gromov, A. Yumachev and S. Danilin, made new long-distance record by flying from Moscow, Soviet Union, to San Jancinto, California, a distance of 6,296 miles.

1938 Two R.A.F. single-engined Vickers Wellesley long-range bombers established new world's distance record for landplanes of 7,162 miles flying from Ismailia, Egypt, to Darwin, Australia.

1939 First commercial trans-Atlantic service begun by Pan American 'Yankee Clipper',

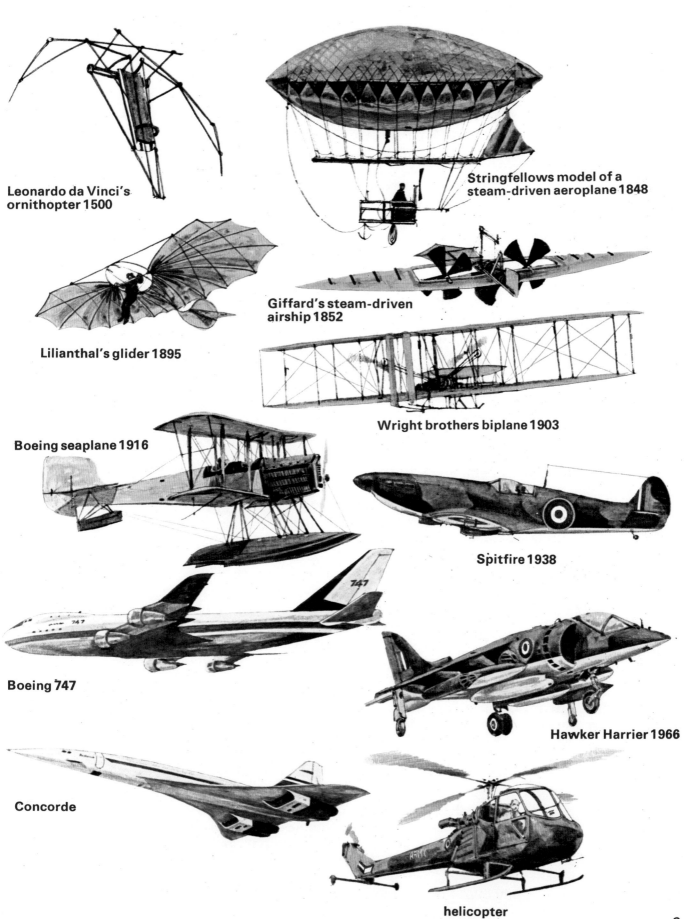

Leonardo da Vinci's
ornithopter 1500

Stringfellows model of a
steam-driven aeroplane 1848

Giffard's steam-driven
airship 1852

Lilianthal's glider 1895

Wright brothers biplane 1903

Boeing seaplane 1916

Spitfire 1938

Boeing 747

Hawker Harrier 1966

Concorde

helicopter

flying by way of New York, Bermuda, Azores, Lisbon, Bordeaux, Marseilles and Southampton.

First British trans-Atlantic air mail service. First jet plane, the German Heinkel He 178.

1941 First flight by British jet plane, the Gloster E.28/39.

1946 Group-Captain E. M. Donaldson, D.S.O., A.F.C., in a Gloster Meteor, raised the world's speed record to 616 m.p.h.

1947 Major Marion E. Carl, U.S. Marine Corps, flying a Douglas Skystreak jet plane, raised the world's speed record to 650.57 m.p.h.

1948 John Cunningham, Great Britain, set new altitude record for heavier-than-air craft in a de Haviland Vampire jet fighter of 59,445.5 feet at Hatfield, Hertfordshire.

1952 B.O.A.C. 'Comet' inaugurated world's first jet-liner service, London to Johannesburg.

1953 Squadron-Leader Neville Duke set up new world speed record of 727.7 m.p.h. in a 'Hunter' at Tangmere.

1955 Colonel H. A. Hanes, U.S.A., set up unofficial speed record of 800 m.p.h. at Palmdale, California.

1956 Peter Twiss flew Fairey Delta 2 at a speed of 1,121 m.p.h. near Chichester.

1957 U.S.A.F. Stratojets make non-stop flight round world in 45 hours 19 minutes.

1969 Anglo-French 'Concorde' made first test flights.

AIRSHIP is a form of aircraft, usually cigar shaped, which is lifted into the air by the buoyancy of the gas filling its envelope. Hydrogen was first used but because of the several disasters caused by fire it was replaced by the dead gas helium. Forward motion is provided by engine-driven propellers slung under the airship. Perhaps the best known type of airship is the 'zeppelin', named after its inventor. Zeppelins were used in the First World War as a bombing aircraft. After the disasters of the zeppelin *Hindenburg* in 1937 and the R101 in 1930, almost all work was stopped.

ALBANIA is a small country of some 11,700 square miles on the Adriatic seaboard with a population of about 2,000,000. It is an agri-cultural country growing maize and wheat. The capital is Tirana.

ALBATROSS is a seabird and can spend weeks or even months at sea, travelling distances of thousands of miles. It has a wingspan of 12 feet which enables it to soar and glide for hours on end. The albatross is found mainly in the southern regions of the earth bordering the Antarctic. It feeds on small sea creatures, especially cuttlefish. Albatross lay one chalky white egg on a simple grass nest or on the bare ground.

ALEUTIAN ISLANDS are a chain of about 150 volcanic islands stretching over the north Pacific Ocean from Alaska to Kamchatka in Asia.

ALGERIA is a republic in North Africa of about 856,000 square miles with a population of some 13 millions, most of whom are ARABS. A large part of the Sahara Desert is in Algeria, and is rich in oil and gas deposits. The capital is Algiers on the Mediterranean coast.

ALLIGATOR is a REPTILE and belongs to the same family as the CROCODILE. It differs from the crocodile in that its upper row of teeth is set outside the lower jaw. The most common alligator is the American alligator which can grow to nearly 20 feet. A close relative of the alligator is the 'caiman', many of which inhabit the rivers of South America.

ALPACA is a South American animal and a close relative of the LLAMA. It is bred for its fine wool from which the cloth 'alpaca' is made.

AMBER is the fossil remains of clear pitch or resin that has oozed out of pine trees. This has been happening for countless ages and the heaps of resin became covered with soil and hardened. The ancient Greeks valued amber highly, and their name for it was 'electron'. They noticed that when a piece of amber was rubbed it had the power of attracting light pieces of material, and so they thought it had magical qualities. It is from this that we get the word 'electricity'. Amber is a yellowish substance and can be easily cut and polished.

An airship is a lighter-than-air craft

The albatross flys thousands of miles

A toad is a cold-blooded amphibian

AMBERGRIS is not a kind of amber, but a substance secreted from the stomach of the sperm whale. It is found floating freely on the surface of the sea and is a waxy, grey substance used in the making of perfume.

AMERICAN REVOLUTION or **AMERICAN INDEPENDENCE** Britain once had an empire quite distinct from what is now known as the British Commonwealth. It consisted of thirteen Atlantic colonies in what is now the United States of America. These colonies had been founded by the Pilgrim Fathers (1620) and others who had come to the New World from Britain to start a new life. Over the years many settlers from Germany, Sweden, Ireland, the Netherlands and many other countries came to these colonies, so the populations became very mixed. Britain, however, was still responsible for the welfare of this 'empire' and some of the measures she introduced angered the colonists who had by now a strong feeling of independence. Many of the new colonists, moreover, had no ties with what the people of British descent still regarded as the 'mother country'. So bit by bit there sprang up a resentment against British rule and a desire to throw off all responsibility to the British parliament in London, and the struggle that followed was the American War of Independence. The first shots were fired against British soldiers by the colonists in Massachusetts in 1774 and the war ended in 1781, although it took another two years before the independence of the thirteen colonies was officially recognized. One of the leaders of this struggle was George Washington (1732-1799) who was elected President in 1793. See U. S. A.

AMPHIBIA are cold-blooded creatures with smooth, naked skins and able to live both on land and in the water. The best known are the FROGS, NEWTS, SALAMANDERS and TOADS. Most have four legs and lay their eggs in water from which hatch 'tadpoles' which breathe with gills as do fish.

ANACONDA is a South American snake and one of the largest snakes, some attaining a length of nearly 30 feet, but usually they are not more than 15 to 20 feet. Their skins are a mixture of blotches of yellow, brownish-green and black,

An anaconda can grow to nearly 30 feet

An Anglo-Saxon village in Southern England

although there are variations. The anaconda is a 'constrictor'; that is, it kills its prey by crushing it in its coils. It feeds on small mammals, birds and, surprisingly, fish for it is an excellent swimmer. See SNAKES.

ANGLO-SAXONS were originally Germanic tribes who settled in Southern Britian after the Roman Occupation (A.D. 450). The legendary Hengist and Horsa led an early invasion which settled in Kent. Traces of the Anglo-Saxon language are still preserved in existing place names; for example Essex, the land of the 'East' Saxons and Sussex, the land of the 'South' Saxons. The names of towns ending with 'ham' and 'ton' come from Anglo-Saxon as does the office SHERIFF. In English history the Anglo-Saxon Per-

iod dates from about A.D. 450 to 1066, the date of the NORMAN CONQUEST.

ANT is an insect. There are a large number of species found in almost every region of the world. They are social creatures; that is, they live in colonies under the earth or in constructed anthills. A single colony is made up of a 'queen' and many male and female workers. The queen lays the eggs and is fed and cared for by the worker ants. The ant grubs spin a cocoon to become pupae; these look like small grains of rice and are often called eggs but they are pupae. The worker ants in a colony each have their own particular jobs - just like workers in, say, a canning factory. Their favourite food is honey or anything sweet, but they also feed

sable antelope

impala

gnu

dik-dik

on a wide variety of other vegetable and animal foods. Some have a protective sting while others squirt out formic acid to ward off their enemies. See TERMITE.

ANTEATER is the name usually given to any ant-eating animal; for example, the AARD-VARKS, PANGOLIN or ECHIDNA, but it is applied to a small group of animals that inhabit the tropical regions of South and Central America. The best-known member of this group is the 'great' or 'giant' anteater. This creature is about 8 feet long, including its striking bushy tail, and is toothless, using its long sticky tongue to lick up the TERMITES on which it feeds. It has powerful claws for tearing open termite hills, and if attacked can put them to good, and fatal, use.

ANTELOPES are found mainly in Africa, Arabia and Syria, a few still live in Asia. They form a large family and include the GAZELLE, KUDU, BUSHBUCK, SPRINGBOK, DUIKER, HARTEBEEST, ORYX and ADDAX. All have hollow horns.

ANTIBIOTICS is that branch of medical science which grew out of the discovery by Sir Alexander Fleming that substances such as PENICILLIN can cure and control many diseases caused by BACTERIA.

APE is a term usually applied to tailless monkey-like animals, in particular the GORILLA, CHIMPANZEE and ORANG-UTAN.

APOSTLE This word is very similar to the Greek word 'apostolos' meaning messenger or ambassador. When used in the New Testament it refers to the twelve disciples whom Jesus chose at the beginning of His Ministry to be His companions and the witnesses of His life, work, death and resurrection. The original apostles were Simon Peter, James, John, Andrew, Philip, Bartholomew, Matthew, Thomas, James (son of Alphaeus), Thaddeus, Simon (the Canaanite) and Judas Iscariot, later replaced by Matthias. The title was also given to Saint Paul and Saint Barnabas.

AQUARIUM in a zoo is where fishes, and sometimes reptiles and amphibians, are exhibited. In the home an aquarium can be 1, a heated tank for tropical fishes or 2, a nonheated tank for temperate water fishes.

ARABS Today the Arabs live in a number of countries in the Middle East and North Africa, mainly SYRIA, LEBANON, IRAQ, SAUDI ARABIA, EGYPT, YEMEN, LIBYA, MOROCCO, ALGERIA and TUNISIA. Little of importance is known of the history of the Arabs before the birth of Mohammed in A.D. 571. It was he who founded the religion of Islam and such was its influence that the Arabs embarked on a series of military expeditions to conquer their neighbours and covert them to their faith. Between A.D. 632 and 656 they conquered Egypt, Syria

The 'great' or 'giant' anteater of South and Central America

The tomb of Tutankhamun and one of the greatest treasures of antiquity ever found

and Persia and later spread to North Africa and thence to Spain. With the rise of the power of Turkey in the 14th century the influence of the Arabs declined. It is only in recent years that the Arab nations have attempted to come together.

ARCHAEOLOGY is that branch of science concerned with revealing the societies and cultures of man that had been—or nearly—buried in the surface of the earth. Scientific archaeology dates from the last century and has revealed in great detail the ways and life of man long before written records were kept. Although digging is an important part of this science, modern archaeology needs many other skills; for example, the knowledge of the scholar to explain ancient languages, the knowledge of modern atomic science to date finds made during digs and expert photography to record the finds. With the coming of the 'aqualung' archaeologists can now excavate the seabed and in regions like the Mediterranean there is much to find—a great deal has already been uncovered. In recent years a new department of archaeology is 'industrial' archaeology; that is, uncovering, preserving and recording industries which have either completely vanished or have been replaced by entirely new methods of manufacture. This form of archaeology deals with man's recent past.

ARCHAEOPTERYX is the oldest known species of bird. Fossil remains were found in rocks in Bavaria and thought to be some 130,000,000 years old. It had true feathers but also many features of a reptile; for example, it had a long tail and three-fingered claws.

ARCHITECTURE is the art and science of building, and covers every type of building, from the humblest cottage to the mightiest palace or biggest block of offices. When some primitive man made the first kind of shelter for himself out of mud and branches of trees he was the world's first architect and builder. This could be said to be the very beginning of what was to become one of civilized man's most wonderful series of achievements—the putting up of fine buildings. Stone Age Man put up crude buildings but the Egyptians were the first people to develop building as an art. Then came the great Greek architects, whose influence on all architecture in the western world can still be seen. Architecture as a subject is subdivided into historical types and styles.

ARCTIC AND ANTARCTIC The Arctic Region of the world is the area surrounding the North Pole and has no exact boundary. On the globe the Arctic Circle is 66° 30′ N. One of the earliest explorers of the Arctic region of the earth was Eric the Red (about A.D. 980). One of the first Europeans was Sebastian Cabot who led an

The archaeopteryx, the ancestor of the bird

expedition to discover a short route to China about 1508. Among the most famous to face the dangers of arctic exploration are Capt. J. Ross (1818), Lieut. J. Franklin (1818), Lieut. E. Parry (1818), A.E. Nordenskiold (1864), Dr. Nansen (1888), Roald Amundsen (1903), Robert Peary (1886) and Commander R.E. Byrd who flew over the North Pole 1926. The Antarctic region of the world is the area surrounding the South Pole and bounded by the 60th southern parallel. Antarctic exploration did not begin until the eighteenth century and one of the first to venture into this inhospitable land was Capt. James Cook (1772). Others who made important voyages were Fabian von Bellingshausen (1819), James Weddell (1823), John Biscoe (1830), Jules Dumont d'Urville (1840), Charles Wilkes (1839), J. Clark Ross (1840), Roald Amundsen (1901), Capt. R.F. Scott (1901) and Sir Ernest Shackleton (1901). The International Geophysical Year (1957-8) saw the start of intensive exploration of all aspects of Antarctica. There are now a number of permanent scientific stations in Antarctica.

ARGENTINA is a Spanish-speaking republic in South America of just over 1 million square miles and a population of over 23 million people. The capital is Buenos Aires. It is mainly an agricultural country, exporting large quantities of meat all over the world. The cattle are reared on the vast pampas which form a large part of Argentina.

ARMADA is the Spanish word for 'battle fleet' and historically refers to the battle fleet Philip II of Spain sent to destroy the English fleet in 1588. The Spanish Armada was defeated by Sir Francis Drake. The story goes that Drake was playing bowls at Plymouth when the Armada was sighted and when urged to break off his game said: "There's plenty of time to win the game and thrash the Spaniards too."

ARMADILLO belongs to a small family of animals native to South and Central America. It is covered with a series of jointed bands of bony armour and when attacked rolls itself up into a ball. They feed at night and mainly on insects, small snakes and rodents.

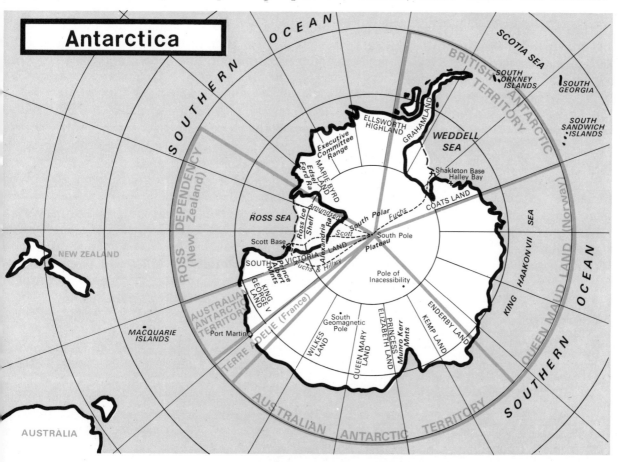

The armadillo rolls into a ball when attacked

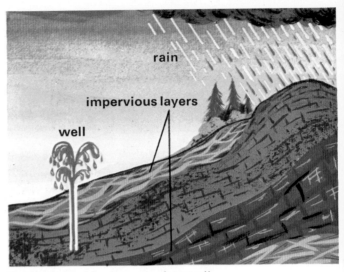

Section showing an artesian well

ARTESIAN WELL is a type of well where water is forced to the surface by natural pressure. This occurs when an inclined water-bearing strata is sandwiched between layers of non-water-bearing rocks; see diagram. The name comes from 'Artois', a town in France.

ARTISTS See TABLE 5, page 188.

ASIA is the largest continent on the earth's surface, being nearly 1/3 of the earth's surface. It is separated from Europe by the Ural Mountains, by the Bering Straits from America, the Suez Canal from Africa, the Arctic Ocean in the North and the China Sea, Sea of Japan and Sea of Okhotsk in the East.

ASS is a relative of the HORSE. It is smaller, has long ears, an upright short mane and 'brays' rather than 'neighs'. There are four different kinds: 1, Somali wild ass, 2, Kian or Tibetan wild ass, 3, Onager or Persian wild ass and, 4, the Mongolian wild ass. When domesticated it is known as a 'donkey'.

ASSYRIA was in ancient times the mountainous northern parts of the land between the rivers Tigris and Euphrates and the seat of the great Assyrian civilization of the 13th and 12th centuries B.C. Its outstanding kings were Assurnasir-pal, Sargon and Sennacherib (Bible, Kings xvii, 13).

ASTRONAUT is a member of the crew of a space-vehicle. The first astronaut was the Russian Yuri Gagarin who orbited the earth in April 1961 and was followed a month later by Alan Shepard of the United States. See SPACE FLIGHT.

ASTRONOMY is that branch of science devoted to the study of the heavens; that is, the planets, moons, stars, meteors, nebulae, etc. Man's interest in the heavenly bodies is as old as man himself. For example, over four thousand years ago the ancient Babylonians prophesied the eclipses of the sun and moon, and the rising and setting of the planets. At about the same time the Chinese were making the first maps of stars and planets. Until the time of Galileo it was believed that the earth was the centre of the universe. Copernicus (1437-1543) showed that the sun was the centre of the solar system and that the planets, including the earth, revolved round it. The telescope of Galileo was an important instrument in proving this theory. In recent times astronomers have been able to use gigantic telescopes like the 200-inch telescope on Palomer Mountain, U.S.A. to peer into the very corners of the universe. A new instrument is the RADIO-TELESCOPE.

ATLANTIS is thought to be a large island in the Atlantic Ocean, west of Africa, which sank into the ocean as a result of some great natural disaster, such as an earthquake. Legend has it that it was the centre of a powerful civilization which conquered great areas of Africa and Europe. It was described in the writings of the Greek philisopher Plato.

ATMOSPHERE is the blanket of air that surrounds the earth and thought to extend some 500 miles into space. Its main ingredients are oxygen, nitrogen, carbon-dioxide and water vapour. There are, in addition, small quantities of the rare gases argon, neon, helium, krypron and xenon. The average pressure of the atmosphere at sea level is 14.5 lbs. per square inch.

ATOLL is a reef made of CORAL surrounding a lagoon. Such formations are found in the Pacific and Indian Oceans.

ATOMIC ENERGY See **NUCLEAR POWER**

AUK is a seabird related to the PUFFIN. It is a 'diver' with webbed feet, short wings and short tail. The 'great' auk, a magnificent seabird, became extinct about 1845.

AUROCHS was a large wild ox which became extinct in the 17th century and thought by some naturalists to have been the ancestor of our modern domestic cattle.

AURORA BOREALIS is the scientific name for the 'Northern Lights'. They appear in Arctic and Northern regions in the form of glowing bands or curtains of different coloured lights. Scientists think it is caused by particles shot into the earth's atmosphere from the surface of the sun. Similar lights are seen in Antarctica and called 'Aurora Australis'.

AUSTRALIA is an island continent of 2,974,580 square miles and is a British Dominion. The Commonwealth of Australia, including the island of Tasmania, is nearly as large as Europe but has only a little over 12 million inhabitants, most of whom are of British origin but there are about 50,000 native Aborigines. Australia is made up of the following states: New South Wales (Cap. Sydney) Queensland (Cap. Brisbane); South Australia (Cap. Adelaide); Western Australia (Cap. Perth); Victoria (Cap. Melbourne); Tasmania (Cap. Hobart). All these capital cities are ports, though Perth is served by the port of Fremantle. An area, largely uninhabited, is the Northern Territory. Its capital is Darwin and another famous town is Alice Springs. The Territory does not yet govern itself in the way other states do. The federal capital is Canberra. Australia

produces more wool than any other country in the world. The country also has rich supplies of gold, iron ore, lead and zinc and has a new and growing steel industry. One of the most important rivers is the Snowy in New South Wales and Victoria. A big new irrigation scheme is being carried out on this river and the Murray which involves taking the river waters through the mountains. The first free immigrants arrived from Britain in 1793, the east coast of Australia having been discovered by Captain Cook about twenty years before. These settlers came to New South Wales which is thus the oldest state in Australia. In 1910, the six states were all united in a federation called the Commonwealth of Australia. See map on following pages.

AUSTRIA is a small republic in central Europe (34,100 square miles), little more than half the size of England, with a population of just over 7 millions. Until 1918 Austria was the centre of the great Austro-Hungarian Empire. The capital is the beautiful city of Vienna on the River Danube. Austria is an agricultural country but iron and steel are also produced. Austria's beautiful alpine scenery attracts large numbers of tourists in summer and skiers in winter.

AUTOMATION is a method of manufacturing things, like engine pistons, without the direct aid of human beings; that is, a process in which raw materials are fed in at one end and finished products come out at the other. Such processes are controlled by electronic means, usually computers programmed to a series of machine operations.

AXOLOTL is a strange creature which looks very much like a large tadpole (6-9 inches) about to turn into a frog. It is the larval stage of a SALAMANDER and remains in this condition throughout its life. Axolotls are native to Mexico where they are found in lakes and ponds.

AZTEC was a powerful civilization of American Indians that lived in Mexico between A.D. 1200 and 1600 until conquered by the Spanish. They were great craftsmen as their buildings and objects excavated by archaeologists show. They were, too, a warlike people. One of their best-known leaders was Montezuma.

SUMATRA
Barisan Range
Palembang
‹rakatau ▲

I N D O   N E S I   S

Bandjarmasin   CELEBES

Djakarta Semarang Surakarta   Macassar
JAVA   Bandung Jigjakarta Surabaja   FLORES
Surabaja   SUMBAWA   TIMOR
SUMBA   TIMOR SEA

Darwin
Daly

KIMBERLEY

Great Sandy Desert

A U S T

Hamersley
Range   Gibson Desert   Ma

WESTERN AUSTRALIA

INDIAN

OCEAN   Great Victo
Desert

Tropic of Capricorn

Kalgoorlie ●

Perth ○   GREAT A
BI

Bunbury ○

Australia and New Zealand

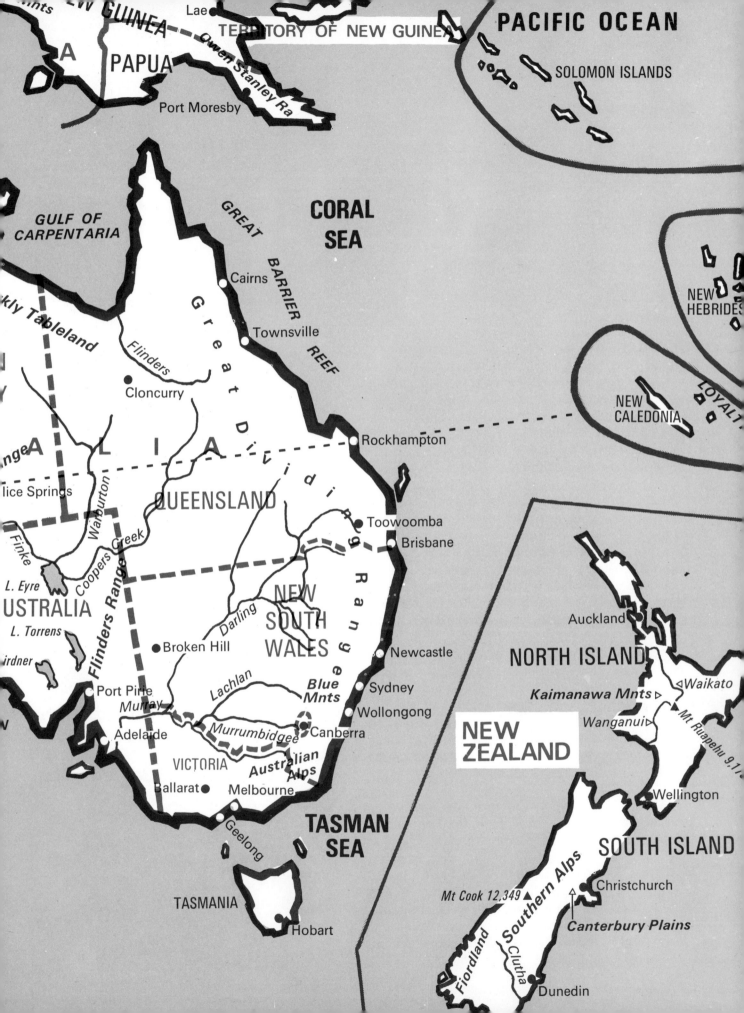

BABOON is a dog-faced monkey native to Africa and Arabia, and considered to be the more intelligent of the monkeys. Baboons live in groups or troops and feed on fruits, roots and small creatures like scorpions and insects. When roused they can be very dangerous—even a lion will steer clear of a male baboon. The most colourful of the baboons is the mandrill. In ancient Egypt the baboon was honoured as the god Anubis.

BABYLONIA was an ancient civilization centred at Babylon in what is now Iraq. It occupied the plain through which run the rivers Tigris and Euphrates. In the Bible it is also called 'Shinar' in Genesis and the 'Land of the Chaldeans' in Jeremiah. Two of its famous Kings were Hammurabi (1792-50 B.C.) and Nebuchadnezzar (605-562 B.C.).

BADGER is a night-prowling animal, lying up during the day in burrows, called 'setts'. The common badger of Europe is distinguished by its white face with a broad black stripe on each side. The American badger is smaller with a dark brown face and a narrow white stripe down the middle. It feeds on roots, bulbs, vegetables, insects, eggs and small creatures like mice.

BALI is an island (2,530 square miles) to the east of Java and is part of INDONESIA. Its population of some 1½ millions mainly work on the island growing rice, coffee and tobacco. Because of its natural beauty it is often called the 'Jewel of the East', in spite of the fact that it has several active volcanoes. The two large towns are Denpasar and Singaradja.

BALLET is a theatrical performance consisting of dancing (the word comes from the Latin *ballo*, to dance) with musical accompaniment and gestures but no dialogue as in an ordinary play. The meaning of a ballet is to convey an idea or tell a story to the audience. Dancing of one kind or another figures, of course, in religious rites since early times, but ballet as we know it today really began in Italy and France during

A mandrill, the most colourful baboon

Artist's impression of Babylonian ziggurat

the seventeenth century, when it formed part of entertainments at royal and noble houses. In classical ballet the short, fluffy skirt worn by the female dancers is called a 'tutu'. The leading dancer is called a 'ballerina' and supporting dancers form a corps-de-ballet. The person who decides what steps shall be used in a ballet is called a 'choreographer'. Famous classical ballets are *Giselle, Swan Lake, The Sleeping Beauty,* and *Coppélia.* Many notable modern ballets have also been produced.

BANDICOOT is a small MARSUPIAL and native to Australasia and New Guinea. There are several different groups, some with short noses, others long noses. One group, the now rare pig-footed bandicoot, is very much like a very small deer. Most feed at night on plant life and small animals.

BANGLADESH is an independent republic in N.E. India and formerly East Pakistan. It is about 55,000 square miles and has a population of over 50 millions. The capital is Dacca. The country is mainly agricultural and its main export is jute.

BANKS are places where money may be kept safely. The word bank comes from the Italian word *banco* or bench because the Italian merchants who made a business of lending money sat at benches or counters in the open market place. The modern business of banking is very complicated but briefly it may be said that bankers make a profit by lending money which people have deposited with them to other people who, when they pay it back, have to pay the bank more than they borrowed from it. This is called 'interest' and the profit to the bank thus comes about because the interest charged to a borrower is greater that the interest the bank credits to a depositor.

BAPTISM is a New Testament word and came from a Greek word meaning 'to dip in water'. John the Baptist was so called because he baptized his followers in the River Jordan; the act symbolized a moral and spiritual cleansing. As the Christian Church developed, infants were baptized and given a name, and thus the alternative name for the ceremony of baptism is christening. Baptism is a sign of admission to the

Christian Church; the Baptist Church follows the ancient practice of allowing baptism only to adults.

BARBARY APE is a monkey and belongs to the macaque family. The natural home of this monkey is North Africa, especially the mountainous regions of Morocco and Algeria. It was taken to Gibralter where it still lives under the protection of the Governor. Its main food is fruit and vegetables.

BAROMETER is a scientific instrument for measuring the pressure of the atmosphere. In its simplest form it consists of a tube of mercury just over 30 inches high, closed at the upper end and open at the lower, see diagram. Any increase in pressure causes the mercury to rise in the tube and any lowering in pressure for it to drop. Another form of barometer is the 'aneroid'

Below, two examples of simple barometers. *Above,* an aneroid barometer for weather forecasting

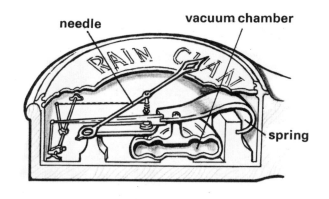

needle   vacuum chamber

spring

ANEROID BAROMETER

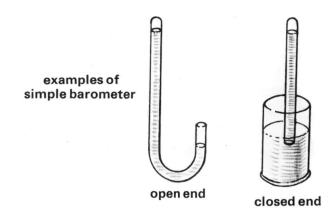

examples of simple barometer

open end   closed end

An American beaver

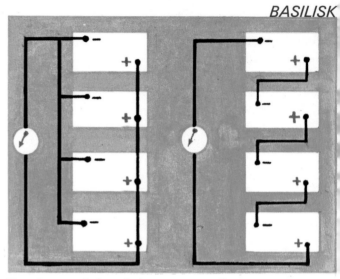

Two forms of electric battery coupling

barometer, see diagram. The most important uses of the barometer is 1, to predict changes in weather caused by changes in atmospheric pressure and 2, to find out heights above sea-level.

BASILISK is a reptile native to the tropical regions of America. It has a crest along its back and tail which it can erect to give it a rather ferocious look, but it is really harmless. When the need arises it can rear up on its hind legs and run over the ground. It is not to be confused with the 'basilisk' of the ancients which was a fire-breathing dragon.

BATS are **MAMMALS** and not birds. Their forelimbs have developed into wings which allow them to fly. Bats are divided into two main groups 1, the insect-eating bats and 2, the fruit-bats or flying-foxes. Most bats fly only at night The zig-zig flight of bats has always interested man. Science has discovered that a bat emits from its mouth a very high-pitched sound (usually called 'ultra-sonic') which is reflected back when it strikes an object ahead of it. This warns the bat to alter its direction of flight and so avoid the object. It is, in fact, a kind of sound 'radar' system.

BATTERY, ELECTRIC consists of two or more electric cells coupled together. When the positive pole of the first is coupled to the negative pole of the second and so on (see diagram) the battery is said to be in 'series'. If like poles are

joined together the battery is in 'parallel'. Series coupling gives a greater voltage while parallel gives a greater current or amperage.

BEARS are very often of large size and heavy build, with a short tail, loose lips, and broad short feet with five toes, all close together, which have long, strong claws. Bears are found all over Europe and Asia, as far as Borneo, only in Morocco in Africa, all over North America and in the northern parts of South America. They feed mainly on plant life—some eat salmon which they are expert in catching. Bears breed once a year and hibernate in the winter. Included in this family are the brown bear, grizzly bear, American black bear, polar bear, Himalayan black bear, honey bear, sloth bear and spectacled bear.

BEAVER is a water-loving animal with a wide scaly paddle-like tail and fully webbed feet which it uses for swimming. There are two species, the European and American. The European beaver lives in burrows in the banks of streams. The American beaver is the more interesting as it is this animal that constructs dams of logs and branches, plastered with mud. These dams are to protect the beaver family from such animals as the coyote and cougar. Their food consists mainly of the bark of willow, poplars and other trees, but they also eat water-lilies, grass and roots.

BEES (HONEY BEES) are winged insects

which feed on the nectar and pollen of flowers. The common honey bee lives in swarms in a hive. Each swarm consists of a single queen, the males or drones and the workers who collect the honey. A swarm can consist of anything from 10 to 50,000 bees and during egg-laying the queen can lay as many as 2,000 eggs per day. During recent years it has been discovered that worker bees perform a kind of figure-eight dance when they return from food gathering which, so it would seem, signals to the other bees a supply of food. The more active the dance the greater is the supply of food.

BEETLES belong to the largest family of all insects. Most beetles can be recognised by their first pair of wings which are a covering curving like a shield over their second pair of wings and abdomen. It is thought that there are at least 250,000 species of beetle in the world.

BELGIUM is a small kingdom (11,800 square miles) in western Europe. Of its population of just over $9\frac{1}{2}$ millions about half are Walloons and speak French and the rest, who live chiefly in the north, speak Flemish, a language very like Dutch. The capital is Brussels, the chief industrial town is Liège and the chief port Antwerp. Belgium is an important industrial country with big engineering and ship-building works. It is also famous for lace and carpets.

BERMUDAS or Somer Islands are a group of islands, about 100 in number, in the west of the Atlantic Ocean and is a British Colony. They have a population of some 52,000 and the capital is Hamilton. Because of the climate it is a very popular tourist resort.

BESSEMER CONVERTER is used in the process of removing impurities from pig-iron in the making of steel. It is named after the inventor Sir Henry Bessemer (1813-98). See IRON.

BIBLE comes from the Greek word *biblios* which simply means 'books'. The Holy Bible is a collection of 66 books divided into two sections: the Old Testament (39 books) which is mainly a record of God's dealings with the Hebrew people and the New Testament (27 books) which tells of the life and teachings of Jesus Christ and the early days of the Christian Church. The Holy Bible is the most widely translated book in the world.

BIGHORN is so called because of its beautiful sweeping horns and is a native of the mountainous regions of the western North America. It is also known as the Rocky Mountain sheep.

BILL OF RIGHTS was a statute passed when William and Mary came to the throne of England in 1689 and has since become an important part of the Constitution of the U.S.A. and individual States. It is concerned mainly to protect the freedom and liberty of a person.

BIOLOGY is the science of living things,

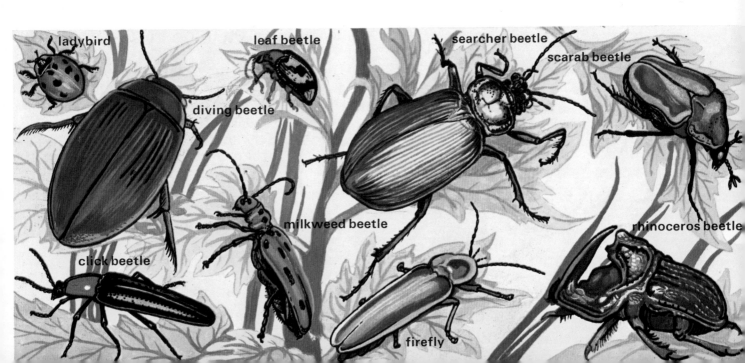

ladybird leaf beetle searcher beetle scarab beetle diving beetle milkweed beetle rhinoceros beetle click beetle firefly

animals and plants, and comes from the Greek words *bios* meaning life and *logos* meaning study. This is a very wide subject and in practice means the study of animals and plants but does not include man. Biology is broken down into narrower subjects; for example, 'histology' which is the study of the cells of which living things are composed, 'genetics' which is the study of heredity or how offspring resemble their parents, 'cytology', the study of how cells are built up and 'physiology', the science of the form and chemistry of organs. As science advances more and more special sciences are developed to handle man's increasing knowledge of living things. See BOTANY and ZOOLOGY.

BIRDS are found throughout the world from the coldest arctic regions to the hottest equatorial jungles. Although all have feathers not all can fly; for example, the ostrich, emu and penguin. The skeleton of a bird is very light, the bones being hollow. The muscles used in flapping the wings are large and make up quite a bit of the total weight of a bird. A bird's feathers are of two kinds; 1, the smaller feathers that cover most of the body and 2, the larger flight feathers in the wings and tail. Every year the feathers are moulted and replaced with new feathers —some birds moult more than once a year. All birds lay eggs in some form of nest and these vary from a single egg to up to 20 like the pheasant.

BISON belongs to the family of wild cattle. It is distinguished by its mane and thick woolly hair over the front of its body and forelegs. There are two species, the European bison or wisent, and the American bison or buffalo.

BLAST FURNACE See **IRON**

BOLIVIA is a republic in the north-west of South America. It is 415,000 square miles, with a population of over 4½ millions. It is a mountainous country in the Andes. About two-thirds of the people are Indians, descendants of the INCAS, and they speak their own languages. The people of European origin speak Spanish. The country takes its name from Simon Bolivar, a great South American patriot. Bolivia has many minerals the chief of which is tin. The capital is La Paz.

BOOMERANG is a hunting weapon used by the primitive people (aborigines) of Australia. It is so made that when it is thrown it will return to the thrower; it is 2 to 3 feet long and about 3 inches wide.

BONGO is an antelope with massive horns twisted into about one complete spiral. It is chestnut in colour and has white stripes running over its body. The bongo lives deep in the forests of Central Africa.

BOSTON TEA PARTY was a protest by American citizens against the importation of tea in December 1773 in Boston. Some fifty men, dressed as Mohawk Indians, boarded an English ship and tipped over three hundred chests of tea into the sea.

BOTANY is that branch of science concerned with the study of plant life. It is subdivided into sections, the most important of which are; 1, the arranging into families and naming of plants; 2, the physical construction of plants; 3, how plants live and reproduce and 4, the distribution of plants throughout the world.

BRAIN AND NERVOUS SYSTEM Almost all animals have a brain, though in the lower animals it is sometimes a slight swelling in the main nerve. In the higher animals it has become a complex organ for sorting out and remembering all the information brought to it by the nerves from the eyes, nose, tongue, skin and the organs of the body. The human brain and that of the higher animals, consists of three parts. The upper part is called the 'cerebrum', and is the area of thinking. Under this comes the 'cerebellum' and the 'medulla', which automatically control the working of such organs as the heart and lungs, and see that the various parts of the body work smoothly together. The surface of the cerebrum consists of the grey brain cells or 'grey matter'. The 'white matter' inside the brain is made up of millions of nerve fibres, like the bundles of wires in a telephone exchange. Running from the brain to every part of the body are nerves whose job is to carry messages to and from the brain. See HUMAN BODY.

BRAZIL is the largest country (3,289,000

Adeline penguin

Little owl

-of-the-rock

goldfinch

puffin

stilt

grebe

jay

square miles) in South America. It has rather more than 88 million inhabitants who are of many different races. The chief river is the Amazon which is navigable through nearly two thousand miles of Brazilian territory. The country has vast forests and is rich in minerals. Its chief export is coffee. The capital is the new city of Brasilia, which is 600 miles north-west of the former capital of Rio de Janeiro. Brazil's second largest city is São Paulo.

BRONZE AGE is the period in history when Man first used bronze for tools and weapons. Bronze was probably discovered quite accidentally, perhaps when some primitive man lit a fire near some copper and tin ores, and noticed the new brownish metal that had formed when they fused. Later it was found that this new metal was harder than tin or copper alone, so it was used for swords, axes and other weapons and tools. The Bronze Age in Europe lasted from about 2000 to 1500 B.C.

BUCKINGHAM PALACE is the home of Queen Elizabeth II; it was also the home of five monarchs who reigned before her. It is one of the 'sights' of London. There was a house on the site in the days of Queen Anne and the Duke of Buckingham lived in it. This house was later bought by King George III and it was this king's son, George IV, who pulled it down and rebuilt it. Neither George IV nor the next king, his brother William IV, lived in it, however, and it was the famous Queen Victoria (1837-1901) who first made it a royal home and called it Buckingham Palace. The Palace has hundreds of rooms and is a storehouse of pictures and other art treasures.

BUFFALO See **BISON**

BULGARIA is a republic in Eastern Europe and borders the Black Sea. It is 43,000 square miles and has a population of just over 8 millions. It is chiefly an agricultural country, producing tobacco, grapes and attar of roses. Recently important industries have developed, particularly steel and coal. The capital is Sofia.

BUOYS are used in sea and river navigation. They are of various shapes and colours, each being designed for a particular duty. Channel buoys mark the approach to the entrance of a channel and are usually pillar or landfall buoys. These are followed by a number of can-shaped buoys to port, and conical-shaped buoys to starboard. Spherical buoys usually denote the presence of an obstruction. Special buoys are used for marking wrecks, quarantine stations, telegraph cables, and as mooring buoys.

BURMA is a republic in south-east Asia of 262,000 square miles and over 26 million inhabitants who are nearly all Buddhists. Most Burmese are farmers, rice being both grown and exported. Her forests produce valuable timber, particularly teak. The country is rich in minerals, the most important of which is oil. Another valuable mineral is ruby. The capital is Rangoon, and Mandalay is an important city.

BURUNDI is a small republic in Africa near the Congo. It is 10,700 square miles and has a population of a little more than 3 millions. It was formerly part of the territory known as Ruanda-Urundi. It is an agricultural country, producing chiefly coffee and cattle. The capital is Bujumbura.

BUSHBUCK belongs to the ANTELOPES and is found in Africa. There are several different kinds, including the nyala. The common bushbuck is a small creature of the forests. Only the males have horns. It has rather a long coat with a crest along its back.

BUSHMEN belong to a tribe in the Kalahari Desert, the great desert region in south western Africa between the Orange River and the Zambesi. They and other negroid tribes are the true natives of the African continent. Bushmen are very primitive, and number probably no more than 30,000. They have long bodies and short arms and legs, bulging foreheads and flat noses, and their average height is about four feet eight inches.

BUTTERFLIES and MOTHS are insects and belong to the group known as 'Lepidoptera', hence the name lepidopterist for a butterfly collector. Although butterflies and moths look very alike they can be told apart. A butterfly always has a narrow waist while moths are more rounded and the antennae or feelers in butterflies are thick, like clubs, at the tip whereas the feelers of moths, although varied in shape, always taper to a point. The life cycle or metamorphosis is very interesting. From the egg stage it changes to a caterpillar, then into a pupa or chrysalis and, finally, into a beautiful adult insect.

This drawing shows the main stages in the life cycle of a butterfly. After the egg has been laid it changes into a caterpillar, then into a pupa or chrysalis and, finally, into a beautiful adult insect

Beautiful butterflies

short-tailed blue ◀

scarce small skipper ◀

◀ white admiral

◀ red admiral

light blue ◀

Camberwell beauty ▶

orange tip ◀

purple hair-streak ▶

danius chrysippus ▶

◀ trodes croesus

Indian imperial ▶

Lulworth skipper ▲

marbled white ▲

27

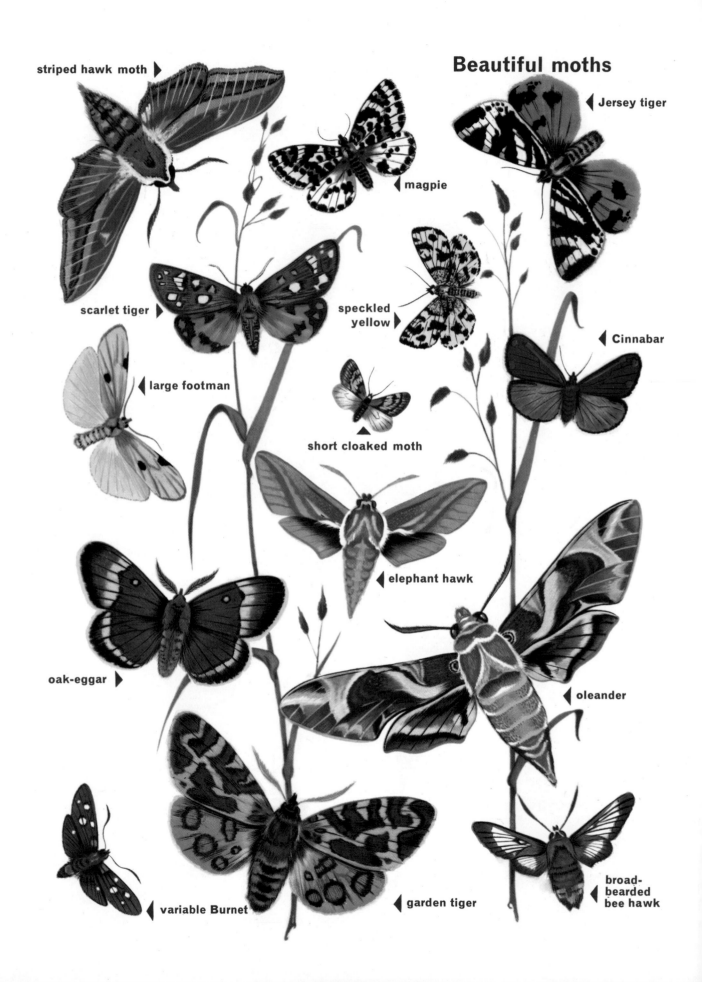

striped hawk moth ▶

Beautiful moths

◀ Jersey tiger

◀ magpie

scarlet tiger ▶

speckled yellow ▶

◀ Cinnabar

large footman ◀

short cloaked moth

elephant hawk ◀

oak-eggar ▶

◀ oleander

variable Burnet ◀

◀ garden tiger

broad-bearded bee hawk

CACTUS is a fleshy plant, usually leafless with sharp spines. Many bear most beautiful flowers, both of shape and colour. Most cacti grow in desert regions and because of their fleshy nature can store water for long periods. They range in size from an inch or so up to 50 feet. In countries like Mexico the prickly pear cactus, one of the most common cacti, is grown to form hedges.

CALENDAR comes from the Roman word *calends* or *kalends,* meaning the first day of the month, and is the way in which a year is divided into months, weeks and days. A year is the time the earth takes to travel once round the sun; this is $365\frac{1}{4}$ days, so every fourth year, or 'Leap Year', is given an extra day at the end of February. The month is based on the movements of the moon and the months were given their names by the Romans. The day is based on the time taken by the earth to revolve once on its own axis. The days of the week have Saxon names, after pagan gods, with the exception of Sunday (Sun's Day) and Monday (Moon's Day); for instance, Wednesday means Woden's Day; Woden (the Norse Odin) was the greatest of the Teutonic gods. The first proper calendar was invented by Julius Caesar and is known as the 'Julian' calendar, the month of July being named after him, but Pope Gregory XIII had it corrected in 1582 to make it more accurate, so the calendar we use today is called the 'Gregorian' calendar.

CALVARY is the name of a hill outside Jerusalem. It was the Latin rendering of a Greek word which in turn was a translation from the Aramaic word *golgotha,* meaning skull. This was the place where Jesus Christ was crucified. A 'calvary' is often the name given to a cross set up by the roadside.

CAMBODIA is a kingdom in south-east Asia and is part of what used to be French Indochina. It is nearly 66,000 square miles, with a population of about 6 millions. The people are mixed, some being like those of MALAYSIA and

Most cacti grow in desert regions

others who came originally from India. They are almost all Buddhists. Nearly all the people are farmers.

CAMELS There are two species, the 'Bactrian' camel of Central Asia and the 'Arabian' camel of the Arabian deserts. The Bactrian camel is a sturdy animal and has longer hair to withstand the cold of the Asian deserts. It has two humps. The Arabian camel has only one hump and is a slimmer and swifter animal. Camels feed on coarse desert vegetation. They have developed humps of a fatty substance on which they live when food is scarce. Their large plate-like feet allow the animal to walk

The one-hump or Arabian camel

easily on desert sand. Camels are close relatives of the LLAMAS.

CAMEROON is a federal republic on the West coast of Africa. It is nearly 184,000 square miles and has a population of about 5 millions. Its capital is Yaounda and its biggest town is Douala. The country produces cocoa, cotton, timber and aluminium for exporting abroad.

CANADA is the largest (3,560,238 square miles) and oldest British Dominion. It lies north of the United States from which it is separated for a considerable distance by five great lakes, one of them, Lake Superior, being the largest fresh-water lake in the world. There are about 21 million inhabitants most of whom speak English except those in the province of Quebec who speak French. The ten provinces of Canada are: Ontario; Quebec; Nova Scotia; New Brunswick; British Columbia; Prince Edward Island; Manitoba; Alberta; Saskatchewan and Newfoundland. Newfoundland with Labrador only joined Canada in 1949. In the north of Canada are two vast almost uninhabited territories, the Yukon and the North-West Territories. Canada's largest cities are Montreal in Quebec and Toronto in Ontario. Other important cities are Edmonton (Alberta), Winnipeg (Manitoba), Hamilton (Ontario) and the port of Halifax (Nova

Scotia). Canada's two most famous rivers are the Mackenzie and the St. Lawrence. Canada is the world's leading supplier of timber and she is one of the chief wheat growing countries in the world. She has many minerals and has more nickel, aluminium, asbestos and platinum than any other country.

CANARY ISLANDS are a group of islands in the North Atlantic Ocean that belong to Spain. The largest island is Tenerife, capital Santa Cruz, and Gran Canaria, capital Las Palmas. The islands export tropical fruits and tomatoes. Their combined land area is 2,807 square miles and population about 900,000.

CAPITOL is the seat of the National Congress of the United States in Washington, D.C. and founded in 1793. It has a magnificent dome based on that of St. Paul's Cathedral in London. It is connected with the Senate-chamber and the House of Representatives.

CAPYBARA is the largest RODENT on earth and a native of South America. Fully grown it can measure over 48 inches long and 20 inches at the shoulder. Capybaras are social animals, moving and feeding in troops. Their main foods are grasses and water plants. They live on river banks and are expert swimmers. For all

A typical English castle of the type built after the Norman Conquest

heir size they are timid creatures, scurrying for cover at the slightest distrubance.

CARNIVOROUS PLANTS should really be called insect-eating plants and consist of a small group of plants that add to their nitrogen supply and other foods by trapping and digesting insects. The best known of these plants are the Venus fly-trap, the sundew and the pitcher plant.

CASTLES are buildings originally built as fortresses. The word 'castle' comes from the Latin *castrum,* fort. The most famous builders of castles, as the word is known today, were the Normans. When William the Conqueror subdued England, he and his followers built castles all over the country because they still feared the Saxon inhabitants. The oldest stone castle in the British Isles is Richmond Castle, Yorkshire; it was built about 1075, nine years after the NORMAN CONQUEST. The largest inhabited castle in the world is Windsor Castle, England, built mainly in the twelfth century. The earliest castles were usually built purely for defence and had very thick, high walls and were often surrounded by a moat. During the fourteenth century, when the land was becoming more peaceful, more and more English castles were adapted to become homes instead of merely forts, and subsequently all large private residences were built as manor houses or palaces.

CATHEDRAL The word *cathedra* means a throne, and in the Middle Ages (from about A.D. 395 to 1500) the church which contained the official seat or throne of a bishop or archbishop was called the 'church of the seat' of *ecclesia cathedralis.* This became shortened to cathedral. Special churches designed to be the centre of a diocese or archdiocese (the domain of a bishop or archbishop) were then built, and such churches in Europe are among the most beautiful buildings ever erected by man. Perhaps the best-known type of cathedral is the 'Gothic' (with pointed arches) built during the twelfth and thirteenth centuries. These magnificent buildings took a long time to build; for instance, Ely Cathedral was begun in 1083 but was not finished until 1533. The world's largest cathedral is that of the diocese of New York; the largest cathedral in the British Isles is the Anglican Cathedral of Liverpool. World-famous cathedrals include those of Notre Dame in Paris, St. Peter's in Rome and England's Canterbury and St. Paul's.

CATS are found all over the great continents of the world from north to south, but do not extend beyond Borneo and are absent from Madagascar and Australia. Their habits are very similar wherever they are found. For preference they kill their own prey, which consists mainly of any mammals or birds they can catch, but many eat frogs, fish, insects and even carrion at times. Usually they catch their prey by stalking or by lying in wait for the animal until it moves within springing distance. Owing to their short jaws, they can never secure their prey with a quick snap, but strike it down or grab it with the paws before seizing it with the mouth—watch your cat catch a mouse. There are a great many species, but apart from the house cat, the best known are the LION, TIGER, PANTHER, LEOPARD, JAGUAR, PUMA and CHEETAH.

CAVY is the name given to the wild kind of guinea-pig found in the forested regions of South America. The best known is the 'Patagonian' cavy. It is very much like a hare and the larger species grow to some 36 inches in length. Cavies live in burrows and are very timid.

CELTS came originally from central Europe, invaded Britain in two waves –the Goidels in the late Bronze Age, and the Brythons and Belgae in the Iron Age. The Celts must have entered Britain in great numbers, for by the time of the Roman invasion almost all the inhabitants of Britain and Ireland used the Celtic language. The DRUIDS were their religious leaders, and the Celts produced fine bronze-work. Some of the Celtic culture was preserved in many parts of the British Isles, notably in their languages –Irish, Gaelic, Welsh, Cornish and Manx. The first three are still widely spoken today.

CENTRAL AFRICAN REPUBLIC is an independent state in Africa just north of the Equator. It was a French colony and was then known as 'Ubanghi Shari'. It is 234,000 square miles but has only $1\frac{1}{4}$ millions inhabitants. The capital is Bangui, near the border with the CONGOLESE REPUBLIC. The country is a member of the French community.

CEYLON is a Dominion within the British Commonwealth. It is an island at the southern tip of India and is 25,330 square miles with over 10 million inhabitants, most of whom work on the land. Tea is the country's main export. Its capital is Colombo. The people of Ceylon are of different origins, the most numerous being the Singhalese, who are Buddhists, and the Tamils, who came originally from India and are mostly Hindus. Ceylon was the first country in the world to have a woman as Prime Minister.

CHAMELEON is a reptile and belongs to the lizard family. There are over 80 known species, most of which are found in Africa and Madagascar. This ponderously slow reptile has split toes specially adapted for grasping, swivel eyes and an extremely long and deadly accurate tongue for catching insects. Much is said about its ability to change colour; in fact, it is not all that important, the range only being from green to yellow to greyish. The average chameleon is under 6 inches long, but there are a few up to 24 inches long, including the tail.

CHAMOIS is a small fleet-footed deer native to alpine regions, especially Austria and Switzerland. Its most noticeable feature is its short hooked horns. An adult measures about 30-36 inches at the shoulder. The 'shammy', a soft leather for cleaning, was originally made from chamois skin.

CHANNEL ISLANDS are a group off the north-west coast of France that have belonged to Britain since the Norman Conquest. There are nine islands, of which the most important are Jersey, Guernsey, Alderney and Sark. Jersey and Guernsey are famous for their breed of cattle. The islands also grow tomatoes, potatoes and flowers for export. There are about 100,000 inhabitants and the islands govern themselves. The Channel Islands total 75 square miles in area.

CHEETAH This beautiful animal is now only found in Africa. Although the cheetah looks very like a leopard it is not a true cat as its claws are more like those of a dog than a cat. The cheetah is thought to be the swiftest animal, being able to run at speeds of 60 m.p.h. and over. They are outstanding hunters and can be trained to do this.

CHEMISTRY All substances—solid, liquid and gas—in the universe are made of elements or compounds of two or more elements. For example, iron is a simple element whereas chalk is a combination of the elements calcium, carbon and oxygen. There are ninety-six natural elements ranging from the lightest, hydrogen, to the heaviest, curium. It is the main job of chemistry to understand the nature of elements, how they combine to form components and, equally important, how components are broken down to simple elements. The two main branches of chemistry are: 'inorganic' chemistry which studies non-living substances, and 'organic' chemistry or the chemistry of living matter.

CHEVROTAINS are small creatures without horns and about the size of hares. They inhabit the forests of tropical Asia and Africa. Being timid and defenceless, they lie up by day in sheltered places, only coming out at dusk to feed on vegetable plants. They are sometimes called 'mouse deer'.

CHILE is a republic in South America which lies between the Andes Mountains and the shores of the south Pacific. It is the narrowest country in the world, stretching from north to south for 2,800 miles and about 100 miles wide. Its estimated area is 290,000 square miles and population about 9½ millions. The capital is Santiago and the chief port Valparaiso. Chile is an important copper producing country and she also has much coal. She owns EASTER ISLAND on which are ancient mysterious stone figures.

CHIMPANZEE is one of the most man-like of the apes. It lives in the forests of West and Central Africa. Chimpanzees spend more time in trees than gorillas, are better climbers, and much more active both in trees and on the ground. When climbing they never leap from branch to branch, but either move along using hands and feet, or swing arm over arm, never letting go with one hand until the other has made a firm grip. When they descend quickly, they drop from bough to bough, checking their fall with their hands as they come down. A fully-grown male measures about 60 inches erect and weighs around 400-500 pounds – its armspread being about 90 inches. There are three forms, the smallest being the 'pygmy' chimpanzee.

CHINA is one of the largest countries in the world being 4,300,000 square miles with a population believed to be about 800 millions. The country is considerably bigger than the United States and is divided into 26 Provinces. These include Inner Mongolia, Manchuria and Tibet. The capital is Peking which has a popu-

The American chipmunk or gopher

lation of more than 4 millions. Shanghai, the chief port, is even bigger with over 6 millions. The most important rivers are the Yangtse, the Yellow and the Canton at the mouth of which is the city of that name. China is rich in minerals, though most of them are not yet fully used. They include coal, copper, lead and zinc, but most of the people are farmers.

CHINCHILLA is a rodent and farmed for its lovely soft silvergrey fur which is much valued for making coats and furs. It is about the size of a squirrel, the head and body being about ten inches long and the tail about five. The chinchilla lives in burrows and its natural home is in the Andes of Chile and Bolivia.

CHIPMUNK is another name for the American ground squirrel or striped gopher found in Asia and North America. Chipmunks differ from

The Great Wall of China is 1,685 miles long

Far East

U S S R

SAKHAL

MONGOLIA

Ulan Bator

MANCHURIA

HOKK

Gobi Desert

Harbin

SINKIANG

INNER MONGOLIA

Mukden

SEA OF
JAPAN

JAPAN

Tsaidam
Swamps

Great Wall of China

Hwang

Peking

Pyongyang
2

HO

Kunlun Mountains

Tientsin

(Yellow River)

Taiyuan

Seoul

1

Fuji
12390

Tokyo

Yokoha

TIBET

CHINA

Tsingtao

YELLOW
SEA

Hiroshima

Gurla Mandhata 25355

Sian

Nagasaki

SHIKOKU

Osaka

Lhasa

KYUSHU

Namcha Barwa 25445

SZECHUAN

Nanking

Shanghai

EAST
CHINA SEA

Chengtu

Hankow

Chungking

Yangtze

Tropic of Cancer

Taipeh

Mandalay

KWANGSI

3

BURMA

Irrawaddy

Salween

NORTH
VIETNAM

CHUANG

Canton

4

Hanoi

PHILIPPINE
SEA

GULF OF
TONKIN

LAOS

HAINAN

SOUTH CHINA SEA

Rangoon

Veintiane

Mekong

LUZON

ANDAMAN
SEA

THAILAND

Manila

PHILIPPINE
ISLANDS

Bangkok

Angkor

5

CAMBODIA

Phnom Penh
Saigon

MINDANAO

GULF
OF SIAM

STRAIT OF MALACCA

MALAYA

Kuala Lumpur

MALAYSIA

Jesselton

SABAH

SARAWAK

6

Kuching

Equator

7

| 1 : SOUTH KO |
| 2 : NORTH KO |
| 3 : FORMOSA |
| 4 : HONG KON |
| 5 : SOUTH VIE |
| 6 : BRUNEI |
| 7 : SINGAPOR |

the ordinary squirrels in that they live in burrows in woods and open spaces.

CIVET has been described as a 'half-cat' and there are several different kinds. The most interesting is the African civet as it is from this animal that we get a substance essential in the making of perfumes. It is about 3 feet long with rather a small head.

CIVIL WAR (U.S.A.) In the entry AMER-ICAN REVOLUTION you can read how the colonists of New England broke away from the mother country and founded a nation of their own. This was in 1783 but by 1861 the American States were quarrelling among themselves; the southern states formed themselves into what they called a Confederacy and wanted to break away from the northern states (the Federalists), one of the principal disputes being about slavery because the south thought it was quite all right for people to own slaves while the north, led by Abraham Lincoln, disagreed. The first shots in the war between north and south –the American Civil War– were fired on 12 April 1861 and, before the Confederates were forced finally to surrender on 12 May 1865, well over 2,000 battles great and small were fought between the opposing forces, with much loss of life and general suffering. The most famous generals in the Confederate army were Robert E. Lee and Thomas 'Stonewall' Jackson; the most famous on the Federal side were Ulysses Grant and William Sherman. In 1865 slavery was prohibited throughout the whole of the U.S.A.

CLOUDS consist of fine droplets of water which have condensed from the invisible water-vapour in the air. Cold air can hold less water-vapour than warm air, so that clouds form when moist warm air becomes chilled. This may happen if it rises to a great height, or if it blows against a cold mountain. The droplets float in the air because they are so small that even the lightest air-currents can blow them upwards as fast as they fall. If the droplets grow too large they fall as rain. A cloud resting on the ground is called a mist or fog.

COAL is the remains of dead fern-like trees and other plants that have lain in the earth's crust for many million years. Most coals are about 300 million years old, but coals only 20 million years old are found in many parts of the world. The wood of trees is made chiefly of carbon, oxygen and hydrogen, and if it is buried so that the air cannot get to it these elements gradually get separated. The gases escape, or combine with sulphur and other substances present in the sap of trees, and only the carbon remains. Pure anthracite coal may contain 90 per cent of carbon.

COLOMBIA is a large republic in the north-west of South America. It is 440,000 square miles and has a population of a little over 18 millions. The capital is Bogota. Colombia grows large quantities of coffee, most of which it exports. Colombia takes its name from Christopher Columbus, the explorer, who discovered it in 1502.

COLOSSEUM was a large arena in ancient Rome, and its ruins can be seen today. It was one of the city's most imposing buildings and had seats, arranged in fifty rows on terraces, to accommodate between 70,000 and 80,000 spectators who flocked from the city and far beyond it to see circuses, chariot races, fights between gladiators and other specially staged events. It is said the Colosseum could be flooded so that mimic sea battles could be presented. This huge arena was begun about A.D. 75 and took five years to complete. It was here that many of the early Christians suffered martyrdom.

COMETS are heavenly bodies that go round the sun like the earth and other planets. Their orbits are very long ellipses, so that they sometimes approach very close to the sun and at others a long way away. The main part of a comet consists of small fragments of rock and iron, very loosely scattered through a big volume of space. You can picture it as a large shower of stones rushing along in the form of a ball. Between the stones, and surrounding the whole, there is a good deal of gas and dust. When a comet approaches the sun, the pressure of the sun's rays forces the gas and dust out of the comet to form a long tail. As this must always point away from the sun, approaching comets have their tails behind them, but when they are travelling away they go tail first.

The giant condor of the Andes in South America and a close relative of the vulture

Above, a mariner's compass. *Below,* a simple gyroscope and basis of the gyrocompass. See article on the GYROCOMPASS on page 68

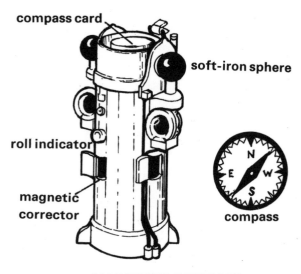

compass card

soft-iron sphere

roll indicator

magnetic corrector

compass

MARINER'S COMPASS

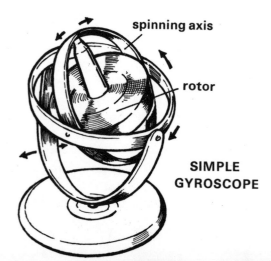

spinning axis

rotor

SIMPLE GYROSCOPE

COMMANDMENTS   They are the foundation upon which the religion of Israel was built and developed; and they have profoundly influenced the ideals of many nations right up to this day.   The story of how Moses received them from God on Mount Sinai, of how Moses found that, in his absence, the Israelites had made a Golden Calf as an object of worship; and how God gave Moses the Commandments a second time, is told in Exodus and Deuteronomy. The Commandments themselves are set out in Exodus, Chapter XX, and Deuteronomy, Chapter V.   Scholars know them by the Greek term 'Decalogue' –The Ten Words.

COMMUNION is the chief sacrament in the Christian Church.   Another name for it is the Eucharist, a word which means thanksgiving in Greek.   The act of taking Communion is to re-enact symbolically the Lord's Supper.

COMPASS is a magnetized needle pivoted to swing freely on a fine point.   Near to the N and S geographical poles of the earth are places where the earth's magnetism is strongest. These places are called the magnet poles.   In fact, the earth behaves as if it had a bar magnet passing through it, with one end near to the North Pole and the other near to the South Pole.   The simple compass comes to rest with one end attracted to the N magnet pole, and the other to the S magnet pole.   We call the end of the needle pointing to the north the 'north seeking' pole, but it is really the S pole of the magnet because it is opposite poles that attract each other.   The compass, then, does not point exactly to the North Pole, but to the magnet pole, and so it is necessary for pilots who steer ships by a magnet compass to know how to allow for the difference.   They are given special charts that tell them how much correction must be made to the magnetic compass.   This makes it possible to find the true geographical north, and so to steer correctly.   A gyrocompass is simply a spinning wheel, see drawing, which is controlled to point to the true geographical North Pole.   In many ways the gyrocompass is better as it is not influenced by the earth's magnetic field.

CONDOR is a vulture.   The Andean condor is the largest living bird having a wing spread

CONSTELLATIONS OF THE NORTHERN HEMISPHERE

1 Pegasus
2 Andromeda
3 Pisces
4 Cetus
5 Aries
6 Triangulum
7 Lacerta
8 Equileus
9 Delphinus
10 Aquila
11 Serpens
12 Sagitta
13 Caygnus
14 Cepheus
15 Cassiopeia
16 Perseus
17 Pleiades
18 Taurus
19 Orion
20 Auriga
21 Camelopardus

22 Lyra
23 Ophiuchus
24 Hercules
25 Draco
26 Ursa Minor
27 Lynx
28 Gemini
29 Canis Minor
30 Cancer
31 Ursa Major
32 Leo Minor
33 Canes Venatici
34 Boötes
35 Corona Borealis
36 Serpens
37 Coma Berenices
38 Leo
39 Hydra
40 Virgo
41 Pole Star

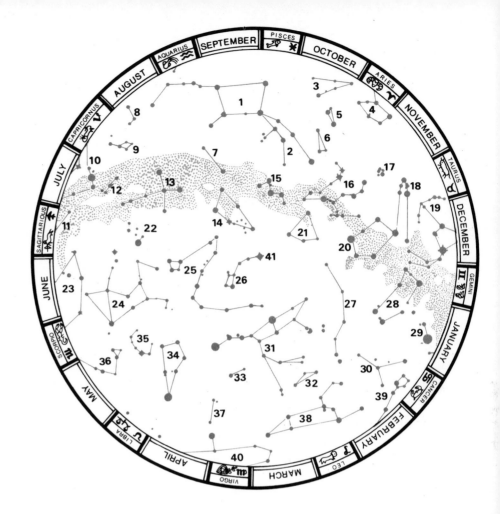

CONSTELLATIONS OF THE SOUTHERN HEMISPHERE

1 Aquarius
2 Cetus
3 Capricornus
4 Piscis Austrinus
5 Grus
6 Sculptor
7 Phoenix
8 Fornax
9 Eridanus
10 Tucana
11 Indus
12 Aquila
13 Saggitarius
14 Pavo
15 Pavo
16 Octaus
17 Hydrus
18 Reticulum
19 Mensa
20 Dictor Dorado
21 Columba
22 Lepus
23 Orion
24 Monoceros

25 Canis Major
26 Puppis
27 Carina
28 Volans
29 Chamaeleon
30 Apus
31 Triangulum Australe
32 Ara
33 Corona Australis
34 Serpens
35 Scorpio
36 Cirinus
37 Lupus
38 Crux
39 Vela
40 Pyxis
41 Centarus
42 Libra
43 Hydra
44 Corvus
45 Crater
46 Sextans
47 Virgo

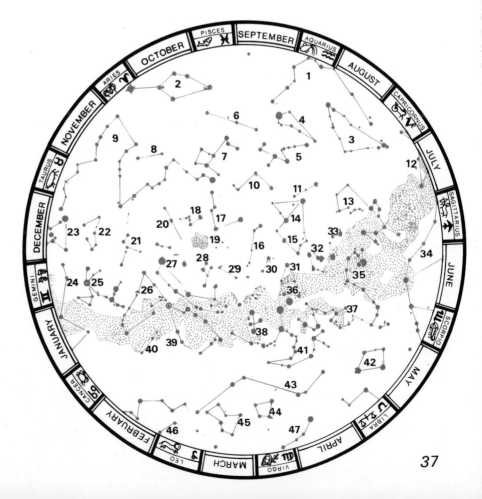

of up to 12 feet. The Californian condor is slightly smaller. Condors live mainly on carrion, that is dead animals.

CONGOLESE REPUBLIC is an African republic that takes its name from the Congo River. It is 905,580 square miles with a population of over 16 millions. The Congo is rich in copper, found in the province of Katanga, which adjoins ZAMBIA. The country is the world's chief supplier of cobalt and has important supplies of uranium. The capital is Kinshasa (formerly Leopoldville).

CONSTELLATION is a group of stars which form a basic shape. From very early times they were given the names of gods, animals, etc. The best-known constellations are the twelve which form the ZODIAC. See page 37.

CORAL In the shallow parts of the warmer seas of the world are tiny creatures called 'polyps' which are capable of building up a hard substance by taking limy matter from the sea and making a skeleton of it; they are busy all the time eating and building and the shapes they build vary considerably, as do the colours –there are corals coloured pink, yellow, green, purple and blue. A huge coral island may begin as just one little polyp which produces other polyps by budding; they go on breeding and working, and so the coral formations grow. The Great Barrier Reef off the coast of Australia is mostly coral.

COSMIC RAYS are extremely small particles which possess a very great amount of energy for their size. For this reason some of them are able to penetrate through the magnetic field of the earth, and pass deep down into coal mines and lakes. Those that do this are called primary cosmic rays. Most cosmic rays collide with atoms in the upper atmosphere, and new particles are created as a result of these collisions. These are called secondary cosmic rays, and like the primary rays have enough energy to go far into the earth. The presence of these particles is detected in the same way as radioactivity, by means of the GEIGER COUNTER, for cosmic rays have electrical effects during their passage from one place to another just as do other radiations.

COSTA RICA is a small republic in Central America on the peninsula which – except for the Panama Canal – joins Central to South America. It is 19,650 square miles and has a population of about 1½ millions. The capital is San José. Its main products are coffee, bananas and sugar cane; recently cattle raising has been introduced.

COTTON is a soft substance like fine wool. It comes from the white fleecy fibre which nature puts round cotton seeds to keep them warm while they are ripening. The cotton plant belongs to the mallow family and its fruit, called a boll, is nothing more than a very light ball of cotton hairs. The bolls are harvested and then 'ginned'; that is, the cotton fibres are separated from the seeds. Oil is obtained from the seeds and used in the making of such things as soap.

COYOTE belongs to the WOLF family and is found in North America. It lives mainly on small animals and is known to attack sheep and for this reason is widely hunted. It is also known as the 'prairie wolf' and 'brush wolf'.

COYPU is very much like a small beaver, with webbed feet but a rat-like tail. It is found in many parts of South America. An adult coypu is about 2 feet long with a 12-inch tail. The fur is used as a substitute for beaver fur and is called 'nutria'. The coypu is also known as a 'beaver' rat.

The coyote is a close relative of the wolf

King Richard I fought in the Third Crusade

CRABS AND LOBSTER See CRUSTACEANS

CROWN JEWELS include the regalia used at the coronation of England's kings and queens and comprise many beautiful and priceless jewels which are lodged in the Tower of London for safety. They are housed in a special case in the Wakefield Tower or Jewel House. After the execution of Charles I the royal ornaments and part of the regalia were sold or melted down by order of Cromwell, but when the House of Stuart was restored with the restoration of Charles II (1660-85) the missing pieces were replaced by copies. The Imperial State Crown, containing 2,783 diamonds together with pearls, sapphires, emeralds and rubies, was especially made for the coronation of Queen Victoria in 1838. The royal sceptre holds the great diamond known as the Star of Africa, with 74 facets, cut from the Cullinan diamond; the collection also contains the famous Koh-i-Noor diamond, five jewelled swords, the Black Prince's ruby (worn by Henry V on his helmet at Agincourt), silver trumpets and other pieces.

CRUSADES In the eleventh century Palestine, or the Holy Land, was invaded by the Turks. Pilgrims to Jerusalem were harshly treated and the Christian nations of Europe decided to raise armies to drive the Turks away. These military expeditions under the banner of the cross were called crusades, and those who took part in them crusaders. Altogether nine crusades took place during nearly two centuries, from 1095 to 1271; only the first, under Godfrey of Bouillon, can be said to have been successful, for it captured Jerusalem, which was made the capital of a small Christian kingdom. But the Turks under their famous commander Saladin won Jerusalem back in 1187 and subsequent crusades (the most notable being that led by England's King Richard I) failed to accomplish anything, and Jerusalem remained in Turkish or Arab hands until the First World War when the British captured it in 1917. Millions of lives were lost during the crusades.

CRUSTACEANS are creatures without backbones but with jointed legs. The best known are the lobsters, crabs, crayfish and shrimps. Lobsters have long bodies with extremely long feelers and fan-shaped tails. Crabs are much rounder, have eyes on movable stalks and five pairs of legs, the front pair usually being grasping claws. Nearly all crustaceans live in water, but there are a few crabs who live on day land.

CRYSTALS All substances are made up of atoms, and these are usually arranged in groups called molecules. The atoms and molecules are rather like building bricks. Sometimes the bricks are all higgledy-piggledy, but in others they are stacked in a heap of flour are not arranged in like building bricks. Sometimes the bricks are all higgledy-piggledy, but in others they are stacked neatly in rows. The molecules of starch in a heap of flour are not arranged in any regular order at all and are like the rough pile of bricks, but the molecules in a sparkling lump of rock salt or sugar are all stacked in neat rows like bricks in a wall. Any substance in which the atoms and molecules are neatly arranged in this way is called a crystal. Most precious stones, including the diamond, are crystals.

CUBA is an island, 44,178 square miles, in the Caribbean with a population of about 8 millions. The capital is Havana. Its chief products are sugar and tobacco. The island was discovered by Christopher COLUMBUS in 1492.

CYCLOTRON is a machine used in studying the properties of atoms by smashing them. It is not easy to break atoms, and the only known method is to bombard them with very fast

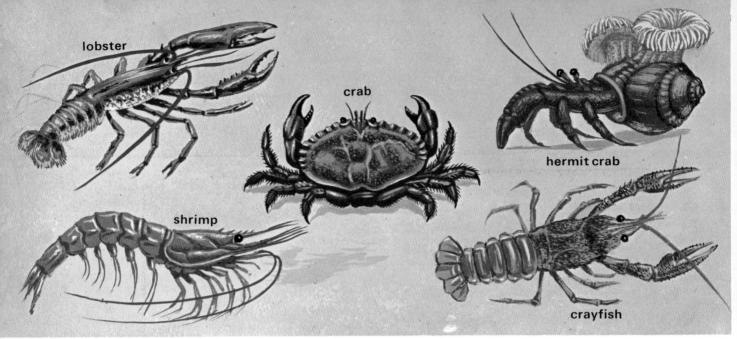

labster

crab

hermit crab

shrimp

crayfish

Various kinds of crustaceans; that is, creatures without backbones, see page 39

particles of their own size or smaller. In an ordinary cyclotron the particles used are protons, deuterons and alpha-particles. They are fired at the atoms they are required to smash like bullets from a machine-gun, only their speed must be very much greater. The particles are forced along between metal plates charged with electricity, but to get up sufficient speed they have to travel a very long way. The metal plates are therefore placed between the poles of a powerful magnet, which makes the particles travel in a circle. As they go faster, the circle widens, so they gradually move outwards from the centre, going round and round in a spiral. When they get to the edge they fly off and hit the atomic target.

CYPRUS is a large island in the Mediterranean of 3,572 square miles with a population of over half a million. Rather more than three-quarters of these are Greek-speaking and Christians, the others being Turkish-speaking and Moslems. The capital is Nicosia.

CZECHOSLOVAKIA is a republic, 53,700 square miles, with nearly 14 million inhabitants. The people speak a Slavonic language related to Russian. About half of them are farmers and the rest are employed in industry. The country is famous for its glass and china. The capital is Prague in the province of Bohemia and another important city is Brno, a big industrial centre.

Seven crystal forms and (below centre) the arrangements of atoms in a crystal of salt

Diagram showing the main parts of a cyclotron. Note the spiral path of the particles

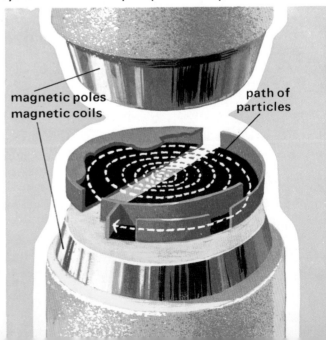

magnetic poles
magnetic coils

path of particles

D

DAHOMEY is a republic in West Africa with an area of about 47,000 square miles and a population of over 2½ millions. The capital is Porto Novo and the main exports are palm products, ground nuts and coffee.

DEER is the name given to those animals that grow antlers (males). These are solid and not hollow as are the horns of antelopes. They usually live in wooded or forested areas and are found in many regions of the world. Among the best-known deer are the fallow deer, red deer, moose, caribou or reindeer and musk deer.

DENMARK is a small kingdom in North Europe and is one of the Scandinavian countries. It is 16,608 square miles in area and has a little over 4½ million inhabitants. The capital is Copenhagen. The country is famous for its dairy produce.

DESERTS are hot, dry regions where little or no vegetation grows and which are rarely inhabited by man or animals. The largest desert in the world is the Sahara in North Africa; it is about 3,250,000 square miles in area. Others are Gobi (Mongolia), Great Arabian (Arabia), Great Australian (Western Australia), Kalahari (South Africa), Atacama (South America), Mohave (U.S.A.) and Thar (India).

DETERGENTS are substances used for cleaning. The word detergent come from the Latin *tergeo,* to wipe. Soap has been in use for more than 2,000 years and is the oldest detergent known, but it cannot be used for every type of cleaning operation because the fats in it can be affected by acids. So chemists have evolved many detergents which are mixtures of various chemicals, each one doing one part of the cleaning job; the chemicals are generally mixed in a mineral (petroleum) oil; these detergents do not use fats, are not affected by acids and can be used in hard or soft water.

DEW consists of waterdrops. When the sun goes down at the end of the day, the temperature drops and the moisture or water vapour in the atmosphere condenses (becomes concentrated) and is deposited in little drops on cool surfaces. When the temperature falls to freezing point, any dew that has fallen may freeze and so we have what is called 'hoar frost'.

DIAMOND is a precious stone in the form of a crystal. It is found principally in South Africa, South America, India and the U.S.S.R. The weight of a diamond is measured in carats. In addition to being used for making beautiful jewellery, diamonds are used in industry. During recent years, scientists have succeeded in

Some people, called nomads, live in deserts. They wander from waterhole to waterhole, their goats and camels feeding on whatever food they can find

making very small diamonds, and it is these which are used in industry. The largest diamond ever found was the Cullinan, named after the chairman of the company who owned the mine where it was found. The stone originally weighed over 1½ lb.; from it was cut the stone known as the Star of Africa, now in the royal sceptre among the British CROWN JEWELS.

DIGESTIVE SYSTEM is that part of the body where food is digested. When food is eaten it is first chewed and passed to the stomach where it is mixed with gastric juices. From here it passes to the small intestine where digestion is completed. The nourishing parts pass to the blood stream and the unwanted parts to waste.

DINGO is a wolf-like wild dog found in Australia. It is about 4 feet long, including its bushy tail and 2 feet at the shoulder. It is a savage hunter and is killed on sight by sheep farmers.

DINOSAURS were giant reptiles that lived about 150 million years ago. There were many different types of dinosaur, ranging in size from about 1ft to 100 feet. Some were plant eaters but some were flesh eaters, especially the terrible Tyrannosaurus, see drawing. The reason why these fantastic animals died out has not yet been explained, but it may well be that they were too big and small brained to adapt themselves to a rapidly changing earth.

DODO was a flightless bird which became extinct about the end of the seventeenth century. It lived on the islands of Mauritius and Réunion in the Indian Ocean.

DOGS have lived with man for a very long time; in fact, it is almost certain that the dog was the first wild animal to be tamed by man. There are many different breeds of dog, each type being originally bred to do special kinds of work. The bulldog with its thick neck and strong jaws was originally bred for baiting bulls. With the exception of sheepdogs, sporting dogs and guard dogs, most are now bred as pets.

DOLPHIN is an air-breathing mammal and not a fish. They are found in most seas of the world and average about 7 feet in length. A

Reconstruction of various dinosaurs, both flesh- and plant-eating

Dogs first bred for various kinds of work but now mainly kept as pets

dolphin has beak-like jaws with many sharp teeth and feeds mainly on small fish.

DOMESDAY BOOK is the name that was given to the survey of England ordered by William the Conqueror, and was so called as it was thought by the people that never again would another such survey be made until the Day of Judgement. It was compiled in 1086, twenty years after the Battle of Hastings, because the Conqueror wanted to know in precise detail what the value was of every piece of farmland and pasture in the country, the numbers of all livestock and who owned them, and so find out how much in tax was due to him as king. The Book is preserved in the Public Record Office in London.

DOMINICAN REPUBLIC is an independent country on the island of Hispaniola in the West Indies. It shares the island with the republic of HAITI. It is 19,322 square miles in area and has a population of 4 millions. The capital is Santo Domingo, for a time called Ciudad Trujillo. It is an agricultural country growing mainly sugar cane, tobacco and coffee.

DORMOUSE is about the same size as an ordinary house mouse but has a furry tail. It is found in hedges and the like and feeds on nuts, especially acorns. In cold regions a dormouse fattens itself up and sleeps through winter.

DREDGER is a special kind of ship used for

The digestive system

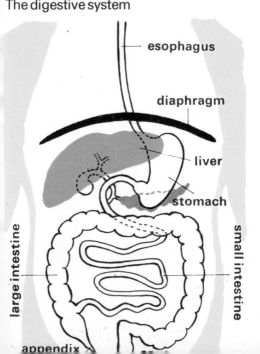

The extinct dodo

A dredger at work

removing mud from rivers, canals and harbours. One type consists of an endless chain of buckets which scoop up the mud and deposit it in a 'hopper' from which it is loaded into a barge and taken away. Another type is the suction dredger which removes the mud by sucking it up a long pipe.

DRUIDS were Celtic priests who held great power in Britain, Ireland and France. Not only did they control the religious life of the Celts but were also law officers and legislators, judges and teachers. The Druids held the oak tree to be sacred and their religious ceremonies usually took place among groves of oak trees.

DUGONG is an air-breathing mammal, like the dolphin, and found in the Indian Ocean and waters off East Africa, Indonesia and Australia. It averages about 8 feet and feeds on sea-weeds.

DUIKER is an antelope-like creature found in South and Central Africa. It lives mainly in wooded and forested areas and feeds on plants, insects and other small animals. The word duiker is the Dutch word for 'diver' and this animal is so named because of its habit of diving for cover when approached.

EAGLE is a bird of prey and belongs to the same family as the buzzard, vulture and harrier. It is a powerful and skilled flyer with a strong beak for tearing flesh. It is found in most parts of the world. Eagles feed on smallish mammals and birds.

EAR is the organ of hearing and has three parts: the external, middle and internal ear. Running from the outer ear is a passage at the end of which is the eardrum –a tightly stretched membrane over the whole passage. When sounds reach the drum it vibrates and these vibrations are passed on to 3 small bones and

from them to another membrane in the inner ear which is shaped like a spiral shell. From there the sounds are transmitted to the brain by the nerves. The inner ear also controls our sense of balance and position.

EARTH is a ball of rock and metal with an equatorial diameter of about 7,926 miles and a polar diameter of about 7,900 miles. Though its origin is not exactly known it was probably once in a molten condition. While in this liquid state the heavy materials were able to sink to the bottom and the light ones float to the top. This is why the earth now has a heavy core of iron and nickel, covered by a thick layer of rocks, the lightest ones being found on or near the surface. The layer of rocks, which is a few thousand miles thick, is called the lithosphere, and most of it is covered by a thin layer of water called the hydrosphere. Above this come the gases of the ATMOSPHERE. Dry land covers approximately 57,469,900 square miles and water about 139,480,800 square miles. The atmosphere extends at its farthest reaches some 900 miles above the earth's surface.

The rocks on the surface of the earth have for millions of years been washed by the sea and exposed to the weather. Some have dissolved in the water, others have been cracked by frost or broken up by the pounding of the waves along the shore. The fragments have then been washed out to sea to settle on the bottom, where they have been hardened again to form a new kind of rock. Rocks formed in this way from sediments are called 'sedimentary' rocks, and examples are sandstone and chalk. The rocks that simply cooled from the molten state are called 'igneous' rocks, and they include such hard rocks as granite.

The earth has never got quite cold, and deep underground it is still so hot that sometimes the rocks become molten again. Then the rocks on the surface are liable to sink in at certain places, or get pushed up in others, and the sedimentary rocks may come up from the bottom of the sea to form dry land. This exposes them to the weather again, and the rivers which now flow over them carve the new surface into the mountains and the valleys that we call 'scenery'; in fact, the shape of the earth is constantly changing.

EARTHQUAKE is a movement in the earth's crust and is caused by rocks moving or slipping deep underground. Earthquakes can also be caused by the eruption of a volcano. It has been estimated that each year there are about 500,000 disturbances in the earth's crust which could all really be called earthquakes, though of course only a fraction of these cause any serious damage or great loss of life.

EASTER ISLAND is a small island, under 50 square miles in area, in the South Pacific 2,300 miles west of the coast of Chile, by whom it is owned. The island has become widely known because of its 'mystery statues' — great stones, shaped in grotesque likenesses of human heads, varying in height from 6 to 37 feet. Experts believe they were carved by the remote ancestors of the present Polynesian inhabitants, but their origin and purpose have never been fully explained.

ECHIDNA is an egg-laying animal found only in Australasia. Its body is covered with spines mingling with long hairs. It is about 18 inches long. Echidnas are very timid creatures and can burrow rapidly into the earth with spade like claws when threatened. It feeds on ants and termites which it licks up with its tongue; it has no teeth. The echidna is also known as the 'spiny anteater'.

ECLIPSE in astronomy is when the moon hides the sun by getting in front of it, or when the moon is hidden in the earth's shadow, see diagram. During a total eclipse the sun's outer rim can be examined by astronomers, especially the solar flares which leap far above the sun's surface.

ECUADOR is a republic in South America of 225,000 square miles and a population of over 5¼ millions of which about a third are descendants of the INCAS. The capital is Quito and the chief river the Upper Amazon. The famous Galapagos Islands belong to Ecuador.

EEL is a snake-like creature found in salt and fresh water all over the world. They range in size from the common eel of about 18 inches to the conger and moray eels of 10 feet and over.

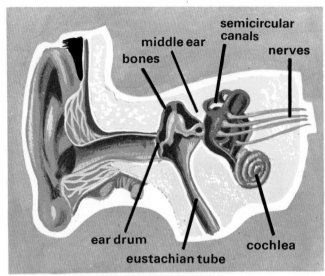

Diagram of the various parts of the ear

Picture showing the progress of an eclipse

The Australian echidna or spiny anteater

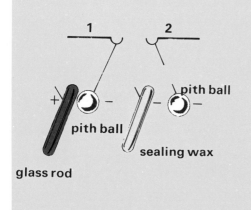

1 pith ball attracted to rod when rubbed with silk

1   2

+ pith ball –   – pith ball –

pith ball

glass rod   sealing wax

2 pith ball repelled by rod when rubbed with fur

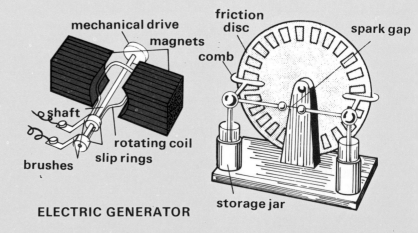

STATIC GENERATOR

mechanical drive

magnets

friction disc   spark gap

comb

shaft

rotating coil

slip rings

brushes

storage jar

ELECTRIC GENERATOR

These drawings show the effect of positive and negative static electricity, an electrostatic generator and a simple electromagnetic generator.

The common eel spawns in a region near the Sargasso Sea in the Atlantic. The young eels or 'elvers' make their way back across the ocean to rivers, streams and ponds, a distance of 3,000 miles and more.

EGYPT is a republic in Northern Africa of 385,000 square miles, mostly desert, and a population of over 34 millions of whom nearly all are Moslems. There are about 1,000,000 inhabitants who belong to the Coptic Church. The capital is Cairo and the chief port Alexandria. The Egyptians are a very ancient people and can trace themselves back to 4241 B.C. Their kings – the pharaohs – built enormous tombs for themselves in the form of pyramids as well as many beautiful statues and temples. Egypt has always been very important—it was the granary of the Roman Empire which Cleopatra (the last Queen of Egypt) used in her attempts to regain control of her kingdom. More recently the Suez Canal has provided a short cut from Europe to the East until it was closed as a result of the war with Israel.

One of the longest rivers in the world—the Nile, in Egypt—flows into the Mediterranean, and much of Egypt's former prosperity came from the immense fertility of the soil which was the result of its annual flooding. In recent years the Aswan Dam has been built to harness the power of the Nile for generating electricity and irrigation of the land.

EIFFEL TOWER is the famous tower in Paris, designed and erected for the Paris exhibition of 1889 by Gustave Eiffel and named after him. It is 984 feet high and built of iron, and has served as both a wireless telegraphy station and a weather-forecasting centre.

ELAND belongs to the cattle family and found in Africa. It has spirally twisted horns like a gimlet. There are two species, the common eland and Lord Derby's eland. The eland is closely related to oxen and can stand as much as 6 feet at the shoulders. It has a heavy dewlap and humped shoulders. Both males and females have horns.

ELECTRICITY is a stream of tiny particles usually known as ELECTRONS. An electric current is a stream of electrons flowing from a negative charge (where there are too many electrons) to a positive charge (where there are too few electrons). The force with which they flow is called the 'voltage', the unit being the volt, and the quantity that flows is called 'amperage', the unit being the ampere.

The Greeks knew of electricity and its name comes from their word for AMBER, but they did not consider it of any real use. It was not until the 16th century that people began to study it scientifically. It was discovered early on that metal was the best way to conduct electricity from the negative to the positive poles. Also that certain materials such as glass, amber and rubber prevented that flow, (these are known as 'insulators'). However it was not until 1840 that electricity was used for power and light; it was not very effective as a source of light until the 1880's, when the modern bulb was invented.

ELECTRON is an atomic particle which carries a negative charge. They exist in all atoms and are like little moons revolving round the centre or nucleus. They were discovered in 1897 by Sir J. J. Thomson. Some radioactive substances, like radium, shoot off electrons which are called 'beta' rays.

ELECTRONICS is the name given to the branch of science which deals with the movement of electrons in space. In the article on ELECTRI-CITY it was explained how an electric current was formed by electrons moving in a metal conductor. Electrons can also move freely in space; for example, in a T.V. set the image on the screen is formed by electrons striking it after passing through a tube from which all the air has been expelled. Another instrument, very much like a T.V. tube, in which electrons move freely is a 'cathode-ray tube', and is one of the most important instruments in modern science. In recent years electronics has been greatly improved by the invention of the transistor, a small device which has replaced the old-fashioned valve or tube.

ELECTRON MICROSCOPE is a type of microscope in which the object to be viewed is exposed to a beam of electrons; in the ordinary microscope the object is exposed to a beam of light rays. In an electron microscope the beam of electrons is focused by means of magnetic lenses (see diagram). The magnified object cannot be seen directly by the eye, but is made visible by means of a 'fluorescent' screen very similar to that used in a T.V. tube. Photographs can be taken by allowing the beam of electrons to fall on a photographic plate. The electron microscope is very important as it enables objects to be seen which are too small for the ordinary microscope. For example, our knowledge of how to cure many diseases is a result of the electron microscope.

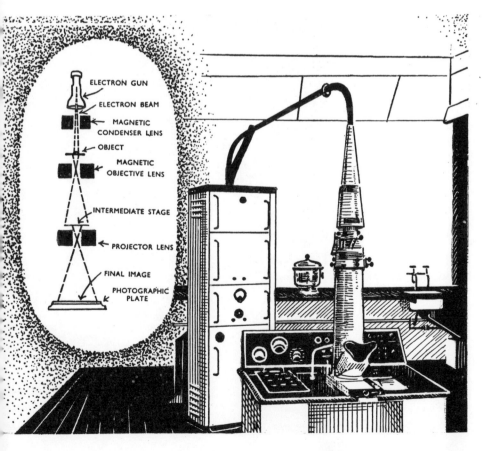

An electron microscope of the type used in science and industry. The cut-out shows the positions of the magnetic lenses and path of electron beam

ELECTRON GUN
ELECTRON BEAM
MAGNETIC CONDENSER LENS
OBJECT
MAGNETIC OBJECTIVE LENS
INTERMEDIATE STAGE
PROJECTOR LENS
FINAL IMAGE
PHOTOGRAPHIC PLATE

ELEMENT In chemistry it is a substance which cannot be reduced to a simpler form. For example, water is made up of two ingredients, hydrogen and oxygen, but chemically hydrogen cannot be composed of any simpler substances; the same applies to oxygen. They are, in fact, what are known as elements, and in nature there are ninety-two. In recent years man has added several more new elements by bombarding RADIOACTIVE SUBSTANCES.

ELEPHANT The most striking thing about the elephant is its tremendous size and very long nose, or trunk. There are two kinds of elephant: one live in Africa and the other in India. The African elephant can be easily recognized by its enormous ears. Both kinds live in herds and feed on fruit, shoots, bark and leaves which they pick by means of their trunks and place in their mouths. The tusks are usually longer in the African elephant than the Indian, and it is for these that it is often hunted. Both types of elephant can be tamed, and some are trained for doing heavy work such as forest-clearing. In India the elephant played an important part in many religious processions.

ELGIN MARBLES are pieces of sculpture which once adorned the Parthenon temple in Athens; they consist of whole figures, reliefs and part of a frieze, and may now be seen in the British Museum, London. They were removed from Greece in 1812 by the Earl of Elgin because at that time the ancient buildings on the Acropolis at Athens were falling into decay. All the pieces are the work of the great sculptor of ancient Greece, Pheidias.

ELK is by far the largest member of the deer family found in North America and Asia, but is now rare in Europe. It has very long legs, a short neck and body, large erect antlers, is coloured brown and feeds on leaves, twigs, mosses, water plants, etc. It is very fond of the water and often spends long periods in rivers or lakes during hot weather.

EMU is the second largest bird on earth and found only in Australia, whose emblem it is. Emus are flightless and grow to a height of about 5 feet. They live in small flocks in open grassland. The female lays 7 to 12 eggs, but it is the

The elk is the giant of the deer family and found today mainly in North America and Asia. It is very rare in Europe.

An equinox occurs when the length of day and night are equal. This happens twice a year. About March 21 in the spring or vernal equinox and September 23 the autumn equinox

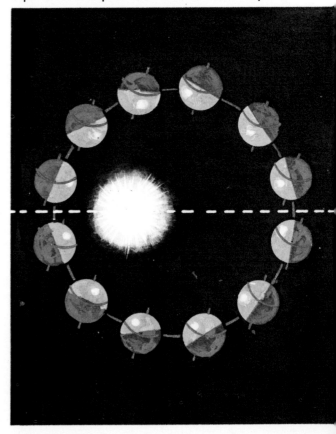

male who sits on the eggs and looks after the young.

ENGLAND is the southern and larger part of the island of GREAT BRITAIN. Its nearest point to the Continent is Dover where the distance across the English Channel is 21 miles. Its greatest length is from Berwick, Northumberland, to the Lizard, Cornwall, which is 425 miles. In England more people are crowded into a smaller space than is the case almost anywhere else in Europe. There are rather more than 44 million people in England. Out of every hundred about eighty live and work in towns.

London, the chief city, is the third largest city in the world and with New York and Rotterdam is one of the three largest ports in the world. It has a population of nearly 8 millions. The River Thames, on which London stands, is the longest river in England and the most important. Birmingham, the second largest city, is famous for its many industries and Coventry nearby is the centre of the car industry. Manchester is the chief commercial city in the north. Liverpool and Southampton are two of the chief shipping ports.

EQUINOX When the sun is on the equator the length of day and night are equal and it is called an equinox. This happens twice a year, the first about March 21 and called the 'vernal or spring' equinox, and the second about September 23 and called the 'autumnal or autumn' equinox.

ESCALATOR is a type of moving stairway used for carrying passengers to and from underground railways, and also in large stores for carrying people from one floor to another. The speed of an escalator depends on how many people have to be carried. Some escalators can carry more than 10,000 persons an hour.

ESKIMOES are people closely related to the North American Indians; they live in the Arctic regions of the world—northern Canada, Alaska, and Greenland. They live mainly by hunting animals such as reindeer, seal, whale, etc. The flesh of these animals is eaten and the skins used for making clothes, tents, boats and many other things which the Eskimo needs. During the winter, Eskimoes live in snow houses called

'igloos', and travel on sledges pulled by Eskimo dogs or 'huskies'. In the summer, Eskimoes live in tents or huts, and when near the sea they travel and hunt seals in KAYAKS, one-man canoes skilfully made from skins.

ETHIOPIA is an empire in Eastern Africa with a seaboard on the Red Sea. It has an area of about 400,000 square miles and population of about 25 millions. The capital is Addis Ababa. The country is agricultural and very mountainous.

EVERGLADES This is the name given to the vast expanse of overgrown marshland in the almost completely flat State of Florida in the U.S.A. It is rich in animal life, especially birds and reptiles.

EXPLORATION From the very earliest times man has been an explorer. Proof of this is the journey of early man from Asia across what is now the Bering Strait to America. The period of great exploration occurred in the fifteenth and sixteenth centuries when Europeans sailed and charted the oceans and continents.

The Table below, although not complete, may help to show something of the story of man's adventure in exploration.

GREAT EXPLORERS AND DISCOVERERS

DATE	NAME	NATION-ALITY	PART OF WORLD
about 500 B.C.	Hanno	Carthaginian	West coast of Africa
985 A.D.	Eric the Red	Norwegian	Greenland
1000	Leif Ericsson	Norwegian	Labrador
1272	Marco Polo	Italian	Far East
1325	Friar Odoric	Italian	Tibet
1484	Diogo Cao	Portuguese	River Congo (Africa)
1488	Bartholomew Diaz	Portuguese	Cape of Good Hope (Africa)
1492	Columbus	Italian	Watling Island and Cuba
1493	Columbus	Italian	West Indies
1497	John Cabot	Italian	North America
1498	Vasco da Gama	Portuguese	India (round Cape of Good Hope)
1500	Pedro Al Cabral	Portuguese	Brazil (South America)
1513	Vasco Núñez de Balboa	Spaniard	Pacific Ocean
1519	Hernando Cortes	Spaniard	Mexico (Central America)
1526	Jorge de Menezes	Portuguese	New Guinea
1527	Francisco Pizarro	Spaniard	Peru (South America)
1541	Francisco de Orellana	Spaniard	River Amazon (South America)

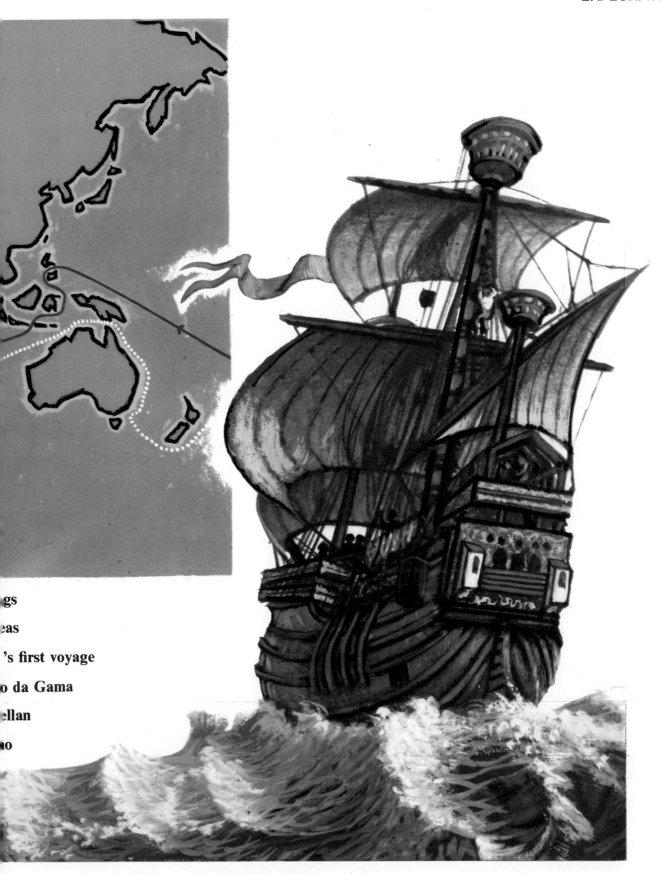

gs

eas

's first voyage

o da Gama

ellan

no

DATE	NAME	NATION-ALITY	PART OF WORLD
1549	St. Francis Xavier	Spaniard	Japan
1596	W. Barents and J. Heemskerk	Dutch	Spitsbergen
1615	W. C. Schouten	Dutch	Cape Horn (South America)
1642	Abel Tasman	Dutch	Tasmania and New Zealand
1762	Karsten Niebuhr	German	Arabia
1768-71	Capt. J. Cook	British	New Zealand and Australia
1795	Mungo Park	British	River Gambia and Niger (Africa)
1822-23	Oudney, Denham and Clapperton	British	Sahara Desert (north Africa)
1828	Capt. C. Sturt	British	Interior of Australia
1851-55	David Livingstone	British	River Zambesi and Victoria Falls (Africa)
1852-55	Heinrich Barth	German	Sudan (North Africa)
1870-73	Przhevalski	Russian	Mongolia
1890-1908	Sven Hedin	Swedish	Central Asia
1909	R. E. Peary	American	North Pole
1911	Roald Amundsen	Norwegian	South Pole
1957	Sir V. Fuchs and party	British	Explored and mapped Antarctic

EYE is the organ of sight, and enables us to observe the world about us. When rays of light from an object reach the eye they pass first through the 'cornea', a transparent membrane in the middle of the eye. Immediately behind this is a chamber containing transparent fluid, and behind this the 'iris', which is the part that gives colour to the eye. The hole in the middle of the iris is the 'pupil'. Next is the lens which has the power of changing its shape to enable light rays to be focused clearly on the 'retina' at the back of the eye. On the retina a small image is produced of the object being viewed. From here messages are sent along the optic nerve to the brain. The blind spot is where the optic nerve enters the eye.

FABLES are stories in which the characters are usually animals but behave and talk as human beings. An important point about a fable is that the story teaches a moral lesson. The most famous writers of fables were Aesop (Greek), La Fontaine (French) and John Gay (British).

FALCONS are birds of prey found throughout the world. They have pointed wings and strong hooked bills. Falcons live on small birds and animals. In the Middle Ages falcons were trained for hunting; the sport was called 'falconry'. The ancient Chinese and Persians also hunted with falcons.

FARMING See **AGRICULTURE**

FERNS are a family of plants which do not flower, and are found throughout the world.

FESTIVALS are days set aside for celebrating

Diagram of the various parts of the eye

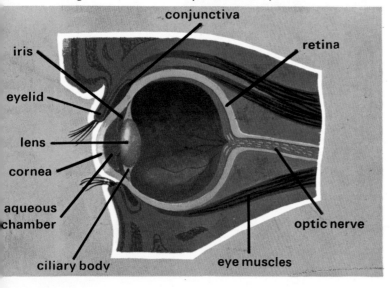

The famous fable of the tortoise and the hare

Peregrine falcon used by hawkers for hunting

Selection of common ferns. Note the wide variety of leaf forms.

a religious event, a great public event, a famous person, etc. Most festivals are of a religious nature and many are also public holidays; for example, Christmas and Easter. Most countries celebrate some form of festival, and many are colourful and exciting. The following are just a few drawn from all over the world.

Sarasvati is a festival to honour the Hindu goddess of wisdom. Children and students play a large part in this festival. It is held early in January.

New Year of the Trees is held in Israel to celebrate the importance of trees in rejuvenating the country. Children parade in special costumes and carry tools used for planting trees. The festival is held late in January.

Lincoln's Birthday is held in the U.S.A. to celebrate the birthday of the great American President, Abraham Lincoln. It is held on February 12.

Butter Festival takes place in Tibet about the middle of February. The interesting things in this festival are the lovely sculptures of Tibetan gods made of coloured butter.

St. Patrick's Day is an Irish festival in honour of St. Patrick, the patron saint of Ireland. There is also a large parade held in New York. It is held on March 17.

Anzac Day commemorates every year the Australian and New Zealand forces that landed at Gallipoli in the First World War on April 25, 1915.

Norwegian Independence Day celebrates the complete independence of Norway from Sweden,

and is a gay public holiday. Held on May 17.

Festival of the Tooth is a religious festival held in Kandy, Ceylon. A tooth of Buddha is paraded with great ceremony through the streets of Kandy. The festival is held early in July and lasts for ten days.

St. Bernadette. This is a pilgrimage to Lourdes in France by people from all over the world to the shrine of the young girl, Bernadette Soubirous. Held between August 16 and 28.

Festival of Light is held in Siam in honour of Buddha. During the ceremony, lamps on little rafts are floated down streams. Held about the middle of October.

Thanksgiving is an important American event held on the last Thursday in November. It celebrates the thanksgiving made by the Pilgrim Fathers for their first harvest in the New World.

Birthday of the Prophet an important Moslem celebration which lasts twelve days in early December.

FEUDAL SYSTEM was a special way in which society was organized during the Middle Ages. It was introduced into England by William the Conqueror and it was really a means of ensuring that the king could raise an army when he needed one. William divided up England between about 170 of his chief followers who thus became powerful landlords; in return for this, these men, who were called 'tenants-in-chief', had to promise to furnish the king with armed soldiers whenever he called upon them to do so. The great barons in turn leased out some of their

flying fish

manta ray

firemouth fish

pompadour fish

angel fish

sunfish

sea horse

eagle ray

lion or scorpion fish

An artist's impression of a typical scene in a market-place of a town in feudal times

land to sub-tenants, who in their turn let it out to peasants or 'villeins'. Each class of society thus owed allegiance to the class above it. The Feudal System really came to an end when it was proved easier to raise an efficient army by hiring troops for pay; this was the beginning of the regular professional army of today.

FIJI ISLANDS are a British Crown Colony that consists of a group of more than 300 islands in the South Pacific, of which 106 are inhabited. The population is over half a million. The capital is Suva on Viti Levu.

FINLAND is a republic in Northern Europe of 130,165 square miles with a population of about $4\frac{3}{4}$ millions. The Finnish language, which is called Suomi, is related to Hungarian and Estonian. The capital is Helsinki. Nearly three-quarters of the country is covered with forest and this fact makes Finland, apart from Russia, the chief timber producing country in Europe. The Aaland Islands in the Baltic Sea belong to Finland.

FIRST-AID is the treatment given to a person immediately after an accident or sudden illness by a person with special training until a doctor or ambulance arrives. Training in first-aid includes understanding the human body and its workings and what to do when any part of it breaks down; it includes knowing what to do if, for instance, someone accidentally cuts a blood vessel or breaks a limb.

FISH are those animals that live entirely in the water. A fish has a long stream-lined body covered with scales, and moves through the water easily by means of its fins and tail. Some of its fins act as keels and some are used for keeping the fish's balance and steering it. It breathes by means of gills, taking in water by opening its mouth, absorbing the oxygen into its blood, and then passing the air out through the gill openings. It should be remembered that WHALES are not fish but MAMMALS as they have to surface to breathe air. There are over twenty-five thousand different kinds of fish in the world.

The largest known fish is the whale shark of the tropics, which grows to a length of 50 feet or more, and weighs several tons. Basking sharks may be up to 40 feet long. The smallest of all fishes is a kind of goby found in the lakes of the island of Luzon in the Philippines. It is only half an inch long, and found in very large numbers.

FLAGS have been used from the earliest times. They are pieces of fabric flown on a staff or halyard as national or local emblems or as naval or military signs. Each country of the world has its distinctive flag, that of Britain being the 'Union Jack', a combination of the flags of St George of England (red cross on white base), St Andrew (white diagonal cross on a blue base), and St Patrick (thin red diagonal cross on a white base). The flag flown at the rear of a ship is called an 'ensign'. The Royal Navy flies a white ensign and the Merchant Navy a red ensign.

FLAGS

ARGENTINA

AUSTRALIA

BELGIUM

CHINA

DENMARK
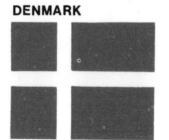

IRELAND
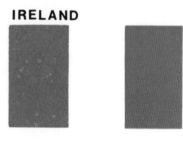

INDIA

ISRAEL

ITALY
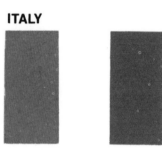

NORWAY
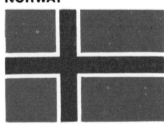

NEW ZEALAND

POLAND

SWITZERLAND

TURKEY

U.S.A.
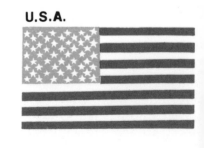

BRAZIL

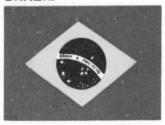

BURMA

CANADA

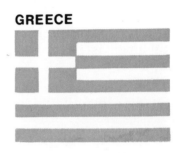

FRANCE

GREAT BRITAIN

GREECE

JAPAN

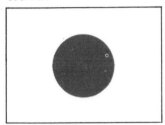

LUXEMBOURG

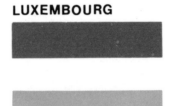

NETHERLANDS

PORTUGAL

SOUTH AFRICA

SWEDEN

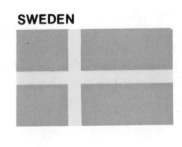

U.S.S.R.

WEST GERMANY

YUGOSLAVIA

FLAMINGO is a wading-bird, and found in Europe, Asia, Africa and Central and South America. It lives in large flocks in shallow lagoons or on the edges of salt lakes, and has beautifully coloured pinkish-white or light scarlet feathers. Its nest is made of mud and is usually built in shallow water. One or two white eggs are laid.

FLAX is a plant which grows to a height of about 16 inches and has a pretty pale-blue flower. Linseed oil is obtained from the seeds, and linen is made from the fibres of the stalk.

FLEA is a wingless, jumping insect which is common in different forms all over the world. It is a parasite, which means that it gets all its nourishment by living on many animals, including man, whose blood it sucks.

FLIES form a large family of insects, of which there are as many as 50,000 different kinds, and are found nearly all over the world. They feed on a large variety of things and spread many diseases. The eggs hatch into tiny, worm-like larvae which will often live on sores, or wounds on human beings or animals.

FLOWERS   See   **PLANTS**

FOLKLORE might be defined as 'learning about people' and in a special sense means studying the stories, legends, superstitions, songs, dances, and so on, of people of long ago, and also the material itself. It applies particularly to the beliefs, etc. of ordinary or country people. Many fairy stories and nursery rhymes as well as many games have their origin in folklore.

FORMOSA, also known as Taiwan, is a mountainous island off the southern coast of China of 13,800 square miles area. The population is about $11\frac{1}{2}$ millions, most of them Chinese. The capital is Taipeh. Formosa's main export is camphor. In the main the country is agricultural but has important fisheries.

FOSSILS are remains of forms of life that lived millions of years ago, preserved in rocks. They may consist of the hard parts of the animals, or simply impressions. The most common fossils are of sea-shells; the largest fossils are

The fox is a swift, alert and cunning animal

The fossil of a brontosaurus, one of the largest dinosaurs. It is from fossil skeletons like this that we can reconstruct exactly how these creatures looked millions of years ago.

A fork-headed tree frog from the tropical forests of Malaya

those of the DINOSAURS, some of which are over 80 feet long.

FOX is closely related to the dog, and is found nearly all over the world. It has a dog-like face, sharp, pointed ears, is covered with thick fur and has a very bushy tail. It is a swift animal, and is very cunning, alert and sharp-witted. It feeds on small animals, birds, eggs and occasionally insects and fruit, according to the country it inhabits. The fur, especially that of the Arctic fox which turns white in winter, is used for making fur wraps, etc.

FRANCE is a republic and the largest country (210,000 square miles) in Europe, except for the Soviet Union. At its greatest length it is 600 miles and its greatest width 540 miles. There are over 50 million people living in France. The capital is Paris on the River Seine. The French language is one of those described as a 'Romance' language. France is the second greatest wine-producing country in the world, especially Burgundy and the area around Bordeaux. France also has many big cities and important industries, and during the years since the war there has been a rapid change from an agricultural to an industrial economy. The chief industrial city is Lyons and the chief port Marseilles, on the Mediterranean.

FRENCH REVOLUTION of 1789-95 took place because of the great poverty that existed in French society and the determination of the leaders of the Revolution to abolish the privileges enjoyed only by aristocrats and the clergy. The motto of the Revolutionaries was 'Liberty, Equality, Fraternity'. Their reasoning was that all men are born equal and should therefore have equal rights. On 14 July 1789 a Paris mob attacked and captured the Bastille, the city's huge, grim prison-fortress; and today is celebrated in France every year as the birthday of French liberty. Many terrible things happened during the French Revolution until at length the extremists were replaced by more moderate men as leaders of the French people, but it may be said that few other events in history have had so much influence on the way of life of present-day.

FRICTION is the force which prevents one surface from freely moving over another surface. In every-day life this force is put to many practical uses; for example, bicycles, motor-cars, locomotives, etc. are brought to rest by the friction between the wheels and brake-blocks. Friction has, of course, many disadvantages, and has to be overcome. One of the best-known ways of doing this is by using oil between the moving surfaces or ball-bearings.

FROG is an amphibian and common over most of the world except for parts of South America, New Zealand and Australia. It feeds on insects and worms, and likes to live in damp, grassy places, spending a lot of time in the water

Europe

ATLANTIC

OCEAN

BAY OF
BISCAY

CAPE FINISTERRE

CAPE ST VINCENT

PORTUGAL

Oporto

Lisbon

Douro

Tagus

SPAIN

Madrid

Guadiana

Sierra Morena

Guadalquivir

Sevilla

Cadiz

Malaga Mulhacen
11420 Murcia

Sa. Nevada

Valencia

BALEARIC
ISLANDS

Cantabrian

Alta Mira

Bilbao

Mnts

Pyrenees

Maladetta
11168

Saragossa

Barcelona

Ebro

Garonne

Nantes

Bordeaux

Lascaux

FRANCE

Loire

Paris

Seine

Massif
Central

Toulouse

Cévennes

Rhône

Lyon
Mt Blanc
15782

Vosges

Jura

Black Forest

Rhine

Geneva

Zürich

Bern

A l p s

Milan

Turin

Po

Venice

Marseilles

ITALY

Florence

A
p
p
e
n
n
i
n
e
s

Rome

Naples

Pompei

CORSICA

SARDINIA

TYRRHENIAN
SEA

Tiber

FAEROE
ISLANDS

NORWEGIAN
SEA

TRONDHE

Jostedals Bre

Galdhöpiggen
8097

SOGNE F

HARDANGER F

Bergen

NORWAY

Oslo

Göteborg

L Väne

SW

Sto

IRELAND

UNITED

KINGDOM

NORTH

SEA

Amsterdam

Brussels

4

3

5

G E R M A N Y

Neanderthal

Bonn

Frankfurt

Hamburg

Elbe

Berlin

Leipzig

Prague

Bohemian
Forest

Moravian
Heights

Munich

7

Innsbruck

Vienna

AUSTRIA

6

Bern

Drava

9

Budapest

Plain of
Hung

DENMARK

Copenhagen

BALTI

Gdan

POL

Wroclav

CZECHOSLOVA

Tatra
8737

Zagreb

Drava

Sava

Danube

Tisza

Belgrade

YUGOSLAVIA

Dubrovnik

Dinaric Alps

ADRIATIC
SEA

Tiranë

10

Pindus Mnts

G
R

IONIAN
SEA

Palermo

Etna
10741

SICILY

MALTA

M E D I T E R R A N E A N

SEA

8

2

1

NORTH CAPE

BARENTS

SEA

Lapland

KANIN
PENINSULA

nekaise
1965

KOLA
PENINSULA

WHITE SEA

U r a l

M o u n t a i n s

OF BOTHNIA

FINLAND

L Onega

L Ladoga

European

Plain

Helsinki

GULF OF FINLAND

Leningrad

Tallinn

ESTONIA

European

Riga

ATVIA

Volga

S O C I A L I S T

R E P U B L I C S

JANIA

Vilnius

Moscow

Minsk

BYELORUSSIA

Central

Volga Heights

Pripet
Marshes

Pripet

Russian

U N I O N   O F   S O V I E T

Desna

Uplands

Kiev

UKRAINE

Volga

MOLDAVIA

Kishinev

Dnieper

SEA OF
AZOV

Crimea

Caucasus

CASPIAN

BLACK   SEA

Elbrus 18480

GEORGIA

Mountains

ARIA

Tbilisi

stanbul

BOSPHORUS

AZERBAIJAN

Yerevan

ns

ARMENIA

Ankara

Sakaria

Mt Ararat
12945

SEA

U

Kizil Irmak

L Tuz

Erciyas
12850

R

K

E

Y

L Van

Euphrates

Toros Mnts

CYPRUS

1	:	GIBRALTAR
2	:	ANDORRA
3	:	BELGIUM
4	:	NETHERLANDS
5	:	LUXEMBOURG
6	:	SWITZERLAND
7	:	LIECHTENSTEIN
8	:	MONACO
9	:	HUNGARY
10	:	ALBANIA

when the weather is hot. There are some kinds of frog which live their lives in trees and known as tree frogs. In the winter it often hibernates at the bottom of ponds. It lays many eggs which are surrounded with a sort of jelly and called 'frogspawn'. These eggs hatch into minute creatures called 'tadpoles' which have a rounded, legless body and a fish-like tail. Eventually the tadpole grows legs, its tail disappears and it becomes a fully-grown frog.

FUNGUS is a plant that does not flower. It lives either on decayed vegetable matter, and called a 'saprophyte', or on living matter, and called a 'parasite'. Fungi (the plural of fungus) rank very low in the plant kingdom, and include moulds, yeasts, rusts, toadstools, mushrooms, etc. Although some kinds of fungi can be eaten, many are very poisonous. Fungi can cause great damage, for example, dry-rot; others are very useful. Perhaps the most useful is the fungus 'penicillin' from which the wonderful drug of that name is obtained.

FUSE is a special kind of wire connected in an electric circuit to act as a safety device. The size of the wire is such that it fuses, that is, breaks down, when the electric current flowing through it is greater than considered safe for the circuit.

GALVANOMETER is a very delicate electrical instrument for detecting and measuring electric currents. A simplified diagram of a galvanometer is shown opposite.

GAMBIA is a narrow strip of land on either side of the River Gambia, and a member of the Commonwealth. It has an approximate area of 4,000 square miles and a population of about 375,000. The capital is Bathurst. The main export is ground-nuts.

GAS In science this word means the state of matter which has no definite shape; that

A selection of fungi found in woods and fields. All are poisonous and must not be eaten.

The gecko belongs to the lizard family

A diagram of a simple galvanometer

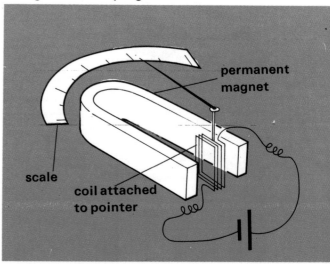

permanent magnet

scale

coil attached to pointer

s, distinct from the other two states of matter, liquid and solid. In ordinary life 'gas' usually means 'coal gas' which is used for heating and cooking. It is obtained by heating coal to a temperature of about 1,000 deg. C., and stored in large tanks called gasometers.

GAUR, sometimes called the 'Indian bison', is one of the largest of the wild cattle and found in the forests of India. It has broad, upturned horns with black tips. The gaur is a vegetable eater, and a quiet animal, except when it is wounded when it is capable of dangerous charges—as many hunters have learnt to their peril.

GAZELLES A group of small delicate ANTE-LOPES of Africa and South Asia. Their natural home is treeless plains and hot deserts, and their sandy brown hides make them inconspicuous in such surroundings. They are notable for their incredible speed and leaps. Gazelles have ringed horns which sweep back into a lyre shape.

GECKO is one of a large family of LIZARDS. Geckos live in trees, houses, in the ground and on the ground, and are insect-eating reptiles active at night. Some—not all—have adhesive pads on their toes which enable them to run up and down walls and over ceilings. Geckos are tropical animals being very common in the Far East.

GEIGER COUNTER is an instrument for detecting and counting atomic particles and radiations. It is one of the most important instruments used in atomic science, and is essential for finding minerals containing radioactive substances.

GEMS are precious and semi-precious stones after they have been cut and polished for ornamental use.

GEOGRAPHY is the science which describes the surface of the Earth and the way in which the various plants and animals that live on it are dispersed. There are two main divisions of geography: physical geography, which deals with the composition of the surface of the Earth and the way in which its living occupants are distributed; and human geography, which is more concerned with economic, political and

A gaur, one of the largest of the wild cattle

social aspects of the subject. For the purposes of geography, the spherical Earth is divided by horizontal (latitude) lines and vertical (longitude) lines. These enable places to be accurately pinpointed. Climate plays a very important part in the science of geography; for example, a region where there is much sun and little rain is usually desert; much sun and heavy rain, tropical forest; little sun and long periods of cold, arctic wastes. These varying climatic conditions influence not only plant and animal life but also how man lives and what he does. See also the entries under GEOLOGY and METEOROLOGY.

Diagram of a simple geiger counter used for detecting radioactive substances

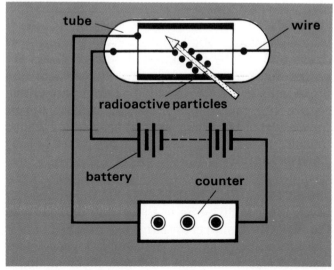

GEOLOGY is the science which studies how the earth came to be formed, how the crust has changed over millions of years, and the materials of which it is composed. Thus a geologist studies rocks, and he describes different kinds of rocks as follows: 'sedimentary' are those composed of mud, sand or lime, because they have been formed mostly out of sediments in the sea; 'aqueous' are those which have been deposited by water; 'stratified', deposited in layers; 'igneous' are those which originally were in a very hot or molten state; and 'metamorphic', which have changed their form by heat or pressure (for instance, slates have been formed from mud, and marble from limestone). See EARTHQUAKE, FOSSIL, VOLCANO.

GERMANY is a large country in Central Europe which since the 2nd World War has been divided into two parts. The German Federal Republic (or Western Germany) has an area of 96,000 square miles and a population of about 59 millions. The capital is Bonn on the River Rhine and other important cities are Hamburg, Frankfurt and Munich. West Berlin also belongs to West Germany although it is completely surrounded by East Germany.

The Democratic Republic of Germany (or East Germany) is Communist and has a smaller area of 41,385 square miles with a population of over 15 millions. The capital is East Berlin and other important cities are Dresden and Leipzig.

GERMS are very small living things consisting of one cell, and usually called 'bacteria'. Although many germs have the power of movement they are considered to belong to the kingdom of plants. Germs are found in millions everywhere, including the human body. Some germs cause and spread dangerous diseases; others are useful, like those which break down waste material into a simple chemical compound which nature rearranges into new materials. Germs have several basic shapes: rod-shaped are called 'bacilli'; those shaped like a ball are called 'cocci'. Germs multiply by simply splitting in two.

GETTYSBURG ADDRESS In the American Civil War (1861-65) a three-day battle was fought at Gettysburg, the capital of Adams County, Pennsylvania, between the Union forces under General Meade and the Confederate forces under General Lee, the latter suffering a disastrous defeat. The battlefield afterwards became a national park with over 400 monuments. In September 1863 the field of Gettysburg was dedicated as a cemetery, and here Abraham Lincoln (1809-65), the first Republican President of the United States, delivered his most famous speech in which he said: 'that this nation, under God, shall have a new birth of freedom—and that government of the people, by the people, for the people, shall not perish from the earth'. The speech at the time did not attract much notice but it has since become celebrated and is known as the 'Gettysburg Address'.

GEYSER is a spring of natural hot water which sometimes gushes out of the earth like a fountain. It is caused by rain water running down through cracks in the earth's crust until it reaches heated rocks; there it boils, generating steam which blows the water above it high into the air. Geysers are found in all volcanic regions of the world but most are found in Iceland, New Zealand and the U.S.A. One of the most famous is 'Old Faithful' (U.S.A.) which gushes a column of hot water to a height of about 170 feet every hour or so, each gush lasting about four minutes and discharging about 12,000 gallons of water.

GHANA is a republic in West Africa, and is a member of the British Commonwealth. Population is about 8½ millions and an area of about 92,000 square miles. The capital is Accra and the country is agricultural.

GIBBON is the smallest member of the ape family. It is a noisy animal and lives in the forests of Malaya, China, Assam and neighbouring regions where it spends most of its time in the tree-tops. It feeds on fruit, leaves, insects, spiders, eggs and sometimes small birds.

GIBRALTAR is a rocky promontory at the southern tip of Spain, 3¾ miles long and ¾ mile wide. The Strait of Gibraltar connects the Mediterranean Sea with the Atlantic Ocean. Gibraltar has a population of over 28,000. It is an important British naval base and has belonged to Britain since 1713.

GILA MONSTER One of the few venomous

A gila monster, a rare and poisonous lizard

A geyser blowing. This is caused by water running down to heated rocks in the earth's interior and steam pressure being generated

A gibbon, one of the most agile monkeys

LIZARDS and found in the desert regions of Arizona and Mexico. A fully grown gila monster can measure up to 24 inches long. It has a yellowish or pinkish skin marked with black bars.

GIRAFFE is the tallest animal in the world. It has a very long neck to enable it to feed on the leaves of the acacia tree, and lives in herds in the open bush country in Africa south of the Sahara desert. Like the camel it can do without water for a long time—even a month! Its only enemy, besides man, is the lion. A close relative of the giraffe is the OKAPI.

GLACIER is a river of ice. High in mountains where great thicknesses of snow gather, the upper layers of snow compress the lower layers which turn into ice. Now, if this ice is resting on a slope it begins slowly to slide, and the weight is so great that a U-shaped valley is ground out. Boulders and stones fall into the glacier and get carried with it. At a point down the mountain slope the ice melts, and the rocks and stones are left in a heap which is called a 'moraine' by geologists.

GLASS is a brittle, transparent substance. Common glass is made by melting together sand, limestone and soda ash. Sand is the main ingredient in all types of glass; and it is the purity of the sand that decides the quality of the glass; for example, fine-quality glass needs the purest possible sand. High-quality glassware is still handblown and decorated, but such things as milk bottles, cheap glasses, etc. are machine-made.

GLIDER is a heavier-than-air machine which is towed into the air and flies—or rather glides—by using the natural air-currents in the atmosphere. During World War II (1939-45), gliders were used for transporting troops and equipment, and one of the most famous exploits in which gliders were used was the Allied raid on Arnhem in the Netherlands on 17 September 1944. The very light type of glider that is used mainly for long-distance soaring is generally called a 'sailplane'.

GNU is a large antelope, sometimes known as the black wildebeest, has horns which project

A gopher or chipmunk is the name of the American ground squirrel. Gophers live in burrows in the earth

sideways instead of forwards. It comes from Central and Southern Africa.

GOAT is a large family of animals found wild in Europe, Africa, Asia and Persia, and is related to the sheep. Our domesticated varieties were descended from the wild goats of Persia and Asia Minor. It has hollow horns which generally curve backwards, and in some species the males have beards. The ibex, markhors and thars belong to the goat family. The Angora and Cashmere goats are valued for their fine, silky hair, others for their milk.

GOLD is a precious metal which from ancient times has been highly valued, especially for ornaments and decorations. It is found in minute quantities throughout the world—even in the sea—and is mined from gold-bearing veins of rocks (called lodes) or from gravel in river beds. The richest gold deposits are in South Africa (Transvaal), America (Rocky Mountains) and the U.S.S.R. (Ural Mountains).

GOPHER or **CHIPMUNK** is the name of the American ground squirrel. They are different from ordinary SQUIRRELS in that they live in burrows in woods and open spaces.

GORILLA is the largest member of the ape family, and lives in the equatorial forests of western Africa. It feeds on fruits and plants, and spends most of the time on the ground, usually only sleeping in trees. Normally it is quite

inoffensive, but if wounded or annoyed it can be a very fierce animal indeed.

GRAMPUS is also known as the 'killer whale'. It feeds on sea-birds, seals, porpoises and fish, and has been known to kill and eat Greenland whales. Its eating capacity can be gauged by the example of one grampus of 21 feet in length which when caught had in its stomach 14 seals and 13 porpoises. See WHALE.

GRAND CANYON In a high plateau of northern Arizona, in the U.S.A., the Colorado River has cut through to form a very deep chasm about 200 miles long and from 4 to 18 miles wide. This great chasm is named the Grand Canyon, and with its treacherous whirlpools and torrents, its gulches and ravines it may be truly said to be an object of awe and wonder. The Grand Canyon was first sighted by white explorers in the second half of the sixteenth century, but the first journey on the Colorado through the Canyon was not made until 1869, by John Wesley Power. The Grand Canyon belongs to the United States national park service. It is a wonderful gorge from the geologist's point of view, for it contains a great number of different rocks.

GRASSES These plants are distributed throughout the world and belong to the family Gramineae. They are easily recognized, but as they lack the well-known parts such as petals and sepals, they are often thought not to be flowering plants. The unfamiliar parts are usually only modifications of more well-known ones in flowering plants. Grasses include sugar cane, wheat, millet, rice, bamboo, rye and barley. Esparto grass is used in the manufacture of high-quality paper.

GRAVITATION Sir Isaac Newton, in pondering over the question of why things always fell towards the earth and why planets followed elliptical paths round the sun, eventually stated the most general law of all physics, one without exception. This law is known as the law of gravitation.

The law states that every body attracts every other body with a force that is directly proportional to the masses of the two bodies and inversely proportional to the square of the distance between them. In fact *every* body attracts *every* other body according to the law of gravitation.

GREAT BARRIER REEF is some 1,200 miles long and is the longest coral reef in the world. It is in the Coral Sea off the coast of Queensland, Australia. It is a wonderland of coral gardens, giant shellfish and beautifully coloured tropical fish.

GREAT BRITAIN is the name given to the chief island of the British Isles. It is made up of the three kingdoms of England, Wales and Scotland. The capital is London on the River Thames in England. It has an area of 87,818 square miles, a greatest lenght of 605 miles and a greatest breadth of 360 miles.

GREECE is a kingdom in south-east Europe about 51,180 square miles and has rather more than 8¾ millions inhabitants. The capital is the ancient city of Athens whose people gave to the world the idea of democracy. The second largest city is Salonika. Among the more famous of the Greek Islands are Rhodes, Crete and Patmos. The Greek people, whose language is descended from that used by the ancient Greeks, are Christians belonging to the Greek Orthodox Church. Most Greeks are peasant farmers who grow and export tobacco and fruit. Currants take their name from the Greek city of Corinth where they were first grown. Greece is also an important seafaring nation.

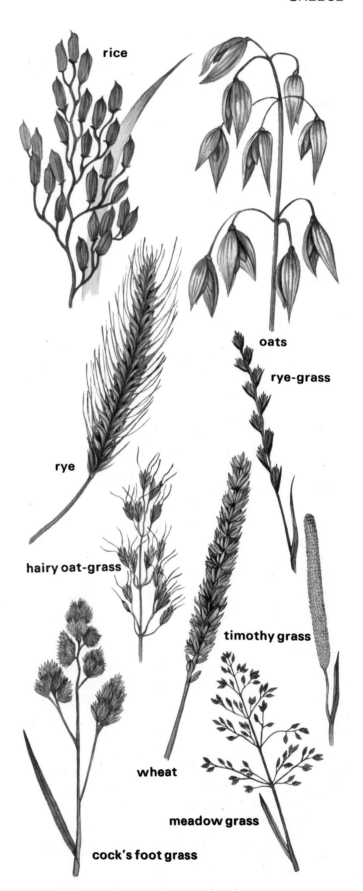

rice

oats

rye-grass

rye

hairy oat-grass

timothy grass

wheat

meadow grass

cock's foot grass

GREENLAND is the largest island in the world except for Australia. It is in the Arctic Ocean and is about 132,000 square miles. Only a small part is ice free and so can be inhabited. There are a little over 34,000 Greenlanders, most of whom are ESKIMOES. Cryolite comes from Greenland and in 1948 important discoveries of lead were made.

GUATEMALA is a republic in Central America which adjoins MEXICO and BRITISH HONDURAS. It has an area of about 42,040 square miles and has about 5 million inhabitants of whom the majority are Indians. The capital is Guatemala City. The country produces coffee, bananas and chewing gum.

GUINEA PIG is the domesticated form of the CAVY. They are rodents, mostly eating grass and have litters two or three times a year. It is said that if you hold them up by the tail, their eyes fall out. In fact they have no visible tail!

GULF STREAM is a warm oceanic current which starts in the Gulf of Mexico, flows through the Straits of Florida, and across the North Atlantic where it slows down to become the North Atlantic Drift. The Gulf Stream is thought to have an important influence on the weather in Britain and other parts of Europe; it warms the seas which wash the coasts of the British Isles, Scandinavia and parts of Iceland, and keeps their harbours free from ice.

GUNPOWDER PLOT was a secret plan to blow up King James I (1603-25) and his parliament. It was organized by some Roman Catholics who were angry at the harsh measures that had been instituted against people of their faith. The aim of the plot was to destroy both King and Parliament on the next day they assembled—5 November 1605. Thirty-six barrels of gunpowder were hidden in the cellars under the Houses of Parliament, and it was the intention that Guy (or Guido) Fawkes should set them off at the appropriate time. The plot was discovered when Francis Tresham warned Lord Monteagle. Guy Fawkes and other ringleaders were caught and executed. Ever since then, on 5th November, bonfires have been lit in which are sometimes burnt stuffed figures (guys), and

fireworks let off in celebration of the fact that the plot failed.

GYROSCOPE is a well-balanced wheel constructed as shown in the diagram for COMPASS. When the wheel spins at a high speed the axis on which it spins tends to remain in a set position no matter how the supporting base is twisted and turned. If the gyroscope is designed in such a way that the spindle points to the true geographic north it can be used as a compass. The gyrocompass used in ships and aircraft is based on this principle. Gyroscopes are also fitted in the lower parts of ships to offset rolling in heavy seas.

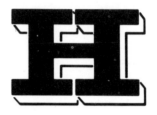

HAIR In human beings hair covers most of the surface of the body, with the exception of the palms of the hands and soles of the feet. It is a form of protection, and there is no doubt that our early ancestors were more hairy than we are today. Most mammals have a covering of hair, and the colder the climate the thicker the coat of hair is.

HAITI is a republic on the island of Hispaniola which it shares with the DOMINICAN REPUBLIC. It is 10,700 square miles with a population of $4\frac{3}{4}$ millions, most of whom are Negroes and French-speaking. The capital is Port-au-Prince. Its chief product is coffee.

HALLOWEEN is celebrated, nowadays more in Scotland and the United States than anywhere else, on 31 October which is the eve of the feast of All Saints. It was once thought that on the night of All Hallows Eve witches, elves and ghosts roamed about. Many games, stories and superstitions are connected with Halloween; it is older than Christianity, having been the eve of the Celtic new year, and in its celebration many pagan and Christian customs have been merged.

HAMSTER is in the same family as the rats and mice, and is found in Central Europe, Asia, Africa, Madagascar and America. It feeds on roots, grain and fruit; and for this reason is treated as a pest by farmers. Hamsters live in groups in burrows which are complete with store rooms and nurseries. It hibernates, or sleeps, during the winter. The golden hamster is a very popular pet.

HARE See **RABBITS AND HARES**

HARP is a very ancient musical instrument. It consists of a triangular-shaped frame with strings running vertically, and is played by plucking the strings with the fingers. The harp is often used in the modern symphony orchestra and is very popular in Wales, Ireland and Mexico.

HARPSICHORD is a musical instrument, rather like a grand piano only smaller. It was much in use in the 17th and 18th centuries. The instrument has a keyboard, and when played, instead of hammers striking strings as in a piano, the strings are plucked by quills. The sound, compared with that of a piano, is rather 'tinny'. Of the many composers who wrote specially for the harpsichord, Bach and Scarlatti are perhaps the best known.

HARTEBEEST is an antelope, and one of the fastest animals in Africa. It has a narrow face, long horns and is from $3\frac{1}{2}$ to 4 feet high.

HAWAII is a chain of islands in the northern Pacific Ocean with a total area of 6,423 square miles. It has a population of 694,000. Its capital is Honolulu and it is the 50th state of the United States of America. Some of the islands are volcanic, while others are formed of coral. One of the volcanoes, Mauna Loa, is the largest volcano in the world and discharges the largest quantity of lava. Pearl Harbour, scene of the famous Japanese attack, is in Hawaii. The chief industries are tourism and agriculture.

HAWK is a European bird of prey, but not related to the eagle or vulture. The most common are the sparrowhawk and goshawk. It lives on small birds, mice, insects, small reptiles, etc.

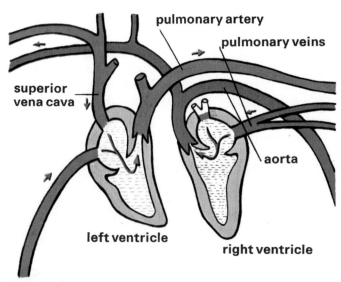

Diagram showing how the blood is pumped by the heart and circulated, see HUMAN BODY

HEART is the organ protected by the rib cage and serves to pump the blood to all parts of the body. It is about the size of a man's clenched fist. How the blood is circulated is shown in the diagram. See HUMAN BODY.

HEAT is something we detect by means of the sense of touch. Scientists call it a form of energy, and measure it with such an instrument as a THERMOMETER. Temperature is a measure of how hot or cold anything is. Heat can travel in three ways:

Conduction is the handing on of heat from particle to particle of a substance when the particles are touching.

Examples of the three forms of heat

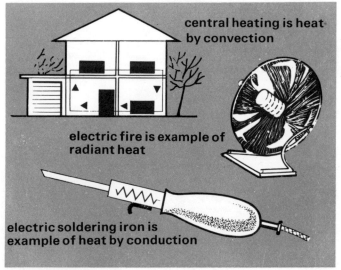

central heating is heat by convection

electric fire is example of radiant heat

electric soldering iron is example of heat by conduction

Convection is the movement in a gas or liquid owing to the hot parts rising.

Radiation is the transfer of heat by means of waves similar to those of light. Radiant heat, as it is called, can travel through a vacuum. The best example of this is the sun's heat which reaches us after travelling millions of miles through empty space.

HEDGEHOG is a short-legged, heavily-built little animal with a pointed snout. It is found in Europe, Asia and Africa, and has sharp spines on its back and sides which serve to protect it from enemies when it rolls itself into a ball. It usually sleeps during the day, coming out at night to hunt for insects, mice, frogs and snails. It hibernates during the winter.

The hippopotamus is a close relative of the pig. It is now found only in Africa. The hippopotamus is a plant eater and feeds mainly in the evening or at night

HELICOPTER is a type of aircraft in which lift and forward movement are provided by a large rotor positioned above the fuselage. The small propeller on the extreme end of the tail is to prevent the aircraft twisting because of the movement of the rotor, and for controlling the direction of the machine. The all-important thing about a helicopter is that it can hover, and ascend and descend vertically; that is, there is no need for long runways. Helicopters are used not only for short-distance transport, but for such jobs as crop spraying, airsea rescue, etc. The great pioneer of this type of aircraft was Igor Sikorsky. The first type of aeroplane to take-off and land nearly vertically was the autogiro, and was designed by Juan de la Cierva.

HIBERNATION is a state of sleep in which some animals pass the winter. Warm-blooded animals store up energy in the form of fat and this lasts them through the winter. In spring they awake from their hibernation and go in search of food. Some animals, like beavers and squirrels, hide away in winter, but do not really hibernate. Such animals do not need to come out of their homes because they store sufficient food to last them through the winter.

HIMALAYAS are a vast range of mountains which stretch for over 1,500 miles eastwards across the northern frontier of India from the borders of Afghanistan to the borders of China. This great mountain system is sometimes called 'the roof of the world'. Its name is pronounced Himalay'a and means 'the abode of snows' or 'the cold place'. The range includes the highest mountain in the world, Mt Everest (29,028 feet). Other high peakes are Kanchen-

junga (28,250 feet), Lhotse (27,890 feet), Nanga Parbat (26,660 feet) and Nanda Devi (25,640 feet).

HIPPOPOTAMUS is related to the pig, but is much larger and is covered with tough hairless hide. Many thousands of years ago it lived in Europe, but is now found only in Africa. It spends most of the daytime by rivers, and is quite happy whether in the water or out, being able to stay completely below the surface for quite long periods. It feeds on vegetable plants.

HOLY COMMUNION is a sacrament which commemorates Christ's last supper with His disciples before His crucifixion. In Roman Catholic churches it is known as the Mass. As recorded in the Gospels and by St Paul, the Communion consists of repeating the action of Jesus in hallowing the bread and wine as tokens of His sacrifice; the bread is broken, thanks are given in prayer for the wine and the bread, and the communicants partake of a little of each. The bread is symbolical of the body of Christ, and the wine of His blood.

HONDURAS is a republic in Central America. It is separated from BRITISH HONDURAS by the south-east corner of Guatemala. It is 43,280 square miles and has a population of about $2\frac{1}{2}$ millions. The capital is Tegucigalpa.

HONG KONG is a British Colony off the coast of China near the mouth of the Canton River. It is only 397 square miles but has nearly 4 million inhabitants. It consists of the main island and some smaller ones together with a small part of the Chinese mainland. The capital

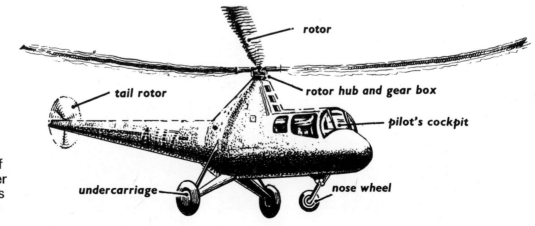

Diagram of a helicopter showing its main parts

rotor

tail rotor

rotor hub and gear box

pilot's cockpit

undercarriage

nose wheel

Welsh mountain pony

New Forest pony

Shire horse

Percheron horse

Arab horse

Mongolian wild horse

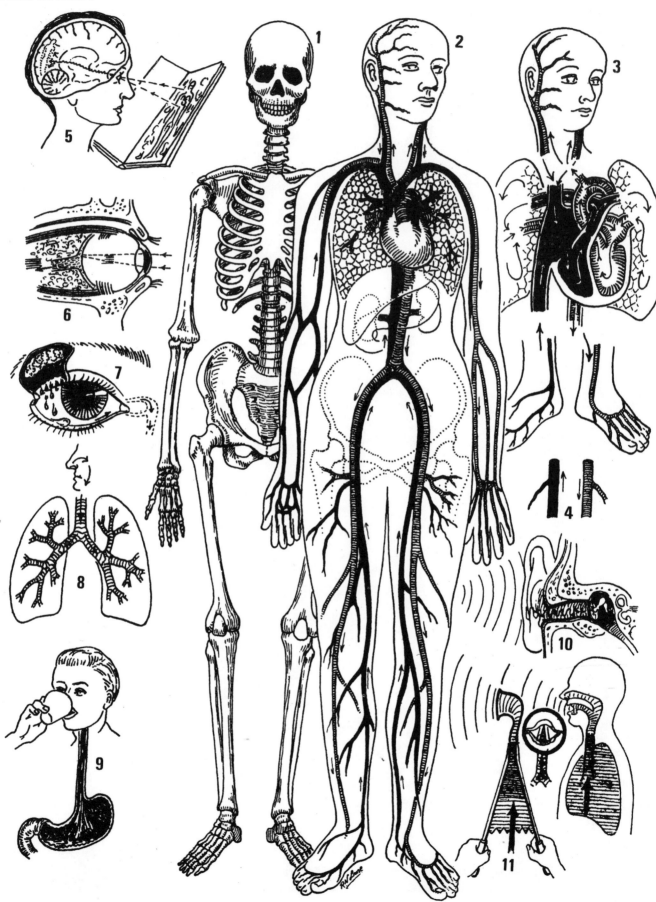

s Victoria. Hong Kong produces large quantities of light goods—toys, shirts, plastic goods and the like.

HORSE This animal has been domesticated or many thousands of years, and is even thought o have been used by man in the late Stone Age. At that time it was a much smaller animal than ur present-day horse. Today there are many different kinds of horses all of which have special eatures according to the sort of work they do. The racehorse is specially bred for speed, and s a very slim, streamlined animal. A hunter, however, is bred for endurance and strength as well as speed, and is solider built and has stronger legs than a racehorse. Cart horses, such as he Shire, Clydesdale and Suffolk Punch, are bred for their great pulling strength. There are also many kinds of ponies, which are much smaller and sturdier than the horse; such as hose from the Shetlands, Hebrides, Orkney slands, Wales, New Forest and Dartmoor. Wild horses are still found in Central Asia and parts of America.

HOUSE OF COMMONS See **PARLIAMENT**

HOUSE OF LORDS See **PARLIAMENT**

HOUSE OF REPRESENTATIVES in the U.S.A. s the lower of two houses in the body called Congress and in whose hands rests the legislaive power of the nation. The upper house in his body is called the Senate. The House of Representatives represents the people, and its 435 members are divided among the states in proportion to population. A redistribution of representatives takes place after each ten-year census. Members serve for two years and are hen eligible for re-election. An elected House of Representatives is also part of the government of Australia. See SENATE.

HUMAN BODY The main components of the human body are illustrated here and to simplify matters—and the body is a very complicated structure—the following descriptions should be read together with the numbered drawing and separate articles:

1 The skeleton or basic framework of the human body, is constructed of 206 individual bones. It consists of a central backbone or vertebral column, a skull at the top to protect the brain, a cage of ribs to protect the heart and lungs, two girdles, and leg and arm bones. The skeleton serves to give shape and rigidity to the body, and to protect internal organs.

2 This shows how the blood is circulated throughout the body. The black lines are veins taking blood back to the heart, and the striped lines arteries taking blood from the heart to the body (4).

3 This shows the heart opened up to illustrate how it is divided up and how blood flows through it. See also HEART.

5 Shows how the eye is connected with that part of the brain concerned with the sense of sight.

6 Section through the eye showing its main parts; see entry on the EYE.

7 The tear gland and tear ducts to the nose.

8 The lungs or organs of breathing. There are two lungs, and each is contained in a membrane called a 'pleura'. The main tube going into the lung is called the 'bronchi'. Inside the lung the bronchi divide and subdivide in the way shown, and end in minute air-sacs which have very thin walls. How oxygen is taken in by the blood is explained in the article on the LUNGS.

9 The passage of food to the digestive system; for fuller explanation see DIGESTION.

10 Section through the ear showing its main parts; see EAR.

11 Section and diagram showing how we speak.

The body also has muscles which allow movement of our bodies—they are sometimes called the engines of the body. There are two kinds of muscle; 1, the kind that operate without our thinking about it; for example, those that control the eyelids and cause us to blink, and 2, the kind that are under control of our will; for example, the muscles in the arms and legs.

The whole body is covered with skin which acts not only as a protection, but contains nerves which send messages to the brain and tell us about our surroundings. The skin by means of perspiration also controls the temperature of the body.

HUNDRED YEARS' WAR began in 1338 when King Edward the Third of England (reigned 1327-77) claimed the throne of France. It ended in 1453. The outstanding events in this long, wasteful war were the Battle of Crecy (26 August 1346); the capture of the Channel port of Calais (1347); the Battle of Poitiers (19 September 1356); the Battle of Agincourt (25 October 1415); and the burning of Joan of Arc (30 May 1431). The Hundred Years' War did not succeed in winning the French throne for England; on the contrary it cost England all her continental possessions except the port of Calais, which had been captured by Edward in 1347 and which remained in English hands until recaptured by the French in 1558.

HUNGARY is a republic in Central Europe through which runs the River Danube. It is about 36,000 square miles and has a population of over 10 millions. The capital is Budapest. The language of the Hungarians is called Magyar. The country has rich wheat-growing lands. It also mines coal, iron and bauxite.

HURRICANE is a West Indian cyclonic storm of great violence (cyclonic means like a cyclone, a system of winds blowing spirally inwards towards a centre of low barometric pressure). The word hurricane is also used rather loosely to describe any wind of extreme violence—say over 75 miles an hour. Just how violent a hurricane can be is indicated by its position on what is called the Beaufort Scale of wind velocities (named after the man who devised it, the English admiral Sir Francis Beaufort); the figure 0 on the scale denotes calm, 4 a moderate breeze, 8 a fresh gale, 11 a storm, and 12 to 17 (the highest force number) various types of hurricane.

HYDRO-ELECTRIC POWER is electric power obtained from water-driven turbines rather like a water wheel, and is a most useful way of harnessing water power to man's needs. The two main methods are: 1, using free flowing water, like rivers or waterfalls, and 2, damming rivers or lakes, and controlling the flow of water over artificial or man-made waterfalls. Some of the biggest hydro-electric schemes in the world are the Hoover Dam (U.S.A.), the Dnieper Dam (U.S.S.R.), Snowy Mountains (Australia), Shannon (Rep. of Ireland), Aswan (Egypt), and Lock Sloy (Scotland).

HYDROGEN BOMB is the latest kind of atomic bomb, and based on the idea of 'atomic fusion'; that is, the energy released by the fusion or joining together of the inner cores of certain light atoms. It is thought that the process of fusion is similar to that which takes place in the sun and produces the great heat which streams from it. Scientists are working to control the tremendous heat and put it to useful purposes such as generating electric power. See NUCLEAR POWER.

HYENA is a member of the cat family, although it looks rather more like a dog. It feeds mainly on the dead bodies of any animals it can find, but will also kill and eat animals such as sheep, goats, and other livestock. There are two main types of hyena, one having a greyish coat with black stripes, and the other a yellowish tawny coat with dark spots.

HYGROMETRY is that branch of METEOROLOGY concerned with the measurement and behaviour of water vapour in the atmosphere owing to the evaporation of water from the surface of the seas, lakes, rivers, etc. The actual quantity of moisture or vapour in the atmosphere is known as 'humidity', and is measured by means of an instrument known as a 'hygrometer' which can also be used for measuring the dew point; the latter is the temperature at which water vapour in the air condenses to water or DEW.

HYRAX is a small rodent-like mammal with hooves whose closest relative is, surprisingly, the elephant. They are fond of rock climbing and are found mostly in mountainous regions of Africa and south west Asia.

IBEX is a wild mountain goat. It is usually brown or grey in colour and has long, curved horns. It is found in mountainous districts particularly in the Pyrenees, Alps and Himalayas.

ICE AGE was a period about 2 million years ago when vast areas of Europe and North America were covered with ice. It is generally thought that man emerged towards the end of this period. The Ice Age actually consisted of several epochs, each separated by periods when the climate became milder, and these various epochs, together with the periods which separated them, are together known as the Great Ice Age. Animals that lived during the Ice Age included the mammoth, sabre-toothed tiger, cave bear and woolly rhinoceros.

ICEBERG is a very large piece of ice which has broken from an ice barrier or glacier, and which floats in the sea until melted by warm oceanic currents. One of the dangerous things about an iceberg is that only one-tenth of its bulk shows above water. It was a huge iceberg that caused the passenger liner *Titanic* to sink in 1912 with a loss of 1,600 lives. Nowadays icebergs can be detected by radar.

ICELAND is an island republic in the North Atlantic not far from the Arctic Circle. It is 40,000 square miles and has a population of 203,500. It used to be linked with Denmark but became independent in 1944. The capital is Reykjavik. The country depends chiefly on its fishing industry. The Icelanders claim that their Parliament, called the Althing, is older than England's and dates back to 930.

IGLOO is an Eskimo snow house. It consists of blocks of frozen snow, built into a dome-shaped structure and furnished inside with plenty of skins. An igloo offers good protection from the fiercest blizzards. When out on long hunting expeditions a skilled Eskimo can build an igloo in less than two hours. Igloos are to be found in the arctic mainland and on the islands of northern Canada where the Eskimoes make their home.

IGUANA is a large lizard found in America, Madagascar and the Fiji Islands. It lives mainly in trees and eats fruit and vegetables, and sometimes worms and insects. It is sold as a food in many parts of America.

INCA was the name of a tribe who in South America founded a powerful empire. About

An iguana is one of the largest of the lizards

An artist's impression of a typical hydro-electric dam. The inset (top left) shows a diagram of a water-driven turbine used for generating electric power by the swift-flowing water from the dam

U S S R

SINKIANG

CHI

Hindu Kush

● Herat

AFGHANISTAN

● Kabul

● Peshawar
Rawalpindi ●

K2 28250 ▲

Kunlun Mountains

● Srinagar

KASHMIR

● Jammu

Tanglha Range

T I B E T

● Kandahar

Jhelum

Lahore ● ● Amritsar
Ravi

Great Himalaya Range

Nyenchen Tanglha Range

● Lhasa

● Quetta

PAKISTAN

Indus

PUNJAB

NEPAL

Kangchenjunga 28146 ▲

● Punakha

Brahmaputra

Thar Desert

● Delhi

Agra ●

UTTAR PRADESH

Mt Everest 29028 ▲
● Katmandu

● Darjeeling

ASSAM

♣ Mohenjo
Daro

RAJASTHAN

● Jaipur

● Lucknow

Chambal

Ganges

● Shillong

● Hyderabad

Jumna

● Patna

**BANGLA-
DESH**

Karachi ○

● Jhansi

BIHAR

**WEST
BENGAL**

● Dacca

GUJERAT

● Ahmadabad

MADHYA PRADESH

Calcutta ●

● Baroda

I N D I A

*Mouths of
the Ganges*

ARABIAN SEA

● Nagpur

ORISSA

♣ Ajanta

MAHAR ASHTRA

Bombay ○

Western Ghats

● Poona

**ANDRHA
PRADESH**

BAY OF BENGAL

● Sholapur

Eastern Ghats

Hyderabad ●

Krishna

Panjim ○

MYSORE

Coromandel Coast

ANDAMAN ISLANDS

Malabar Coast

● Bangalore Madras ●

KERALA

● Mysore

MADRAS

CEYLON

Trivandrum ○

NICOBAR ISLAN

Colombo ○

○ ○
MALDIVE ISLANDS
○

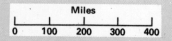

India

The Red Indians of the North West Coast region of North America carved totem poles out of fully grown trees and painted them in very bright colours

A.D. 1200 they settled and founded the town of Cuzco in Peru, and about 200 years later they began a career of conquest under their leader whose name was Inca Pachacuti, and it was from him that the tribe took their name, which was also applied to the great civilization which they developed. The Incas built many magnificent temples, where they worshipped a creator-god, and they were also very skilled in the arts of pottery and weaving. The Inca empire was overthrown by the Spaniards who invaded South America in the 16th century.

INDIA is a large republic in the south of Asia. It has an area of 1,261,800 square miles and a population of more than 537 million. It is a part of the British Commonwealth and its capital is Delhi. Other large cities are Calcutta, Bombay and Madras. The population are mostly Hindus although there are Moslems, Christians and Buddhists. The main industries are tea, cotton, jute and steel.

Civilisation in India dates back to 4000 B.C. and the caste system dates to 1500 B.C. Buddha was born in India in 600 B.C. Hindu literature and art reached its peak in 400 A.D. Britain did not take an interest in India until the 18th century when the East India Company was set up to develop trade in tea and spices. It rapidly took control and ruled India until after the Mutiny of 1857 when Britain took over the East India Company. Queen Victoria was proclaimed Empress of India in 1887 and India remained a major part of the British Empire until her Independence in 1947.

INDIANS (AMERICAN) This title includes the Indians of Central and South America. The native aborigines of North America are usually referred to as 'Red Indians'. Some scholars think the title 'Amerinds' would be a better one. When Columbus landed in the New World on 12 October 1492, he found there some strange-looking people with copper-coloured skins, and because he thought he had reached India he reported back to the king of Spain that these people were 'Indians'. It is possible that the Red Indians came from central Asia, for they

Sioux

Ojibwa

Hopi

Blackfeet

resemble the Mongolian peoples with their high cheekbones and lank black hair. The American Indians comprised many different tribes whose appearance, way of life and language showed considerable variety. The names of some of the more famous tribes are familiar to readers of the novels of Fenimore Cooper and to those who watch 'Western' films: Sioux, Algonquins, Mohicans, Blackfeet, Iroquois and Apaches. The United States has for many years given the Redskins their own reservations, and their affairs are looked after by a special government office, though this does little to atone for the savage and shameful way in which the white man got the better of his Redskin enemies.

INDONESIA is a republic in south-east Asia that is made up of several large islands and many smaller ones. The country is 735,000 square miles with a population of 118 millions. The largest islands are Java, Sumatra, the Celebes and most of the large island of Borneo. Since 1963 the west part of NEW GUINEA, called the West Irian, has been part of Indonesia. The capital is Djakarta, formerly called Batavia on the island of Java. The country is rich in minerals, including tin, coal and petroleum. It also produces rubber, tobacco and rice.

INDUSTRIAL REVOLUTION was the period in English history which began about the second half of the 18th century and ended about the second half of the 19th century. It was during this period that the world saw the introduction of machines driven by steam power, the spinning machine, and the power loom. The Industrial Revolution brought with it not only a tremendous growth in industry but also a big increase in population and the birth of new towns. Other countries soon followed Britain in building up their industries as a result of the many new inventions. A point to be remembered about the Industrial Revolution is that it marks a period not only of discoveries and inventions but also of important social changes and human relationships.

INOCULATION is the injection into the body of a virus (the smallest kind of germ) to prevent the catching of certain diseases. Children are inoculated against such diseases as typhoid, smallpox and whooping cough. So inoculation is first and foremost a preventive measure and it has undoubtedly saved many lives. Inoculation against smallpox is generally referred to as VACCINATION.

INQUISITION was the inquiry made by the Roman Catholic Church, especially during what are called the Middle Ages (from the 5th to the 15th century). Its purpose was to track down and punish any person who was suspected of doubting or disbelieving the teaching of the Church. This was called 'heresy' and was considered a crime. The Inquisition was most active in Spain during the time of King Ferdinand and Queen Isabella towards the end of the 15th century, and thousands of persons, not a few among whom were possibly quite innocent, were executed, while others suffered terrible tortures. The Spanish Inquisition was finally abolished in 1820.

INSECTS There are more than a quarter-of-a-million different kinds of insects in the world, and they are very numerous in tropical regions. The body of an insect is made up of three parts: the head, the thorax, or middle part, and the abdomen. It has one or two pairs of wings and three pairs of legs which are attached to the thorax. One pair of antennae, or feelers, are attached to the head, and most insects have large compound eyes. They breathe through a system of tiny air tubes which run all over the body. Nearly all insects lay eggs which hatch out into grubs or caterpillars, and which eventually turn into adult insects. See ANT, BEE, BEETLE, BUTTERFLY.

INTERNAL COMBUSTION ENGINE is a type of engine driven by the power obtained from burning fuel in a cylinder. The most common type is that used in a motor-car. Most internal combustion engines work on what is called the 'four-stroke cycle', and clearly illustrated in the diagram. The gas engine, diesel engine and jet engine are also internal combustion engines. See JET ENGINE.

INVENTION All about us are devices which ease man's labours, and generally make life more pleasant; for example, television, motor-cars, washing machines, electric lights, etc. All such things are the result of invention by one man or a team of men and/or women. Invention is not something new; in fact, invention is one of the things which distinguishes man from all other animals. See TABLE 7, page 191.

INVERTEBRATES include all animals without a backbone. But whereas those animals having a backbone are built more or less to the same pattern, the invertebrates make up a very mixed collection. On the one hand there are the microscopic protozoa, consisting of a single cell, very simple creatures in every sense. On the other hand, they include the insects which in many ways are more highly organized than some of the vertebrates. In between these we find the sponges, sea-anemones and corals, earthworms, starfish, oysters, slugs and snails, crabs and lobsters, and a host of others.

Apart from many insects and most spiders, the invertebrates live in water, either in the sea or in rivers and lakes, or in damp places. Except for some of the slugs and snails, they breathe by gills, and their chief danger lies in becoming dried up. The protozoa are found in large numbers in the seas and in fresh water, others live in damp earth and many live inside plants or in the bodies of other animals, where they often cause disease. Sponges are found in the seas and fresh waters, and sea-anemones, jelly-fishes and corals are found only in the seas, although a few minute jelly-fishes and the fresh-water hydra are found in rivers and lakes. All these animals have no nerves or their nervous system is of the simplest form. They have no brain, and if they have any sense-organs at all they are very simple, just a few pigment spots to serve as eyes. As we pass up the animal scale of invertebrates, through the worms, starfish and sea-urchins, the mollusca and the crustacea to the insects and spiders, we find a progressively better nervous system, more of a brain, and elaborate senses, such as eyes and antennae.

IONOSPHERE is an electrified region in the atmosphere some 40 to 400 miles above the earth's surface. The electrification of this region is caused by radiations from the sun. It is very important to radio communication as it is this region which reflects radiowaves. If this region were not present radiowaves would be lost in space.

Left, diagram of a four-stroke engine and *right,* main parts of a four-cylinder engine

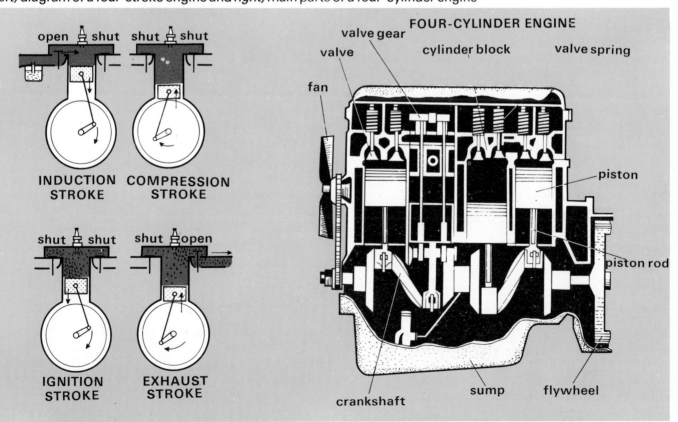

INDUCTION STROKE

COMPRESSION STROKE

IGNITION STROKE

EXHAUST STROKE

FOUR-CYLINDER ENGINE

valve gear
valve
cylinder block
valve spring
fan
piston
piston rod
crankshaft
sump
flywheel

jellyfishes

spider crab

sea squirts

sponge

starfish

bristle
worms

sea anemones

scallop

sea snail

edible crab

IRAN, also called PERSIA, is a large kingdom in the MIDDLE EAST. It is about 628,000 square miles and has about 28 million inhabitants, nearly all Moslems. The capital is Tehran and the chief port Abadan. Most of the country is desert but the country is rich in petroleum. It also produces cotton and is famous for its carpets.

IRAQ, once known as Mesopotamia, is in the Middle East and is 'that land between the rivers'. The rivers are the Euphrates and the Tigris. Iraq is 170,000 square miles and has about 9½ million inhabitants who are all Arabs. The capital is Baghdad, the city of the Arabian Nights. The ruins of the ancient biblical city of Babylon are also in Iraq. The chief oil wells are around Kirkuk and Mosul and the chief port is Basra on the Persian Gulf.

IRELAND, REPUBLIC OF or EIRE as it is also known, is a republic in the island of that name. It has an area of 26,500 square miles and a population of about 3,000,000, most of whom are Roman Catholics. The capital is Dublin. The republic was set up in 1921 after many years of agitation for their own government. It is an agricultural country and much visited by tourists.

IRON and **STEEL** Iron is a silvery-white metal. It is very abundant in the earth's crust and is mined on a very large scale. The Iron Age was the period from 1000 to about 500 B.C. when iron first became widely used for making tools and weapons, being capable of taking a keener edge than the softer bronze. In a modern blast furnace, iron ore is mixed with coal,

An artist's impression of an Iron Age village protected by a stockade

limestone and coke and heated to a very high temperature, about 1,200 degrees Fahrenheit (648 Centigrade). Steel has become the world's most precious metal in a special sense because all the machines which produce our everyday needs—everything from a pin to a printing-press—are all made wholly or partly of steel. It is an alloy of iron and carbon, with varying proportions of other minerals.

IRON AGE In archaeology, this is the term used to describe the last of three stages or periods in the development of man. These stages really

Left, loading Bessemer converter, *centre,* converter blowing and *right,* pouring molten steel. The purpose of the converter is to remove impurities.

the converter blowing

pouring the molten steel into ingots

represent phases of material culture. The first was when man made use of stones as tools or weapons—the Stone Age, which lasted a very long time and may have started about a million years ago. It lasted so long that scientists have divided it into Old, Middle, and New Stone Ages. Then man discovered copper and learnt how to mix it with tin to make bronze, so the next period is called the Bronze Age and it was during this period that recorded history began; in Europe it began roughly about 1900 B.C. Then iron began to be used, so the third period is called the Iron Age, and it dawned in Europe about 500 B.C.

IRON LUNG is a machine in which a patient is placed (perhaps when suffering from infantile paralysis) to make breathing possible. It is, in fact, a machine that gives artificial respiration. The air pressure in the iron lung is changed about twenty times every minute, and it is this change in pressure which causes the lungs of the patient to take in and expel air.

IRRIGATION is the watering of land by means of canals to enable plant life to grow where it would not do so otherwise. It is necessary only in regions where little or no rain falls. Although practised in Egypt from the very earliest times, it is now being used more widely in many countries which have little rain, so as to assist the growth of food materials and so help to feed the world's increasing population. The longest irrigation canal in the world is the Karakumskiy Kanal in the U.S.S.R. It stretches for 546 miles.

ISLAND is any area of land completely surrounded by water. The following is a list of the world's best-known islands:

NAME	BELONGS TO	AREA SQ. MILES
Baffin	Canada	197,800
Banks	Canada	26,000
Borneo	Indonesia and Britain	287,000
Ceylon	Dominion in Commonwealth	25,300
Corsica	France	3,360
Crete	Greece	3,230
Cuba	Republic	44,000
Cyprus	British Colony	3,570
Devon	Canada	20,500
Ellesmere	Canada	77,400
Formosa	Nationalist China	13,800
Gottland	Sweden	1,200
Great Britain		88,100
Greenland	Denmark	840,000
Hainan	Republic of China	13,000
Iceland	Republic	40,500
Ireland	Republic and United Kingdom	31,800
Isle of Man	United Kingdom	220
Isle of Wight	United Kingdom	147
Jamaica	British Colony	4,400
Japan:		
Hokkaido		30,000
Honshu		88,000
Shikoku		6,800
Kynshu		13,700
Java	Indonesia	48,800
Luzon	Philippines	40,400
Madagascar	France	228,000
Mindanao	Philippines	36,500
Newfoundland	Canada	42,700
New Zealand:		
North Island		44,200
South Island		58,100
Sakhalin	U.S.S.R.	29,700
Sardinia	Italy	9,300
Sicily	Italy	9,900
Southampton	Canada	16,100
Sumatra	Indonesia	163,500
Tasmania	Australia	26,200
Tierra Del Fuego	Chile	18,500
Victoria	Canada	80,400

The forecourt of St. Peter's, Rome, and the Mother Church of Roman Catholics

ISRAEL is a Jewish republic which is 10,430 square miles, and has nearly 3 million inhabitants. The people speak Hebrew. The great majority are Jews, the rest being Moslems. The Israelies regard the New City of Jerusalem as their capital but larger towns than this are Tel-Aviv and Haifa. The chief product is citrus fruit and the chief mineral phosphates from the Dead Sea.

ITALY is a republic in southern Europe. Included in Italy are the large islands of Sicily and Sardinia. It is 324,000 square miles and has 54½ million inhabitants. The capital is Rome, on the River Tiber, once the centre of the great Roman Empire. Amongst the cities famous in history are Venice and Florence whilst Naples and Genoa are today the chief ports. Milan and Turin are the chief industrial cities. Most Italians are peasant farmers and the chief crops are wheat, from which macaroni is made, grapes and olives. Most of the people live on the plains of Lombardy because the mountains of peninsular Italy make farming and industry difficult. Italy has few minerals but since the Second World War great quantities of natural gas have been discovered and this has greatly helped the country's industries. Other minerals found in Italy are sulphur and mercury. The country is also famous for its marble.

JACKAL is a wild dog which resembles both the wolf and the fox, and lives in southern Asia, Africa and eastern Europe. It has a thick, coarse coat and bushy tail. It feeds on hares, birds, mice, vegetables, and any dead animals which it can find.

JACOBITES The name comes from *Jacobus,* which is the Latin form of James. The Jacobites were those who supported James II of England (reigned 1685-88) and his descendants. King James made vain efforts to re-establish the Roman Catholic faith and had to leave the

The jackal is a wild dog and, as this picture clearly shows, is very like a wolf and fox

country. His son, James Francis, tried to regain the throne back but he was defeated along with his 'Jacobite' followers at the Battle of Sheriffmuir in Perthshire, Scotland, in 1715. His son, Charles Edward Stuart, tried in turn to gain the English throne but was likewise defeated, this time at the Battle of Culloden Moor, near Inverness, Scotland, in 1746. Thus the Jacobite cause was lost.

JADE is the name of a very hard gem stone. It is used for making beautiful objects such as small bowls, statues, necklaces and other things. An even rarer and more valuable form of jade is called jadeite ('precious' jade, or Chinese jade). Jade is held in high esteem, especially among the Chinese and Japanese. Its colour ranges from a delicate green to white.

JAGUAR is a member of the cat family, and is a very good climber. It is a fierce animal, and resembles the leopard with its tawny coat which is marked with spots. Although it usually feeds on monkeys, deer and other small animals, it will, if driven by hunger, attack cattle, horses, and even man. It is found in South, Central and North America.

JAMAICA is one of the largest of the West Indian Islands and a Member of the British Commonwealth. It is little more than 4,410 square miles and has a population of nearly 2 millions. The capital is Kingston. The next most important town is Montego Bay. The country produces sugar, rum, bananas and bauxite. Jamaica was discovered by Christopher Columbus in 1494.

JAPAN is an island kingdom in the Pacific Ocean made up of four large islands and many smaller ones. The country is 142,810 square miles, but has 103 million inhabitants. The capital is Tokyo, the largest city in the world. Other big cities are Osaka, Nagoya, Kyoto and Yokohama, the chief port. Japan is the most important industrial country in Asia. She is the leading ship-building country and also produces textiles and manufactures goods like toys, bicycles, motor-cars and transistor radios.

JAVA is an island in south east Asia and a part of the republic of INDONESIA. The capital Djarkarta is on Java. Products are rubber, tea and rice. Java was, at one time, part of the Dutch East Indies.

JELLYFISH is the common name for the sea creature known as the 'medusa', and is related to the sea anemone. There are a number of different kinds, many of them being amongst the most beautiful animals in the sea. Jellyfish catch their food with long stinging tentacles. The Portuguese man-of-war is a jellyfish, and its sting can be very dangerous—swimmers should avoid it at all costs.

JERBOA is a rodent about the size of a rat. It has very long hind legs and a long, tufted tail. It lies in burrows during the day and feeds during the night. Jerboas walk or trot on their hind legs and can move at great speed by means of long leaps, in some cases up to several yards in length. They are to be found in North Africa and from Central Asia to China.

JET ENGINE is a type of internal combustion engine that gives its power directly to the machine it is driving, instead of through a chain of gears, a propeller and the like. The principle used in a jet engine is Newton's 'reaction', and is better known as 'recoil'. When you fire a gun the bullet shoots out of the barrel, and the butt kicks or recoils back. In a jet engine hot gases are shot out of one end, and the machine to which it is fitted moves in the opposite direction. The speed at which the machine moves forward depends upon its weight, and the speed of the hot gases shooting out of the rear. The greater the quantity of hot gases shot out, the greater the power of the engine. What should be remembered is the fact that movement is *not* a result of the hot gases pushing against the atmosphere.

Inside an engine (see drawing) is an impeller: it is a form of pump, which forces large quantities of air into the engine and past jets of burning fuel. The air mixes with the burning fuel, expands rapidly and rushes out of the rear jet. On its way out it blows round a turbine wheel which works the compressor pump. In some types of engine it turns a heavier turbine which is able to work a propeller. This type of engine is known as a 'turbo-prop'.

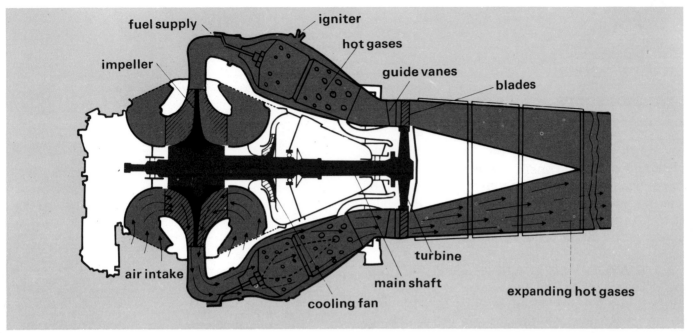

Diagram showing the main components of a typical jet or gas turbine engine

JORDAN is an Arab kingdom through which the River Jordan flows. It is about 30,000 square miles and has a population of nearly 2 millions. The capital is Amman. The country is mainly agricultural and produces phosphates from the Dead Sea which are used as fertilizers and exported.

JURY This word comes from the old French word *jurée,* meaning an oath. A jury is a body of men and women (usually twelve in number) who are sworn (that is, they take an oath) to try a case in a court of law before a judge. They have to give a verdict on a crime after hearing all the evidence; they pledge themselves to bring in a verdict that is true and just and upon which the members of the jury must be agreed. The entitlement to trial by jury is one of the most cherished rights of the Anglo-Saxon nations. The Normans and later rulers of England developed the jury system.

JUTES were a tribe of Anglo-Saxons from Germany who settled in Kent during the 5th century A.D. It is thought that Hengist and Horsa may have led the invasion.

The jaguar of America is very like a leopard

The Portuguese man-of-war is poisonous

KALEIDOSCOPE is an optical device which, if tapped or rotated, gives an endless number of beautiful coloured patterns. It is made of a tube with an eyepiece at one end, and at the other end a compartment containing bits of coloured glass and two inclined mirrors. The kaleidoscope was invented by Sir David Brewster in 1817 and the name comes from Greek words meaning 'to look at beautiful forms'.

KANGAROO lives in Australia and New Guinea. It travels by taking huge leaps over the ground, and for this reason its hind-legs are very big and strong, while the fore-limbs, which are only rarely used for movement, are quite short and weak. The kangaroo has a pouched stomach where the female carries her baby until it is old enough to fend for itself. One kind of kangaroo lives almost all its life in trees. A close but smaller relative of the kangaroo is the WALLABY.

KAYAK is an ESKIMO canoe. It is made of a very light wooden frame over which skins are stretched. A kayak usually takes only one person and is propelled with a double-ended paddle.

KELP is a kind of brown seaweed which grows to great lengths; one type found off the western shores of America grows to a length of 400 feet. The name 'kelp' is also used for the ash which is left after burning seaweed, and from which iodine used to be obtained.

KENYA is a large republic in East Africa. It is 224,950 square miles and has a population of nearly 11 millions. The capital is Nairobi and the chief port Mombasa. The country is famous for its coffee; tea and cotton are also grown.

KESTREL is a small bird of prey. It is found in many parts of the British Isles, Europe and Asia. It does not build a nest, and feeds on frogs, mice, insects and small birds. It can be trained for hawking.

KINGS AND QUEENS OF ENGLAND
(827 to 1603)

	Acceded	Died
Saxons and Danes		
Egbert	827	839
Ethelwulf	839	858
Ethelbald	858	860
Ethelbert	858	866
Ethelred	866	871
Alfred the Great	871	901
Edward the Elder	901	925
Athelstan	925	940
Edmund	940	946
Edred	946	955
Edwy	955	959
Edgar	959	975
Edward the Martyr	975	978
Ethelred II	978	1016
Edmond (Ironside)	1016	1016
Canute	1017	1035
Harold I	1035	1040
Hardicanute	1040	1042
Edward the Confessor	1042	1066
Harold II	1066	1066
House of Normandy		
William I	1066	1087
William II	1087	1100
Henry I	1100	1135
Stephen	1135	1154
House of Plantagenet		
Henry II	1154	1189
Richard I	1189	1199
John	1199	1216
Henry III	1216	1272
Edward I	1272	1307
Edward II	1307	1327
Edward III	1327	1377
Richard II	1377	1399
House of Lancaster		
Henry IV	1399	1413
Henry V	1413	1422
Henry VI	1422	1461
House of York		
Edward IV	1461	1483
Edward V	1483	1483
Richard III	1483	1485
House of Tudor		
Henry VII	1485	1509
Henry VIII	1509	1547
Edward VI	1547	1553
Jane	1553	1554
Mary I	1553	1558
Elizabeth I	1558	1603

(1603—PRESENT)

	Acceded	Died
House of Stuart		
James I (James VI, Scotland)	1603	1625
Charles I	1625	1649
Charles II	1649*	1685
James II	1685	1688
William III and	1689	1702
Mary II	1689	1694
Anne	1702	1714
House of Hanover		
George I	1714	1727
George II	1727	1760
George III	1760	1820
George IV	1820	1830
William IV	1830	1837
Victoria	1837	1901

* Restored to throne in 1660 after fall of Commonwealth.

KINKAJOU lives in South and Central America. It has soft brownish fur and a very long tail. It is a very good climber, and spends most of its time in trees, feeding at night on vegetables and small animals.

KIWI is a flightless bird and is a native of New Zealand. It is covered with hair-like feathers, has tiny wings, a long, slender, curved bill and no tail. It lives in the thick undergrowth of forests where it spends most of the day, coming out at night to search for earthworms and grubs, as well as berries, shoots, seeds, etc. It nests in a burrow or hole lined with sticks, ferns, leaves or grass, and usually lays two eggs which are white or greenish in colour. It gets its name from the cry it makes which sounds rather like 'kiwi'.

KNOTS It is a good thing to know how to tie knots properly. It can save much time and trouble and sometimes can even save lives. People such as sailors, cowboys and steeplejacks know only too well what can happen if a knot slips. The best knots are those which can be made quickly, which hold firmly without slipping, yet do not blind so tightly that they can be untied only with great difficulty. Other forms of knots are called hitches or splices. The word 'knot' is also used by sailors to measure the speed of a ship, and is the number of nautical miles travelled in one hour; a nautical mile is 6,080 feet.

KOALA is known as the Australian bear, although it does not really belong to the bear family and is, in fact, a MARSUPIAL. It usually lives in eucalyptus trees, and eats the leaves at night, spending most of the day curled up asleep on a branch. It is covered with greyish-white fur, but has no tail. The young koala bears stay in their mother's pouch for about three months after they are born, and are then carried on

The kestrel of Europe and Asia

The kinkajou of South and Central America
The flightless Kiwi is found in New Zealand

89

her back until they are old enough to look after themselves.

KOMODO DRAGON is the largest lizard in existence today. It grows to up to 12 foot in length and is found on the island of Komodo belonging to INDONESIA.

KOOKABURRA is an Australian bird which lives mainly in open forest country, and lays its eggs in a hole in a tree or a burrow. It is about 18 inches long, has a slightly hooked bill, and feeds on insects, rats and mice, lizards, snakes, eggs and small birds. It has a strange call that sounds rather like a laugh.

KOREA is a republic of about 85,260 square miles on a peninsula in north-east Asia which borders China and the Soviet Union. Since the end of the Second World War the country has been divided, the dividing line being the 38th parallel. North Korea is rather larger than the South but has only 12½ million inhabitants, the South has about 30 million. The capital of South Korea is Seoul; that of North Korea Pyongyang. The main exports are fish products, textiles, iron and some tungsten.

KUDU Perhaps the most magnificent ANTELOPE in Africa. The males have twisted horns of up to 60 inches long, the females are hornless. A male stands about 6 feet at the shoulder and weighs anything up to 700 pounds. The coat is greyish-brown with vertical white stripes down the body. Kudus usually live in harsh, scrubby regions. There are two species, the 'greater' kudu and the 'lesser' kudu, the latter being a remarkable jumper, covering over 30 feet in a single leap.

LAKES The table below gives the size of most of the world's best-known lakes. The lakes are arranged in order of greatest area.

LAKES OF THE WORLD

(Arranged in order of area)

NAME	COUNTRY	AREA IN SQ. MILES
Superior	U.S.A.-Canada	31,820
Victoria	Africa	26,820
Aral	U.S.S.R.	24,630
Huron	U.S.A.-Canada	23,010
Michigan	U.S.A.	22,400
Chad	Africa	20,000
Nyasa	Africa	14,200
Tanganyika	Africa	12,700
Baikal	U.S.S.R.	11,580
Great Slave	Canada	11,170
Erie	Canada	9,950
Winnipeg	Canada	9,400
Maracaibo	Venezuela	8,296
Ontario	Canada	7,540
Ladoga	U.S.S.R.	7,000
Balkash	U.S.S.R.	6,680
Onega	U.S.S.R.	3,800
Eyre	Australia	3,500
Rudolf	Africa	3,500
Titicaca	Bolivia-Peru	3,200
Reindeer	Canada	2,440
Torrens	Australia	2,400
Koko-Nor	China	2,300
Vanern	Sweden	2,150
Bangweolo	Africa	2,000
Van	Turkey	1,450
Balaton	Hungary	230
Geneva	Switzerland	220
Windermere	Britain	11

LAOS is a kingdom in south-east Asia with an area of about 90,000 square miles and a population of some 2½ millions. The capital is Vientiane.

LAPLAND is not a separate country but is a district, stretching across the North of Norway, Sweden, Finland and the Soviet Union, in which Lapps live. The district is considerably larger than Great Britain but there are only about 100,000 Lapps. They are wandering people, or nomads, who have domesticated reindeer for their food and transport.

LATHE is a machine for shaping metal, wood, plastic, etc. It consists in the main of a rotating chuck in which the object to be machined is held, and a stationary bed which carries a fitting to hold a cutting tool. The fitting is so made that the cutting tool can move across the object or along it. In modern engineering workshops there are many types of lathe, each designed to carry out a special kind of work. The most common used in a workshop are the centre lathe and capstan lathe.

The komodo dragon is the largest of the lizards now living on earth

LAVA is molten rock discharged from a volcano, and a stream of lava is a very thick fluid saturated with gases and steam. When lava is thrown up by a volcano it may flow at first as fast as fifty miles an hour but it usually slows down as it gets farther from the cone of the volcano to a speed of less than one mile an hour. Scientists recognize two kinds of lava—basic and acid; basic lavas come from the deeper levels of the earth; acid lava cools more quickly. Then there is lava which has small crystals embedded in it; this is called porphyry. A flow of lava from a major volcano, such as Vesuvius, near Naples in Italy, can do a fantastic amount of damage. Not only this, but it can completely change the landscape.

LEAD is a heavy metal, but soft enough to be cut. It is used in the making of paints and glass and for covering electric cables and roofs. Lead was known to the ancient Egyptians and is mentioned several times in the Bible. All the compounds of lead are poisonous, and workers, such as painters, glaziers, plumbers and printers, need to exercise special caution if quantities of this metal are being used.

LEAGUE OF NATIONS was formed in 1920 because of the terrible destruction of life during the First World War (1914-18). The idea of the League was to stop war as well as all disputes which seemed likely to lead to war, and at first it did much good work, especially for the health and welfare of people. But the League was not powerful enough to stop disputes between nations, and country after country lost faith in it

and withdrew their membership. The Second World War (1939-45) proved that the League was indeed unable to prevent wars, and its work came to a standstill. In April 1946 it held a final meeting and its work was taken over by a new organization called the UNITED NATIONS. Credit for the idea, admirable in itself, for setting up the League of Nations must go to Thomas Woodrow Wilson who was Democratic President of the U.S.A. from 1913 to 1921.

LEATHER is the tanned or dressed hides or skins of such animals as cows, sheep and horses. Tanning is a very skilled and complicated job, but the main steps in the process are soaking the skins in a solution containing salt; treating with slaked lime (except sheep skins); scraping off the hair with a special knife or in a machine; and tanning the hide or skin (which at this stage is called a 'pelt') with a special solution. Brown leather is tanned with what is called 'tannic acid'. White leather used for gloves and the like is tanned with alum.

LEBANON is a small Arab republic of about 4,300 square miles bordering the eastern shores of the Mediterranean, an area sometimes called the Levant. The country has a population of over $2\frac{1}{2}$ millions. About half the people are Christians and the other half Moslems. The capital is Beirut. Lebanon grows and exports fruits. Before the First World War Lebanon was part of the Turkish Empire. It then became a French Mandated territory under the LEAGUE OF NATIONS but became a republic during the Second World War.

LEECH is a blood-sucking worm that lives in water. It is usually found in freshwater ponds or streams in temperate regions of the world although in the tropics they are found in moist vegetation. They have suckers at each end of their bodies, the one at the head end being equipped with teeth.

LEMMING is a rodent, and closely related to the vole. It is about 6 inches long, and is a tortoiseshell colour, resembling a small guinea-pig. It is found mostly in Scandinavia where it lives in a burrow. Every so often hordes of lemmings make their way across country, and if they reach the coast, instinctively go into the sea where thousands are drowned. It is not yet known why they do this strange thing.

LEMUR is a monkey-like animal. It is mostly found in Madagascar. Lemurs live in forests where they usually sleep during the day, and come out at night to feed on fruit, eggs, insects, etc.

LENT in the Christian Church lasts for forty days, beginning with Ash Wednesday and ending with Easter Sunday. It is intended to a be a period of fasting (doing without food or some kinds of food) in commemoration of Christ's fast in the wilderness as described in the Gospel of St Matthew, chapter four verse two. In the Latin

The night-feeding lemur found in Madagascar

Church, Lent formerly lasted for thirty-six days; the extra four days were added in the fifth century. The Roman Catholic Church strictly observes this spring fast; the English Church also observes it but gives no official directions about abstaining from food. The 'Lent' term is the name usually given to the spring term at universities.

LEOPARD is a member of the cat family. It is a very sleek animal with a handsome spotted coat. It is found in Africa, Ceylon, Borneo and the East Indies. It is more agile than the lion or tiger, and is a good tree climber. It hunts

Five examples of the principles of levers

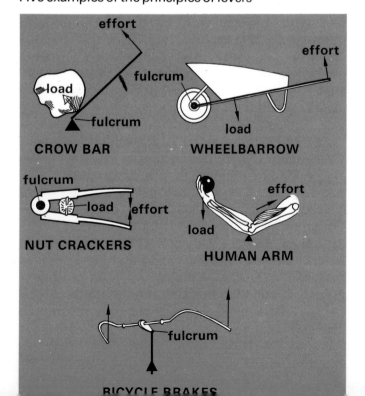

CROW BAR

WHEELBARROW

NUT CRACKERS

HUMAN ARM

BICYCLE BRAKES

The leopard has a sleek, handsomely spotted coat

and kills various animals for food, mainly at night.

LEVERS   A good example of a simple lever is a crowbar.   To lift something up it is necessary to have the crowbar supported at one point called the fulcrum.   The force to be applied by the person using the lever must be further from the fulcrum than the resistance to be overcome. See illustration of how they are best arranged.

LIBERIA is an independent English-speaking negro republic in West Africa.   It is 43,000 square miles and has a population of $1\frac{1}{4}$ million. The capital is Monrovia.   The country produces rubber, cocoa, coffee and iron ore.   The country was founded in 1820 as a home for American negro slaves.

LIBYA is a large Arab kingdom on the Mediterranean coast of Africa.   It is 810,000 square miles but has a population of only about $1\frac{3}{4}$ million.   The country is divided into three divisions—Tripolitania, Cyrenaica and the Fezzan. There are at present two capitals—Tripoli and Benghazi—but a new capital is being built at Beida in Cyrenaica.   Most of the country is desert and until the discovery of oil a few years ago was one of the poorest countries in the world.

LIECHTENSTEIN is a tiny principality on the upper Rhine with a population of about 22,000 in an area of about 65 square miles.   The capital is Vaduz.   There is some industry.

LIFESAVING (SWIMMING)   Every swimmer should learn how to save the life of another person who may get into difficulties in the water. So important is this considered in Britain that there is a Royal Life Saving Society with headquarters in London, and the Society's bronze medal is awarded to anyone over the age of fourteen who reaches a set standard of efficiency. There are special techniques which swimmers are advised to adopt when endeavouring to save life.   Sometimes the person who is in danger of drowning becomes panic-stricken and may seize and pull down the person who comes to the rescue; to avoid this happening, the rescuer should if possible always approach from the rear; he then gets his arm round the neck and under the chin of the drowning person and tows

him backwards to safety, using his legs and his free arm to do the back-stroke.   A swimmer who practises lifesaving should also learn the art of giving artificial respiration.

LIGHT is wave-motion which, when it strikes the eye, causes the sensation of sight; in other words, we see by means of light.   Light has a range of wave-lengths from the very short to the very long.   Light that affects our eyes has a wave-length from $\frac{1}{40,000}$ inch to $\frac{1}{80,000}$ inch.   All light travels at the same speed, which is 186,000 miles per second!

White light is made up of a number of different coloured lights.   This can be easily shown by passing a beam of light through a triangular prism and making a SPECTRUM.   Light travels in straight lines, unless reflected by a polished surface like a mirror.   When light passes from, say air to water, it is bent or refracted.   This can be shown by placing a pencil in a glass of water, when the pencil will appear to be bent at the point it enters the water.   This is an important property of light, and used in the making of all types of lenses.   The study of the behaviour of light is called 'optics'.

LIGHTHOUSES have been used from earliest times to warn ships of rocks and other dangers. The early type of lighthouse was no more than a bonfire on a high tower, and it was called a 'fire-beacon'.   The last fire-beacon in use was at Flat Holm in the Bristol Channel; it was discontinued in 1822.   The famous Pharos lighthouse, so called because it was built on the small island of Pharos, near the city of Alexandria in Egypt, was erected about 285 B.C. and became one of the seven wonders of the world. It is believed to have been about 400 feet high with its light visible for about thirty miles.   It was destroyed by an earthquake.   The oldest English lighthouse was probably one built by the Romans at Dover.   Though wood fires were used originally for lighthouses, they were later replaced by coal burnt in iron baskets then big candles were used, but the results were not satisfactory; then oil lamps and then gas.   Nowadays the majority of lighthouses are powered by electricity; in fine weather they send out an intense and penetrating white light, and in foggy weather a yellow beam is often found to be better.   The efficiency of lighthouses was greatly

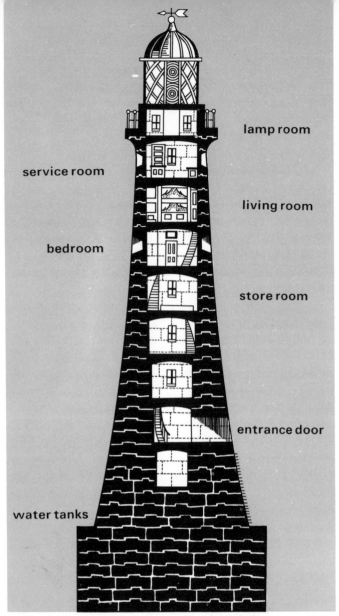

lamp room

service room

living room

bedroom

store room

entrance door

water tanks

Diagram showing the main parts of a lighthouse

A male lion has a striking mane

improved by a French scientist named Augustin Fresnel who died in 1827. It was his idea to surround the light in a lighthouse with lenses and prisms so that its power was increased and the rays of light concentrated into a beam like a search-light. Some lighthouses are called 'occulting' which means that their light flashes at intervals, the flash lasting longer than the interval between each flash; a 'flashing' light is one which shows itself for a *shorter* period than the interval between each flash. The most powerful lighthouse in the world is the Creac'h d'Oeussant lighthouse off Brittany, France; it was completed in 1959, is 159 feet high, and its light is equivalent to the luminous power of 500 million candles. The tallest lighthouse anywhere in the world is in Japan; it is a steel tower 348 feet high near Yamashita Park in Yokohama.

LIGHTNING Primitive man was terrified by thunder and lightning, thinking that these phenomena were signs that the gods or evil spirits were angry with him. But of course the ancients did not know about electricity, and it was not until the middle of the eighteenth century that Benjamin Franklin, the American scientist, showed that lightning was really just a very big electric spark and that thunder was simply the loud crack made by this enormous spark. Certain clouds, called by scientists cumulo-nimbus, are charged with electricity; we call them thunder-clouds. These clouds have tiny particles of ice whirling about inside them, and this generates great friction which causes the electrical charge to build up. Eventually the charge becomes so great that the electricity leaps through the air; it heats the air and produces a great spark which can be as much as five or ten miles long. See THUNDERSTORM.

LINEN is a material made from the fibres of the stalk of a plant called flax, which the Romans called *linum*. It is one of the fibres which have been used by man since very early times: mummies found in ancient Egyptian tombs were wrapped in linen bands. The Bible speaks of princes being dressed in 'purple and fine linen'. Linen has great strength when stretched, and for this reason it is excellent for sail-cloth. The valley of the Nile in Egypt was the original home of flax and linen, and linen was regarded in those times as a symbol of purity and was the only material that the ancient Egyptian priests were allowed to wear. The chief centres of linen manufacture (in which the flax fibres are soaked, combed, straightened, spun into yarn and woven) are Belfast in Northern Ireland, Dunfermline in Scotland, and Leeds in Yorkshire, England.

LION is the biggest member of the cat family. It is found in Africa and parts of Asia. It differs from the rest of the cat family in that the males have a mane, and a tuft of hair at the tip of the tail. A lioness has no mane; in fact, it is a much sleeker animal. It often hunts for food in groups by day and night, and is the main enemy of such animals as antelopes, zebras, wild pigs and the like.

LIZARD is a reptile. There are about fifteen hundred kinds of lizards, the most important being the geckos, iguanas, molochs, flying dragons, slow-worms and monitors. A true lizard is usually covered with scales, and has four well-developed limbs ending in toes, but there are exceptions to this; such as the slow-worm which has no limbs. Most of the lizards lay eggs which are buried in sand and hatched after a few weeks, although some young are born without eggs.

LLAMA Although this well-known animal does not have a hump, and is a much smaller animal, it is related to the camel. It is provided with a thick, fleecy coat to keep it warm in the high mountains of South America where it lives in large herds. A close relative of the llama is the alpaca.

LOBSTER See **CRABS**

LOCOMOTIVE is an engine driven by steam, oil or electricity, and used on railways for pulling carriages or wagons. The first locomotive to be built was 'Locomotion', and designed by George Stevenson. It pulled the first public train between Stockton and Darlington on September 27, 1825.

Locomotives are classed according to their wheels; for example, a 'Britannia' locomotive is a 4-6-2. This means that it has 4 bogie wheels at the front, 6 driving wheels that are coupled together, and 2 rear wheels. The wheels on the tender are not included.

LOOM is a machine for weaving fabrics. There are many types of loom, ranging from the simple home-made loom to the large and complicated machines which can weave the most intricate patterns. But the basic principle is the same in all types of loom. A number of threads are wound on the yard beam of a loom; these threads are called the 'warp'. A continuous thread is then passed backwards and forwards, under and over the warp; this thread is called the 'weft' (in olden days it was known as the 'woof'). The pattern of threads thus produced is similar to a simple darn.

LUNGS are the organs by which we breathe. There are two lungs, one each side of the chest. Air is drawn in through the mouth and nose, and passes to the lungs along the windpipe or 'trachea'. The trachea divides into two branches inside the chest. One of these branches, called a 'bronchi,' goes to each lung. Inside the lung the bronchi divide and subdivide, finally ending in minute air-sacs. Lying very close to the air-sacs are tiny blood vessels, the 'capillaries'. It is these that take up oxygen in the air and pass it to the blood. See HUMAN BODY.

LUTE is a musical instrument which was widely used in the 16th and 17th centuries. It has a very soft sound. Lutes are still made for those members of an orchestra or music group who wish to play old music on the instruments for which it was originally written. The lute was plucked, not played with a bow,

Diagram of the lungs, see HUMAN BODY

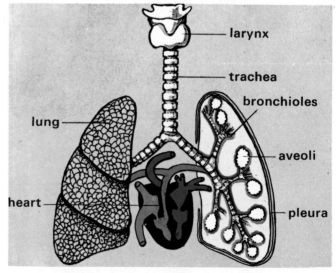

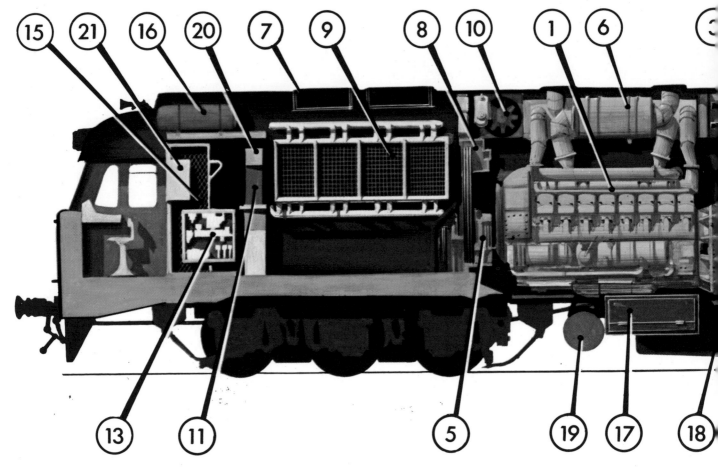

Diesel-electric locomotive. 1, diesel engine; 2, alternators; 3, rectifier; 4, exciter; 5, compressor; 6, silencer; 7, radiator fan; 8, electromagnetic coupling; 9, radiator; 10, coding fan; 11, traction motor blower; 12, filters; 13, brake cubicle; 14, air equipment; 15, electric equipment cubicle; 16, water tank; 17, batteries; 18, fuel tank; 19, air reservoir; 20, thermostatic controls; 21, electronic equipment; 22, train lighting controls; 23, traction motor; 24, transmission.

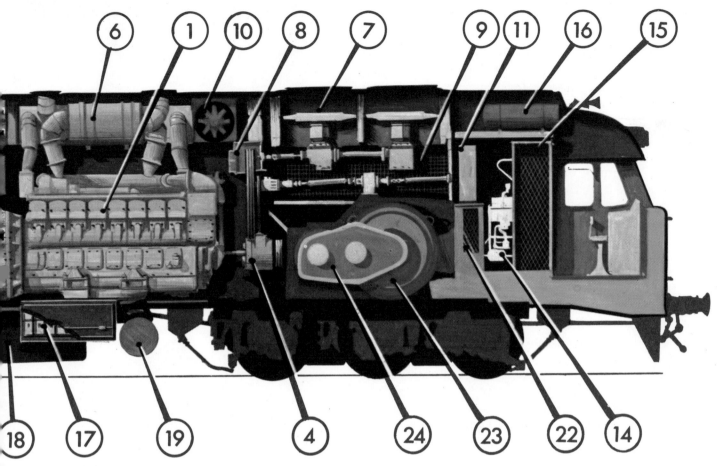

Steam locomotive. 1, blast pipe; 2, smoke box; 3, tube leading superheated steam to cylinders; 4, superheater header; 5, superheater tubes; 6, feedwater valve; 7, firetubes; 8, regulator valve; 9, regulator rod; 10, safety valve; 11, firebox stays; 12, firebox; 13, locker; 14, coal space; 15, water pick-up head; 16, main water filler inlet; 17, piston valves; 18, piston; 19, slide bars; 20, crosshead; 21, connecting rod; 22, reversing gear; 23, coupling rod; 24, firebricks; 25, water tank; 26, water pick-up.

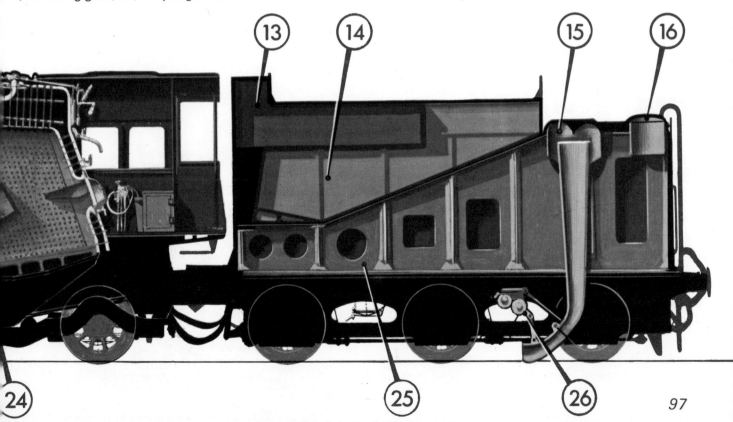

and it was introduced in medieval times by the Saracens by way of Spain, along with the mandolin and the guitar. In shape the lute is like half a pear.

LUXEMBURG is a Grand Duchy that borders Belgium, France and Germany. It has an area of 1,000 square miles and a population of about 340,000. Its capital is also named Luxemburg. It is rich in iron and coal and has a flourishing steel industry.

LYNX is a member of the cat family. It is larger than the domestic cat, has a short tail, tufted ears, and a fringe of whiskers on each cheek. It is now rare in Europe, but is found in Asia, India, Africa and North America. It feeds on small animals and birds.

LYRE The Greek god Hermes (Roman Mercury) was supposed to have invented the ancient musical instrument called the lyre by putting strings across the empty shell of a tortoise. Afterwards the tortoise was held sacred in honour of Hermes. This harp-like instrument was much in favour with the ancient Greeks. It consists of a body with two horn-like pieces rising from it, and a cross-piece between the horns, from which the strings are stretched to the lower part. The body was hollow, to increase the sound produced by plucking the strings with a stick of ivory or polished wood, or with the fingers. The number of strings was increased gradually from only three to sixteen.

MACHINE TOOL This term is generally used to describe the machines which make things in a factory. For example, a LATHE is a machine that is equipped with cutting tools to shape metal and wood. Other kinds of machine tools are boring machines, drilling machines, shaping machines, milling machines, etc.

MACH NUMBER is the measure of the speed of a high-speed aeroplane compared with the

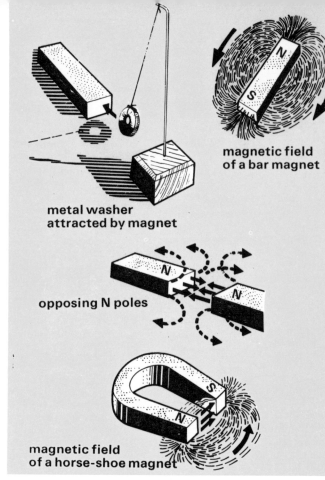

magnetic field of a bar magnet

metal washer attracted by magnet

opposing N poles

magnetic field of a horse-shoe magnet

Diagram showing how magnets attract and repel, and various kinds of magnetic fields

A mammoth, an extinct member of the elephant family that once roamed over wide areas of the earth

speed of sound. Thus, an aeroplane travelling at a speed of Mach 2 is travelling at twice the speed of sound.

MADAGASCAR is the fifth largest island in the world and lies off the east coast of Africa in the Indian Ocean. It has an area of 228,000 square miles and a population of over 6½ millions. The capital is Antananarivo (or Tananarive). The country is mainly agricultural producing coffee, sugar, sisal and rice. MICA is mined there. Madagascar became independent in 1960 as the Malagasy Republic.

MAGNA CARTA was a charter which the barons made King John sign at Runnymede in 1215. It laid down certain rights which the King had to grant. The Magna Carta has been called the 'keystone of English liberty'.

MAGNETISM The word magnetism comes from the name Magnesia, a place on the Aegean coast and known to the ancient Greeks. The ancients knew that there was a sort of iron ore in Magnesia possessing unusual properties –in fact, properties we now call magnetic.

One property of a magnet is that if it is made in the form of a needle and suspended freely from its middle, it always sets itself in a line running approximately north and south; and the same end always points north. So there is evidently some difference between the two ends, which are called the poles. The end pointing north is called the 'north pole', and that pointing south is called the 'south pole'. Another property of magnets is that the north pole of one magnet will repel the north pole of another, and the south pole of one magnet will repel the south pole of another. But if the poles are of opposite polarity, then they attract each other. Yet another property of a magnet is that it will attract pieces of iron or iron-alloy to it. The reason for this is that all round the magnet the magnetic force is acting, and when into this magnetic 'field' a piece of iron is put, some of the energy goes into the iron and makes it magnetic for the time being. And the way in which this happens is such that the pole of the temporary magnet that is nearest the actual magnet is of opposite polarity to it. See COMPASS.

MALARIA is a disease caused by a female mosquito which injects a germ into the human bloodstream. Quinine was at one time used as a remedy, but in recent years such manmade compounds as 'mepacrine' are taken. Since the end of the Second World War much work has been done to clean up the areas where the malaria-carrying mosquito breeds.

MALAWI is a republic in Central Africa and member of the British Commonwealth. It has an area of 45,400 square miles and a population of over 4½ millions. The capital is Zomba. Main exports are tea, tobacco and cotton.

MALAYSIA lies in the Malay peninsula of south-east Asia and part of the island of Borneo. It is a member of the British Commonwealth and achieved independence in 1957. It has an area of 27,380 square miles and a population of about 10½ millions. The capital is Kuala Lumpur and the main products are rubber, timber, pepper, agricultural crops and also tin.

MALI is a republic in north-western Africa with an area of about 465,000 square miles and a population of nearly 5 millions. The capital is Bamako and the main export is groundnuts. The ancient town of Timbuktu lies within Mali's boundaries.

MALTA is a small island in the Mediterranean. It is 95 square miles and has a population of about 330,000. Included with Malta are the smaller islands of Gozo and Comino. The Maltese language is descended from that of the Phoenicians who colonized the island. The people claim to have been Christians since St. Paul was ship-wrecked on the island. The capital is Valletta.

MAMMALS are animals, the females of which bear their babies alive, and feed them with their own milk. Also, most mammals have a coverinf of hair; an exception, of course, is the whales which are almost hairless. Compared with other classes of the animal kingdom, mammals have a highly developed brain. Mammals are a very large class of animals, ranging from the platypus to man.

MAMMOTH As you can see from the drawing, the now extinct mammoth was a member of the elephant family. It used to roam over most parts of Europe, Asia and North America, had gigantic tusks which curved inwards, and grew a woolly coat covered with long, coarse hair in the winter. Skeletons of this animal (several have been found preserved in ice in places in Siberia) show that it often grew to a size much larger than that of the African elephant.

MANATEE An aquatic mammal some 7 feet long weighing about 450 pounds. They have broad flat tails and their forelimbs have become little more than flippers. They are essentially vegetarian and peaceful. Their enemies are crocodiles and sharks. They give birth to one or two babies, born under water. Manatees are found in the coastal waters of West Africa, Caribbean and Central America.

MANDRILL is a MONKEY, closely related to the BABOON. However, they have short tails and are found mostly in the forests of West Africa. The male mandrill has bright blue and crimson on his muzzle and hind-quarters.

Magnificent temple built by the ancient Maya people

The lion marmoset, so named because of its mane

MARATHON is the name of a plain in Greece and it was here that the Athenians repulsed a Persian attack in a famous battle in 490 B.C. News of the great victory was brought to Athens by an athlete named Pheidippides, who ran the whole way non-stop and collapsed on reaching the capital. The distance was afterwards measured and found to be 26 miles 385 yards and when the ancient Olympic Games were started again in 1896 a 'marathon' race was included in the events in commemoration of the historic run, and has been a feature of them to the present day. The fastest time for the marathon is 2 hours 8 minutes 33·6 seconds by an Australian in 1969.

MARMOSET is a small New World monkey found in South America. The pygmy marmoset is the smallest primate in the world. Marmosets can be tamed as pets, and are very friendly little animals. They bite if they are teased or take a dislike to someone.

MARMOT is a large burrowing rodent found in the Alps, Himalayas and North America. They hibernate in winter and have 2 to 4 young per litter.

MARSUPIALS are animals, the female of which has a pouch in which the young is kept and nourished after birth. These include such animals as the kangaroo, wallaby, wombat, bandicoot, tasmanian wolf, banded anteater, pouched moles, platypus, opossums, and koala bears. Most of these animals are found only in Australia; the exception are the opossums which are also found in America. Most of these are described in this book under the animal's name.

MASQUE was a kind of entertainment popular at the royal courts of the 16th and 17th centuries. It consisted of a play in verse, with some music and dancing, and the players wore masks, hence the name. The story was usually based on a legend. A famous masque is *Comus* by the English poet John Milton (1608-74); it was first staged at Ludlow Castle, Shropshire, in 1634.

MAYA was the name of a great American-Indian civilization in Central America before the conquest of that country by the Spaniards in the 16th century. The Maya people built magnificent stone temples decorated with beautiful carvings. They had some knowledge of astronomy, and had composed an accurate calendar. The Maya were an agricultural people; the main plant grown was maize.

MENSURATION is that branch of mathematics which deals with the measurement of lengths, areas and volumes. The area of a square is the units in length multiplied by the units in breadth, and if the measure is in inches, the area is written as so many square inches; for example, the area of a square 4 inches long by 4 inches broad is 16 square inches. A cube with four-inch sides has a volume of 4 × 4 × 4 = 64 cubic inches.

METALLURGY is the science of metals. It studies how metals can best be extracted from ores, the physical properties of metals; that is, strength, wear, etc., and what metals are best suited to special needs. Although metallurgy has always been an important subject, it is now even more so because of the advances in such fields as jets, rockets and atomics. For example, one of the big jobs in rocket flight is to find metals which will stand up to the terrific temperatures of the rocket motors.

METEOR is a smallish stone which enters the earth's atmosphere at a speed of about 50,000 miles per hour. Because of the resistance of the air, meteors flame and burn away before reaching the earth's surface. Meteors generally enter the earth's atmosphere in swarms. A very large meteor may get through the earth's atmosphere without being entirely burnt up, and land on the earth's surface; it is then called a 'meteorite'. One of the largest of such meteorites was the 'Great Siberian' which has been estimated to have weighed about 200 tons; it devastated an area of thousands of square miles, and destroyed and uprooted about 80 million trees.

METEOROLOGY is the scientific study of the weather. The weather at any moment depends mainly on how hot or cold the air is and its pressure. Hot air holds much more water vapour than cold. Therefore, if hot air takes up water, and is then cooled, water is deposited either in fine drops making a cloud, or larger drops which fall as rain—they can also take the form of fine ice-crystals which fall as snow. On the other hand, if cool air is warmed, it takes up more water, and there is no rain. Again, if the air pressures at different places are unequal, air moves from the areas of high pressure to areas of low pressure. This movement of air is wind. The rotation of the earth affects the direction of winds. The most important side of meteorology is weather-forecasting.

METRONOME is an instrument with an inverted pendulum which can be set to beat so many times to the minute and thus give the right speed at which a piece of music should be performed. The instrument makes an audible 'tick-tock'. The word metronome comes from two Greek words meaning 'measure' and 'law'.

MEXICO is a large republic in the central part of America. It is 758,000 square miles and has a population of nearly 50 millions. The people are Spanish-speaking. Apart from those of European descent there are many Indians, descendants of the AZTECS, Tolecs and MAYANS. The capital is Mexico City. Mexico is rich in minerals, particularly in silver, gold, lead and petroleum. The country also produces cotton and coffee.

MICA is a mineral which can be parted in the

form of thin flat sheets. It is used in industry for such things as stove windows where the material has to be both transparent and yet heat-resisting. There are large mica mines in India, U.S.A. and U.S.S.R.

MICROPHONE　See **RADIO**

MICROSCOPE is an optical instrument which enlarges objects too small to be clearly seen by the human eye. The simplest form of microscope is a magnifying glass. See ELEC-TRON MICROSCOPE.

MIGRATION Certain birds and animals migrate; that is, travel from one country to another at special times of the year. Exactly how and why they do this is not clear, but it is almost certain that the journeys they make have to do with food and breeding. Birds migrate very great distances; for example, the Pacific golden plover flies from Alaska, where it nests, to Hawaii, in winter, a distance of 2,400 miles. One of the most famous migrations was that of the caribou (the North American reindeer) from their summer to winter feeding grounds; another was that of the American bison (often called buffalo) of which herds numbering millions also travelled hundreds of miles, following the same routes year after year.

MILITARY AND NAVAL EVENTS The table below gives some of the battles on land and sea which have been important in shaping the course of history.

GREAT BATTLES AND WARS

(490 B.C. to the Present)

DATE	EVENT	
490 B.C.	Battle of Marathon	Athenians defeated Persians
431-404	Peloponnesian War	Between Athenians and Spartans
264-146	Punic Wars	Between Rome and Carthage
55	Invasion of Britain	Roman army led by Julius Caesar
A.D. 70	Jerusalem destroyed	Roman Emperor Titus
410	Rome sacked	Visigoths led by Alaric
450	Saxon invasions of Britain	Hengist and Horsa
1066	Battle of Hastings	Harold defeated by William
1314	Battle of Bannockburn	Robert Bruce defeated English
1346	Battle of Crecy	Edward III defeated French
1415	Battle of Agincourt	Henry V defeated French

1455-84	Wars of the Roses	Between Houses of York and Lancaster
1513	Battle of Flodden Field	English defeated Scots
1588	Spanish Armada	Defeated in English Channel by navy led by Sir F. Drake
1690	Battle of the Boyne	William III defeated James II
1704	Battle of Blenheim	Marlborough defeated French
1706	Battle of Ramillies	Marlborough defeated French
1775-83	American War of Independence	
1798	Battle of the Nile	Nelson defeated French fleet
1805	Battle of Trafalgar	"　　"　　"　　"
1805	Battle of Austerlitz	Napoleon defeated Russians and Austrians
1815	Battle of Waterloo	Wellington defeated Napoleon
1853-56	Crimean War	Britain, France and Turkey against Russia
1857	Indian Mutiny	Revolt against British
1870-71	Franco-Prussian War	Between France and Prussia
1879	Zulu War	Between British and Zulus
1899-902	South African War	Between British and Boers
1914	Battle of Tannenberg	Germans defeated Russians
1914	Battle of Ypres	German advance held
1914	Battle of Marne (Ist)	"　　"
1916	Battle of Verdun	
1916-17	Battles of the Somme	"　　"
1916	Battle of Jutland	Between British and German fleets
1917	Russian Revolution	Tsar overthrown
1918	Battle of the Marne (2nd)	German defeat
1918	Zeebrugge	Attack on German submarine base
1935	Abyssinia	Attacked by Mussolini
1936	Spanish Civil War	
1939	Poland	Attacked by Hitler and start of Second World War
1940	Battle of Britain	Defeat of German Air Force by R.A.F.
1941	Russia	Attacked by Hitler
1941	Pearl Harbour	American naval base atacked by Japanese Air Force
1942	Battle of El Alamein	Rommel defeated by Gen. Montgomery
1942	Battle of Guadalcanal	Gen. MacArthur attacks Japanese
1943	Battle of Stalingrad	Start of German defeat in Russia
1944	Normandy landing	Invasion of Europe
1945	Hiroshima and Nagasaki	Attacked with first atom bombs

GREAT MILITARY AND NAVAL LEADERS

Name	Lived	Nationality	Main Event(s)
Alexander the Great	356–323 B.C.	Greek	Conquered Persia, Syria, Egypt, Phoenicia, and marched into India
Alexander of Tunis, Earl	A.D. 1891-1969	British	Second World War—North Africa
Alexander Nevski	1218-63	Russian	Defeated the Teutonic Knights on Lake Peipus
Attila	406–453	Hun	Conquered great part of Roman Empire
Baden-Powell, Lord	1857–1941	British	Defended Mafeking in Boer War
Beatty, Earl	1871–1936	British	Battle of Jutland—First World War

Name	Dates	Nationality	Notes
Bonaparte, Napoleon	1769–1821	French	Victories over Russia, Austria and Prussia—defeated at Waterloo and Trafalgar
Bruce, Robert	1274–1329	Scots	Defeated Edward II at Battle of Bannockburn
Caesar, Julius	102–44 B.C.		Extended Roman Empire to Germany, France and Britain
Caractacus	about A.D. 50	British	Fought Romans at Wallingford and Colchester—captured and taken to Rome
Charlemagne	742–814	Frankish	Defeated Saxons, Lombards, Saracens in Spain and Hungarians —christianized countries he captured
Clive, Robert, Baron	1725–1774	British	Battle of Plassey (India)
Cortes, Hernan	1485–1547	Spanish	Conquered Mexico
Cromwell, Oliver	1599–1658	British	Formed the 'Ironsides', and won battles of Marston Moor and Naseby
Drake, Sir Francis	1540–96	British	Defeated the Spanish Armada
Eisenhower, D. D.	1890	American	Supreme Commander of Allied Armies that defeated Germany in 1945
Foch, Marshal	1851–1929	French	First World War—Battles of Ypres and Vimy Ridge
Garibaldi, G.	1807–82	Italian	Helped make Italy a free and independent country
Gaulle, General De	1890–1970	French	Leader of Free French army in Second World War
Genghis Khan	1162–1227	Mongolian	Conquered large part of Asia
Gordon, General	1833–85	British	Siege of Khartoum
Grant, General	1822–85	American	Led the armies of the north in the Civil War
Haig, Earl	1861–1928	British	First World War—Battles of Somme and Passchendaele
Hindenburg, Paul	1847–1934	German	First World War—defeated Russians at Tannenberg
Jackson, General	1824–63	American	Battle of Harper's Ferry—American Civil War—known to his troops as 'Stonewall'
Kitchener, Earl	1850–1916	British	Battle of Omdurman and Boer War
Lawrence of Arabia	1888–1935	British	Led the Arabs against the Turks in First World War
Lee, General	1807–70	American	Led armies of South in Civil War
MacArthur, General	1880–1964	American	Defeated Japanese in Pacific in Second World War
Marlborough, Duke of	1650–1722	British	Defeated French at Blenheim, Ramillies and Malplaquet
Marshall, General	1880–1959	American	Chief of Staff of the U.S. Army in Second World War
Montgomery,	1887	British	Defeated Rommel at El Alamein, Normandy in 1944, and led army to the Rhine
Mountbatten, Earl	1900	British	Reconquest of Burma from Japanese
Nelson, Viscount	1758–1805	British	Defeated French fleet at Battle of Trafalgar
Petain, Marshal	1856–1951	French	Battle of Verdun in First World War
Roberts, Earl	1832–1914	British	Campaigns in Africa and India—especially Boer War

Robert Bruce, leader of the Scots at Bannockburn

Name	Dates	Nationality	Notes
Rommel, General	1891–1944	German	Commanded the Afrika Korps with great success until defeated by General Montgomery
Sherman, General	1820–91	American	Destroyed Atlanta by fire after capturing it from South
Smuts, Field-Marshal	1870–1950	S. African	Fought with Boers against British. In First World War commanded British forces in E. Africa
Suvarov, General	1729–1800	Russian	Led Russian army in Napoleonic Wars
Tito, Marshal	1892	Yugoslav	Led Yugoslavia against German invader in Second World War
Wavell, Earl	1883–1950	British	Defeated Italians in Cyrenaica in Second World War
Wellington, Duke of	1769–1852	British	Defeated Napoleon at Waterloo

Diagram showing the main parts of a microscope

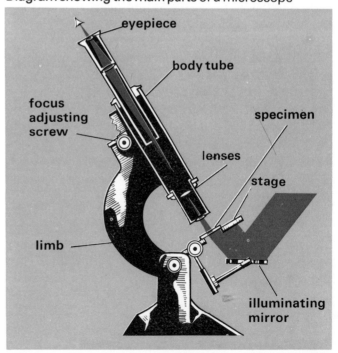

eyepiece

body tube

focus adjusting screw

specimen

lenses

stage

limb

illuminating mirror

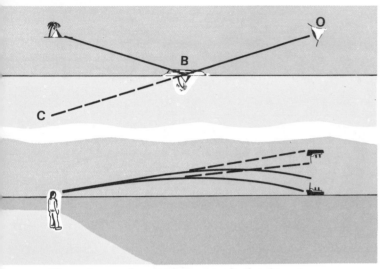

Top, mirage of an oasis as seen in the desert
and *below,* a mirage as seen at sea

Below left, drawing of the inside of a snail,
one of the commonest of the molluscs

MIRAGE is an image of something reflected in the sky, and seen especially over deserts. The image is usually upside down, and this is caused by the bending of light. Travellers in hot desert regions have reported seeing pools of water where, in fact, none have been found to exist. What they have seen is the reflection of a pool miles away out of sight on the other side of the horizon. The rays of light, passing upwards from the pool, strike a layer of denser air which acts as a mirror and directs the rays of light down again through the hot light air next to the sand. A mirage can also occur at sea, when the inverted image of a ship or ships may appear in the air.

MOLE is a small, furry animal which is found in many parts of the world, and is specially suited for underground life. Its front legs are equipped with strong claws for digging, and with them it burrows under the ground in search of grubs and earthworms. It makes its nest underground, and here, on a bed of leaves and grass, the young moles are born in the spring.

MOLLUSCS are found in most parts of the world, and can live either on land or in water. They are usually protected by a shell, have a tongue with horny teeth, and crawl along by means of a muscular foot. Typical molluscs are shell-fish, snails, slugs, soft-bodied cuttlefish and the octopus.

MONACO is a tiny principality on the Medi-terranean and joined with France. Its Sovereign Prince is Prince Rainier who married the film star, Grace Kelly. It is only 2 miles long and half a mile broad, and has little over 24,000 inhabitants. It is best known for its Casino at Monte Carlo.

MONASTERY is a building in which monks live; that is, men who have vowed to devote their lives to the service of God. The first monks were simple hermits who lived in small caves. The word monk comes from a Greek word meaning 'living alone', because the early monks led individual, solitary lives. The first monastic organization dates from the year 305 when St. Anthony set up a monastery near Memphis, on the Nile. St. Benedict (born about the year 480) laid down strict rules for his followers (called Benedictines); he held that the best discipline is work, which is the foundation of goodness. Other famous orders of monks are called Carthusians, Cistercians, and Dominicans. Inmates of a monastery serve under an abbot or prior. In England the monasteries were dissolved during the years 1536-40 by order of Henry VIII (reigned 1509-47).

MONEY When early man ceased hunting and settled down to farm and make tools, weapons and so on, he obtained the things he needed by what is called barter. This means that if a man wanted, say, an axe, he might offer his pigs or his corn in exchange to a man who made axes but had no pigs or corn. So each man got what he wanted in a fair exchange. However, as populations increased and life became more civilized, this bartering became very clumsy, so pieces of precious metal were used instead. Thus, a man who wanted, say, a horse, would give a piece of gold or silver to a man who had horses for sale, and this man in turn might buy with the money something that he wanted from another man. So money began to circulate. Gradually each country came to have its own coinage, and laws were passed about the size, weight and purity of the pieces. The oldest coins were made in Greece and China in the 7th century B.C.

The place where coins are made is called a mint. Most money used in trade and industry is kept in banks, and it is through the banks that large sums of money are paid in and out. The word bank comes from the Italian word *banca,* meaning a bench, because the old Italian merchants who acted as bankers usually conducted their business at benches. The world's earliest bank notes were issued by a Swedish bank in 1661 but paper money is an invention of the Chinese, who are believed to have used it as early as the 7th century A.D.

MONGOLIA or Mongolian People's Republic, is a vast desert country to the north of China. It is about 600,000 square miles but much of it consists of the great Gobi Desert. The population is only a little more than a million. The capital is Ulan Bator.

MONGOOSE lives in India, Africa and Spain. It has a long body covered with coarse hair, short legs and a bushy tail. It is a fierce little animal, and lives in a burrow or hole, feeding on rats, mice, various reptiles, birds, eggs, etc. It is well known for the fearless way in which it will attack and kill the most deadly snakes, especially the cobra.

MONKEYS There are two main groups of monkeys, one of which is found in America (New World monkeys), and the other in Africa and Asia (Old World monkeys). The New World monkeys are distinguished from the monkeys of the Old World by not having cheek-pouches, the nostrils are sometimes set widely apart, and they often have a tail which is prehensile; that is

adapted for grasping or seizing. The Old World monkeys usually have cheek-pouches, and the tail is never prehensile. Typical New World monkeys are the squirrel monkeys, howler monkeys, woolly monkeys, marmosets and spider monkeys. The best known of the Old World monkeys are the baboons, macaques and langurs. The chimpanzees and gorillas belong to the ape family.

MONSOON is a word from the Arabic language, and means 'season'. Generally it means the rainy season (June to September) in India and near-by countries. But the word is, in practice, given to the winds that change with the season in India and elsewhere. There are summer monsoons and winter monsoons and over parts of Asia the monsoons directly affect the agriculture and day-to-day life of the inhabitants of those regions. Rain can be very heavy during the summer monsoon, whereas the winter monsoon is a drying wind, bringing only slight rain.

MOON is the heavenly body that revolves round the earth. It is approximately 238,860 miles from earth, and about 2,160 miles in diameter. Because of the movement of the earth only one face is ever seen from the earth. The moon has no atmosphere similar to our own, and no form of life exists on it. Scientists are now studying the rock samples brought back by American astronauts and hope to discover how the moon was formed and how old it is.

MOOSE See **ELK**

MOROCCO is a kingdom in North Africa that is 180,000 square miles and has a population of a little more than 15½ millions. The capital is Rabat, with Tangier as the summer capital. The largest city is the port of Casablanca. The country produces phosphates, manganese, iron ore, lead and zinc and is famous for its fine leather work. The people on the coast are mostly Arabs and those in the Atlas Mountains chiefly Berbers.

MORSE CODE is a system of signalling invented by an American, Samuel Finlay Breese Morse (1791-1872), with the help of Alfred

Vail. The Code can be signalled by telegraph or a high-powered lamp; it consists of dots and dashes which represent letters of the alphabet, numerals, punctuation marks, and the more usual phrases. It is in international use for both civil and military purposes. The length of the dash is three times that of the dot. A hand-operated key can transmit the Morse Code at about twenty-five to thirty words a minute; the speed by lamp is about half that rate. Here is the Code:

A	.-	N	-.	1	.----
B	-...	O	---	2	..---
C	-.-.	P	.--.	3	...--
D	-..	Q	--.-	4	....-
E	.	R	.-.	5	.....
F	..-.	S	...	6	-....
G	--.	T	-	7	--...
H	....	U	..-	8	---..
I	..	V	...-	9	----.
J	.---	W	.--	0	-----
K	-.-	X	-..-	Begin message:	-.-.-
L	.-..	Y	-.--	End message:	.-.-.
M	--	Z	--..	Repeat message:	..--..

MOSQUITOES are a kind of fly that have long, slender bodies, long legs and scale-covered wings. The eggs are laid in or near water, and the larvae which hatch out from them always start their life in the water, where they feed on minute particles of food. There are more than 1,500 kinds of known mosquitoes, many of which are very dangerous because of the way in which they spread diseases; such as, malaria and yellow fever.

MOSS is a non-flowering plant which grows like a mat on rocks, ground, trees, etc., where it is damp. Mosses, like ferns, increase by means of spores, and not seeds.

MOTHS See **BUTTERFLIES**

MOTOR-CAR or **AUTOMOBILE** is any self-propelled vehicle, usually with four wheels. The first true model was made by a Frenchman, Nicholas Cugot, in 1770. It was steam-driven, had three wheels and a speed of 2½ m.p.h. There were many who experimented with steam-driven carriages, but advance was slow until the invention and development of the INTERNAL COMBUSTION ENGINE. The men mainly responsible for this were the Frenchman Etienne Lenoir (1860) and two Germans, Nikolaus Otto (1860) and Gottlieb Daimler (1885). In Britain the main pioneers were H.J. Lawson, F. Lanchester, Herbert Austin, William Riley, J.D. Siddely, C.S. Rolls and Henry Royce, W.R. Morris (later Lord Nuffield) and W.D. Bentley. In the United States there were C. and J. Duryea, E. Hayes, D. Buick, Henry Ford, R.E. Olds and G. Selden.

MOUFLON belongs to the sheep family, and is found in its wild state in the mountains of Sardinia and Corsica. It is one of the few remaining wild sheep in the whole of Europe. The mouflon is rather a small animal, standing about 28 to 30 inches high at the shoulder. It has a reddish-brown coat, and the ram has curved horns of up to 30 inches long. In

A mosquito, the carrier of many diseases

A selection of common mosses

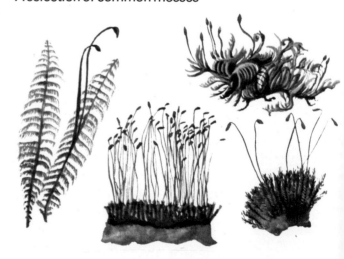

Benz 1888

Rolls Royce 1907

Ford Model 'T' 1908

Bentley (4½ litre) 1930

M.G. 1947

Citroen 1938

Wolseley 1950

Jaguar 'T' Type 1961

Lotus Formula 1 1972

winter it has a whitish coloured mark on its back.

MOUNTAIN is an area of land rising high above the normal level of the earth. There is no special height for a mountain. The following list gives the heights of some of the highest and best-known mountains:

NAME	HEIGHT IN FEET	COUNTRY
Everest	29,028	Nepal/Tibet border
Kara Koram	28,250	Kashmir
Nanga Parbat	26,660	Kashmir
Minya Konka	24,900	China
Stalin	24,590	U.S.S.R.
Aconcagua	22,830	Argentina
McKinley	20,300	Alaska
Kibo	19,560	Africa
Demavend	18,600	Iran
Elbruz	18,480	U.S.S.R.
Popocatapel	17,880	Mexico
Kenya	17,040	Africa
Ararat	16,950	Turkey
Ruwenzori	16,800	Uganda
Mont Blanc	15,780	French/Italian border
Matterhorn	14,700	Swiss/Italian border
Jungfrau	13,650	Switzerland
Grossglockner	12,420	Austria
Ben Nevis	4,400	Britain

MOVIES is a slang name for motion pictures, otherwise the cinema, where examples of the cinematographic art are shown. The word cinema comes from the Greek *kineo,* to move. Some of the earliest attempts at making moving pictures were made as early as 1870 when a series of photographs showing someone performing a simple action were mounted on the blades of a paddle wheel. When the wheel was a turned at a certain speed the pictures could not be seen separately, but gave the impression that the viewer was looking at one moving picture. Famous names in the development of motion-picture techniques were William Friese-Green, John Rudge, Thomas Alva Edison and George Eastman. The secret of the success of moving pictures lies in what

The mouflon, one of the last of the wild sheep

The musk-ox of the arctic regions

The twins Romulus and Remus were suckled by a wolf and are the mythical founders of Rome

is called 'persistence of vision'. The screen actually shows a succession of still pictures presented at the rate of twenty-four a second; they follow each other so smoothly and quickly that an impression of continuous movement is given; and this is because the eye retains for a short time an impression of a picture even after it has disappeared from view.

The story of the cinema has been one of constant progress and improvement, the most important development being the sound film, which was introduced in 1929; then followed coloured films, and the three-dimensional and wide-screen films, as well as stereophonic sound when the sound comes from different parts of the screen.

While the great majority of 'movies' are made for the sole purpose of providing entertainment to cinema-goers (as well as earning money for all those connected with their making!) there are many films which are made solely to convey important information or provide specific forms of training; such films may be said to spread knowledge, enlightenment, truth, help, and understanding between peoples, and as such deserve an honourable mention whenever films are discussed.

MUSEUMS are buildings where rare objects of great value and interest are preserved and exhibited. The first museum in the world was the Ashmolean Museum, Oxford; it began with the collection of curiosities presented to the University of Oxford by Elias Ashmole in 1677. The British Museum in London was started in 1759 and the present building, which was built in 1823, has a total floor area of more than seventeen acres. An even larger museum (and the largest in the world) is the American Museum of Natural History in New York City; it has twenty-three acres of floor space. There are large and important museums in most countries.

MUSK-OX is a short-legged, heavily-built animal which lives in Greenland, north-eastern Canada and some of the Arctic islands. It is about 4 feet high, has thick horns which curve down and outwards, and has a very long, shaggy, brownish coloured coat. It gets its name from its peculiar musk-like smell.

MUSTANG is a small, half-wild horse of America. It has descended from domesticated horses which escaped from captivity.

MYTHOLOGY is the study of myths; that is, stories recording a people's beliefs on the origin of life, gods, heroes, etc. From the very earliest times men have created stories to explain things that influenced their lives. For example, in ancient Rome a thunderstorm was thought to be the result of the anger of the god Jupiter, who when roused aimed thunderbolts at the earth.

NAMES The word name is defined as that by which a person, thing or place is called or known, and it is the same or similar in several languages: Latin *nomen,* German *name,* Old English *nama.* Of personal names, the oldest recorded are believed to be those inscribed on remains of buildings found in the Middle East, such as those on Sumerian tablets dating from about 3,000 years before Christ. Names were often bestowed on persons on account of their appearance, peculiarities or occupation; thus we have names such as Long, Short, Brown, Black, Farmer, Carpenter, and so on. A person can bear a family name and also one or more individual names; the former are called surnames and the latter christian names or forenames. The commonest name in the world is Mohammed or Muhammad (it can be spelt in a variety of ways). John and William have been the most popular forenames in Britain for hundreds of years. In Britain, America and most continental countries, a wife changes her surname on marriage to that of her husband. In Scotland and Ireland, names often begin with M', Mc or Mac (meaning in Gaelic 'son of') while 'O' before an Irish name stands for grandson.

NARWHAL This animal is a cetacean, mean-ing it belongs to a group of mammals that live in water, breathe air and are fish-like in form. This group includes the toothed whales. So the narwhal is a kind of whale with one large projecting tusk (occasionally two) in the male. Its name is thought to come from old Danish words meaning 'dead whale' because the narwhal is of a pallid, lifeless colour, like a corpse. It is found mainly in the Arctic Ocean, and a fully grown specimen may be about 16 feet in length.

NATURAL HISTORY means the study of animals and plants in the wild. This is different from biology which is the study of animals and plants in the laboratory or in captivity. Natural history is a most rewarding study, and one which is most suitable for young people. To be successful one must have 1, patience to watch animal life; 2, care in moving so as not to disturb the animal being observed; 3, a notebook to write down all things observed. Any young person keen on natural history should join the junior branch of their local Natural History Society.

NEON is a gas found in very small quantities in the atmosphere. When an electric discharge passes through neon gas it gives off a rich reddish glow, and for this reason is used for advertising at night.

NEPAL is a small independent kingdom in the Himalayas on the north-east frontier of India.

The narwhal is a kind of whale with one long projecting tusk in the male

It is 54,360 square miles and has a population of nearly 11 millions. Mount Everest is in Nepal. The capital is Katmandu. There are peoples of different races and religions in Nepal, one of the most important groups being the Gurkhas whose bravery as soldiers is almost legendary.

NEST Generally we think of a nest as a place where birds lay their eggs and rear their young. However, other animals make nests for bearing and bringing up their young. The most unusual perhaps is the stickleback's nest. Birds' nests are the most interesting, and by their variety show that birds are clever builders. If you are a bird watcher be extremely careful not to disturb a nest. Also, don't try counting the eggs in a nest where you have to reach to your full extent. The slightest slip and a nest is disturbed and more often than not the mother bird will desert the eggs.

NETHERLANDS, or HOLLAND, is a kingdom in Western Europe. It is 13,500 square miles and has a population of over 13 millions. The seat of government is at The Hague, the chief city is Amsterdam and the chief port Rotterdam. Much of the Netherlands has been re-claimed from the sea and the Dutch are at present re-claiming an even larger area. The Netherlands is a rich agricultural country and is famous for its cheeses and flower bulbs.

NEW GUINEA is the second largest (347,450 square miles) island in the world. It lies in the Pacific Ocean, north of Australia. The island is divided into three parts. The west part belonged to the Netherlands until 1963 when it became part of Indonesia. It is now called south-eastern Irian. The part which is called Papua is looked after by Australia. The third part in the north-east is now an International Trust Territory of the United Nations and is looked after by Australia. British Papua (New Guinea) is nearly as large as France. The population is about 2 millions. The capital is Port Moresby. The island produces gold, rubber and timber.

NEWFOUNDLAND is an island off the east coast of North America at the mouth of the Gulf of St. Lawrence and a province of CANADA discovered by Cabot in 1497. It has a population of about 515,000. The capital is Saint John's. Included with Newfoundland is Labrador. The most important industries are fishing, manufacture of wood pulp for paper and the mining of iron, copper, zinc and gypsum. Gander is one of the important airports on the North Atlantic air routes.

NEW ZEALAND is a British Dominion. It consists of a group of islands in the South Pacific Ocean, the two larger being North and South Island. These two islands are 104,000 square miles. The capital is Wellington on North Island, other important towns being Auckland, also on North Island, and Christchurch. New Zealand is also famous for its meat and dairy produce. The population is over $2\frac{3}{4}$ million, most of whom are of British descent but there are also a number of Maoris, the original inhabitants of the islands. New Zealand rules a number of Pacific Islands, including the Cook Islands. She also is responsible for uninhabited land in the Antarctic Ocean. New Zealand was discovered by Tasman in 1642 and was explored by Captain Cook in 1769.

NEWSPAPER The first printed newspaper in Britain was published in 1622 and was called *The Weekly News from Italy, Germany, etc.* *The London Gazette* was the first regular newspaper; it appeared in 1665. The country with the largest number of newspapers is said to be the U.S.S.R. with nearly 8,000, of which the government newspaper Izvestia has a daily circulation of about 8,700,000. Single issues of the British Sunday newspaper *The News of the World* have, however, reached a sale of 9,000,000 copies.

NEWT is an AMPHIBIAN which looks rather like a lizard and is often found in ponds. The male of the crested newt has a wide, flattened tail and a fin running from head to tail. Newts are quite colourful during their breeding season. They hibernate in winter.

NIAGARA FALLS are on the Niagara River, between Canada and the United States, and about 22 miles north-west of Buffalo City, New York State. At one time the Niagara Falls were thought to be the highest in the world at 162 feet, but that was before the discovery of such cataracts as the Victoria Falls in Rhodesia (340 feet) and the Angel Falls in Venezuela (3,212 feet total drop). But because of their scenic splendour the Niagara Falls are still held by many people to be the grandest of all such cascades. The Niagara Falls are really two waterfalls: the Horseshoe Falls are in Canada and the American Falls are in the U.S.A. They are separated by Goat Island, in the centre of the river. A number of people have lost their lives in trying to go over the Falls in barrels or to swim the rapids, but in 1859 a tight-rope walker named Blondin crossed the Falls on a rope with someone else on his back!

NICARAGUA is a republic and the largest country in Central America. It is 57,140 square miles, but has fewer than 2 million inhabitants of whom most are of mixed Spanish and Indian origin. The capital is Managua. The country exports cotton, coffee and gold.

NIGER is a republic in Africa and takes its name from its chief river, the Niger. It is 484,000 square miles but has a population of only about 4 millions. The capital is Niamey. Except for a small area near the capital the country is mostly desert.

NIGERIA is on the west coast of Africa and is 357,000 square miles. There are about 66 million inhabitants who belong to three African racial groups—the Hausas, the Ibos and the Yorubas. The capital is Lagos, other important towns being Ibadan and Kano. Like NIGER the country takes its name from the River Niger. It produces cocoa, cotton and palm oil. The chief minerals are coal, tin and columbite and recently oil has been discovered.

NOMADS are people who wander from place to place, either in search of food, or because of the wandering habits of the animals they rear (the word comes from the Greek and means to drive to pasture). Many people in Central Asia

Top, a diagram showing how fission, a chain reaction, is set going. This process is not only the basis of the atomic bomb but atomic or nuclear power.

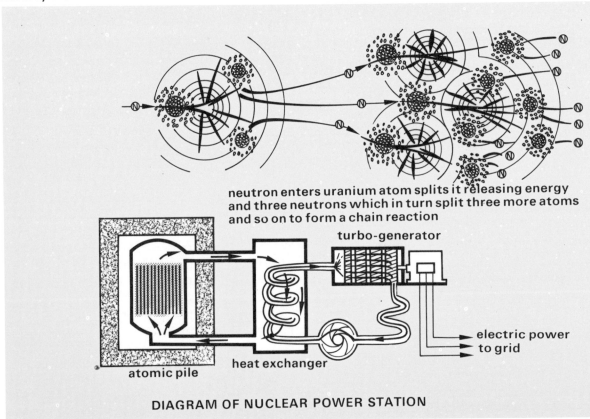

neutron enters uranium atom splits it releasing energy and three neutrons which in turn split three more atoms and so on to form a chain reaction

turbo-generator

electric power to grid

atomic pile

heat exchanger

DIAGRAM OF NUCLEAR POWER STATION

The Russian ice-breaker 'Lenin' and an example of a peaceful use of nuclear power.

are nomads, particularly the Mongols who breed camels, goats and sheep.

NORMAN CONQUEST   The first stage of the Norman Conquest of England took place in 1066 when Duke William of Normandy landed at Pevensey, in Sussex, and fought the celebrated Battle of Hastings with King Harold II.   The previous king of England, Edward the Confessor (1042-66) had, so the story goes, promised the throne to Duke William; but when Edward died the throne was seized by Harold, who was Edward's brother-in-law and the son of the most powerful nobleman in the land, Earl Godwin of Wessex.   The Battle of Hastings saw the death of Harold and was followed by William's march on London where he was crowned king.   He promised to retain the law of England but soon made many changes, introducing Norman methods and institutions.   William gave orders for the compilation of the famous DOMESDAY BOOK —a survey of the entire land and its livestock— which took about six years to complete.

The most important result of the Norman Conquest was that the country became united under a strong and absolute monarchy, whereas previously there had been much quarrelling between various petty kings and nobles.

NORWAY is a kingdom in Northern Europe and one of the Scandinavian countries.   It is 125,000 square miles but much of the country is near the Arctic and cannot produce food. There are only a little over $3\frac{3}{4}$ million inhabitants. The capital is Oslo.   Norway is a very beautiful mountainous country and its forests produce timber for export.   Norway has a large merchant navy and her fisheries are important.

NOSE is the organ through which air passes to the lungs, and which is sensitive to smells. It is made partly of bone, and a softer bone-like substance called 'cartilage'.   When breathing, the nose acts as a filter, particles of dust and dirt being held in the sticky substance, known as 'mucus', which is present in the nose.

NUCLEAR POWER comes from the nucleus or central part of an atom.   It is extremely small; occupying only about one million-millionth of the volume of the whole atom.   In the nucleus of any atom, tiny particles are bound to each other by 'nuclear forces' of enormous strength, and the only way to separate them is to bombard them with highspeed protons, neutrons or other particles that are naturally radioactive.   Such elements—and uranium is only one—keep shooting out particles on their own, without the assistance of any outside force.   The most useful particles for bombarding atoms are neutrons, because they have no electric charge.   Electrically-charged particles like protons have to smash their way through the barrier of electrons surrounding the atoms, but neutrons having no electical charge are not affected by electrons and slip through quite easily.   When they strike the nucleus they may do one of two things.   They may stick on to it, converting it into another form of the same element, or they may knock particles out of it and change it into a different element.

When two or more things are strongly bound together and then forced apart, the force which bound them is released. It disappears, but it is not destroyed. It escapes in some form or other; very often it takes the form of heat. The nuclear forces may escape in the form of intense radiations, even more powerful than X-RAYS, or in the form of mechanical energy carried by protons, neutrons and other nuclear particles travelling away at very high speeds. This is the atomic energy that is released in the form of heat in an atomic pile, and it can be used to heat the boiler of a steam-engine which will then drive an electric generator. Each smashed atom produces an enormous quantity of energy for its size, but it is very very small and to get enough to be useful many millions of millions of millions of atoms have to be smashed every second. You might think that this would mean consuming several tons of 'fuel', but atoms are so minute that the weight of a million million million of them is only about one six-millionth of an ounce! Nuclear reactors—are surrounded by a concrete shield several feet thick to absorb the dangerous gamma-rays and other radiations that are produced in enormous quantities when the pile is working. Such a pile may contain many tons of uranium, but every pound weight of uranium consumed gives as much heat as 1,500 tons of coal. Some modern nuclear reactors use pure U-235 or plutonium, and run at a high temperature. Others, known as 'breeder reactors', are designed especially to produce large quantities of fresh nuclear fuel, generally plutonium.

NYLON is a man-made material, sometimes called a 'synthetic' material. The raw materials from which it is made are coal, air and water. In addition to being used for making various articles of clothing, nylon is used for brushes, combs, buttons, climbing ropes and countless other items.

OCEAN is a vast area of sea. The oceans and seas make up three-quarters of the earth's surface.

OCEANS AND SEAS OF THE WORLD

NAME	AREA IN SQ. MILES	GREATEST DEPTH IN FEET
Pacific Ocean	70,000,000	35,400
Atlantic Ocean	31,530,000	30,150
Indian Ocean	28,350,000	24,000
Arctic Ocean	5,500,000	17,900
Malay Sea	3,137,000	21,340
Mediterranean Sea	1,145,000	14,400
Bering Sea	878,000	13,420
Okhotsk Sea	582,000	11,160
East China Sea	480,000	10,500
Hudson Bay	472,000	1,500
Sea of Japan	405,000	10,200
Andaman Sea	305,000	11,000
North Sea	220,000	2,000
Red Sea	178,000	7,250
Caspian Sea	170,000	3,000
Baltic Sea	158,000	1,300

OCELOT This animal belongs to the CAT family and lives in Central and South America.

An octopus and close relative of the squid

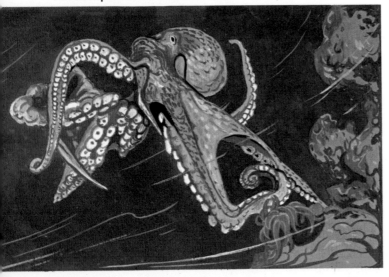

The okapi lives in the jungles of Central Africa

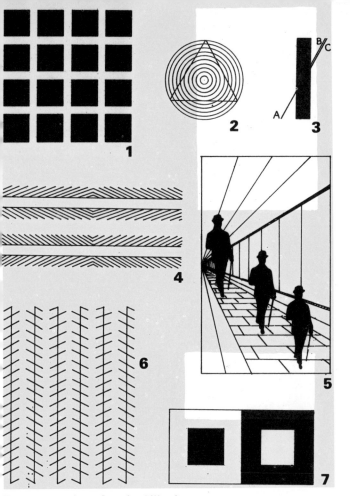

Four examples of optical illusions

United States to Argentina, and feeds on fruits, insects and birds. You may have heard the expression 'playing possum' meaning that someone is pretending to be dead or not paying any attention, and this arose because of the opossum's habit of pretending to be dead if an enemy is in the vicinity. There is also an Australian opossum but it is not a true opossum, and really belongs to the phalanger family, another group of marsupials.

OPTICAL ILLUSIONS Strangely enough, we cannot always believe exactly what we see. You may think that this doesn't make sense, but if you look at the illustrations on the opposite page you will see that it is true. In Fig. 1 you can see 16 black squares separated by white bands. When you look at it you will notice that there is an illusion of shadows where the white bands cross. In Fig. 2, although the sides of the triangle are perfectly straight, they appear broken in the middle because the background of circles makes the acute angles appear larger than they really are. In Fig. 3 the line AB is straight, and not AC; the illusion is due to the fact that the thick black band appears narrower than it really is. The four lines in Fig. 4 are really parallel; they appear to be crooked because of the oblique lines which give a disturbing effect to our sense of direction. In Fig. 5, although the man who is farthest away appears to be the biggest, all three figures are in fact exactly the same size! In Fig. 6 the lines appear to slant in different directions but they are really parallel. In Fig. 7 the black square is slightly larger than the white one, but it appears smaller because a white object on a black ground always appears larger than a black object on a white ground.

OPTICS Branch of physics concerned with the study of light. See LIGHT, MICROSCOPE and TELESCOPE.

ORANG-UTAN is a member of the ape family, and closely approaches man in appearance. Its name comes from the Malay language and means 'man of the woods'. The body is bulky and covered with long, reddish-brown hair. The orang-utan has short legs but its arms are so long that they reach the ankles when the animal is standing upright, and when it walks along it can place its knuckles on the ground. This

It can be recognized by its large, pink nose, fairly short tail and tawny coat which is marked with black spots or streaks. It is a savage animal and feeds on small animals and birds.

OCTOPUS is a sea creature. The giant octopus of the North Pacific Ocean has been known to grow to a width of 32 feet. The octopus has a roundish body and eight arms, called tentacles, each of which has two rows of suckers along it. It uses these arms when moving across the sea bed and also for catching crabs and other shell-fish on which it feeds. When attacked, the octopus can squirt out an inky fluid that blinds the attacker and enables the octopus to escape. The octopus has been known to seize human swimmers and pearl divers. It is related to the cuttlefish and squid.

OKAPI is a rare animal, related to the giraffe. It lives in the dense forests of Central Africa and feeds on leaves. Only the male okapi has horns.

OPOSSUM This animal is a MARSUPIAL (pouched) found throughout America, from the

animal is found in swampy forests in Borneo and Sumatra, islands in the Malay Archipelago, Indonesia, and is quite at home among trees. It is vegetarian, feeding mainly on fruits.

ORCHESTRA is a group or band of players of musical instruments; it can vary from a handful of players to a full symphony orchestra of more than a hundred performers. A symphony orchestra is divided into four sections: strings, woodwind, brass and percussion; the last-named group are those instruments which are played by being struck, such as drum, cymbals, triangle and xylophone. See TABLE 1, page 183.

ORGAN is a musical instrument in which the keys are connected to pipes which are made to sound by forcing air through them. Large modern organs may have as many as five keyboards with thousands of pipes, the wind being supplied by an electrically driven pump. Two great composers for the organ were J.S. Bach and Handel.

ORYX is a large African antelope found in deserts. Both male and female have long horns and long tufted tails.

OSTRICH is the largest living bird. An adult male ostrich stands about 8 feet high. Although the ostrich is unable to fly, it can run very fast on its long, powerful legs. It is found in the desert and on the open plains of Arabia and Africa, where it has now been largely farmed. Its eggs are laid in a shallow hole scooped out of the sand.

OTTER is found almost all over the world, except in Australia. Although it spends quite a lot of time on land, it is completely at home in the water. It has webbed feet, a flattened head with small eyes and ears, a thick, powerful tail, and almost waterproof fur. It feeds on fish as well as small animals, insects and birds. It lives in a burrow, hollow or rock crevice called a 'holt'.

OWLS can be found in all parts of the world. They feed on small animals, insects, birds, reptiles, fish, worms and snails, which they hunt at night and seize with their sharp, curved claws. The owl has a fairly large head, the beak is hooked, and the eyes are big and 'wise-looking' which has given rise to the familiar expression 'as wise as an owl', though owls are not necessarily wiser or cleverer than some other animals. Among the best-known owls are the tawny owls, short-eared owls, little owls and barn-owls.

OXYGEN is the most abundant of all the elements, and composes about one-half the crust of the earth. Besides being the essential element in water and the atmosphere, it is present in all living things. Ozone is a special form of oxygen.

PAKISTAN is a republic in the Indian subcontinent. It was divided into two parts—West Pakistan, which is by far the larger, and East

An adult male ostrich stands about 8 feet high

Pakistan now BANGLADESH. The country is 310,400 square miles and has a population of about 45 millions. The capital is the new city of Islamabad, near Rawalpindi. Its former capital was the important port and city of Karachi. Another famous and older city is Lahore. Pakistan also grows and exports cotton and tea.

PALESTINE, or the Holy Land, is the name given to the ancient land of the Bible. Since 1947 it has been divided between ISRAEL and JORDAN.

PANAMA is a Central American republic through which runs the Panama Canal. Panama is 31,900 square miles with a population of little under 1½ millions. Most of the people are of mixed Spanish and Indian descent. The capital is Panama City. The country produces bananas, cocoa, coffee and rubber.

PANDA The giant panda, which lives in the bamboo forests of China, resembles a bear and is black and white, with large black patches over its eyes. The smaller panda, or cat-bear, resembles a raccoon; it is reddish and black in colour, has a white face striped with red, and a ringed tail; it lives in the Himalayas and southern China. The smaller panda is only about 3½ feet long, including its bushy tail. The giant panda, when fully grown, is about half the size of a polar bear and weighs about 22 stone.

PANGOLIN, also called the 'scaly anteater', feeds on white ants and has a long tongue to enable it to eat them easily, and very powerful limbs for tearing down their nests. It is covered with large, spiny scales that cover the whole body except the underparts which are soft and hairy. These scales give the pangolin protection from enemies. When attacked, it can roll itself up into a ball in the same way as a hedgehog does. The pangolin is found in Africa and Asia.

PAPER The ancient Egyptians made a kind of paper from the papyrus plant, and in fact the word paper comes from this. However, paper as we understand it now was brought to Europe by the Moors, who had learnt about it from the Chinese. The first paper-mill in Britain was started about the beginning of the sixteenth century. Today the best type of paper is made from pure rag; paper of lower quality is made of a mixture of rags and wood pulp, and the paper on which newspapers are printed is made entirely of wood pulp. Paper has been called 'the raw material of literature'.

PARAGUAY is a republic in central South America and lies on the river of the same name. It has no sea-board. The country has an area of about 157,000 square miles and a population of just over 2 millions. The capital is Asuncion, one of the oldest cities in South America and the centre from which the Spaniards colonised. Most of the country is covered by jungle but cattle rearing is carried out on the grassy plains that make up the rest.

PARLIAMENT is the body which makes the laws of the land. In Britain it is headed by the sovereign and consists of two Houses or Chambers: the House of Lords and the House of Commons. The name parliament has been in use since 1265 to describe people who are selected to help the sovereign rule the country. The word itself comes from the French *parler*, to talk, and so some people scornfully refer to a parliament as 'a talking shop'. The date mentioned above, 1265, is important in English history, for it was then that Simon de Montfort, leader of the barons, summoned a meeting not only of the noblemen and knights but also citizens and ordinary people to represent the cities and boroughs. The year 1295 marks another important development in parliament, for it was then that Edward I made the rule that the people as well as their rulers should have a voice in governing the country. Since the time of this 'Model Parliament', as it came to be called, parliament has had a continuous history.

The House of Lords is not elected by the people at general elections; its members are really the descendants of William the Conqueror's Great Council and are called peers, and they hold hereditary titles or are specially created 'life peers'. The House of Commons is elected by people voting at each general election. The parliament of the United Kingdom meets in the Palace of Westminster, to which the separate parliament of Northern Ireland (subsidiary to the Imperial Parliament with regard to certain major powers) sends a fixed number of twelve representatives.

PARNASSUS was the name of a mountain in ancient Greece. The modern name for it is Liakoura. It was held sacred to Apollo and the Muses. The Greeks believed in a legend of a great flood, similar to that mentioned in the Bible; in their version, however, when Zeus caused the waters to subside, the ark built by Deucalion (the Greek Noah) came to rest on Mount Parnassus.

PARROTS are found wild in Africa, America, Asia and Australia. They feed mainly on fruits and seeds. Their feathers are usually brilliantly coloured and they have a curved, hooked beak and fleshy tongue. Parrots have a remarkable ability to imitate the human voice, and so people like to keep them as amusing pets. They belong to the same family as cockatoos, macaws, parakeets, and lovebirds.

PARTHENON is the magnificent temple of the goddess Athene on the Acropolis in Athens. One of the most beautiful buildings in the world, it was built in the years 454-438 B.C. and its construction was supervised by Pheidias, most fa-

The Parthenon in Athens, and temple of Athene

mous of Greek sculptors. The giant statue of the goddess herself, in ivory and gold, which formerly stood inside the temple, was his own work. The Parthenon was made in glistening marble and decorated with the most marvellous coloured sculptures. Carvings from the frieze, called the ELGIN MARBLES, which ran round the outside can be seen in the British Museum in London. The building was exquisitely proportioned; it was built in what is called the Doric Order of architecture, and the Doric column is said to be the most perfect detail of architecture ever evolved, because of its beauty and extreme simplicity. For over 2,000 years the Parthenon stood in all its glory on the summit of the great rock at Athens; then, in 1687, disaster overtook it. Athens was under Turkish domination and the Venetians were attempting to win it back; the Turks had no respect for the Parthenon and had turned it into a storehouse for gunpowder; a Venetian bomb fell on it and the resultant explosion left the Parthenon in ruins, much as the visitor sees it today.

PASSOVER is a Jewish feast and commemorates the deliverance of the Jewish people from the Egyptians. It is observed by the eating of unleavened bread (without the substance used to make dough ferment and rise) and reading from the Book of Exodus on certain days.

PEARLS are found inside the shells of oysters. The pearl is formed when a foreign body, such as a grain of sand, gets inside the oyster's shell and the oyster tries to get rid of the irritation caused by this foreign body by covering it with thin layers of a fine substance which it secretes. Thus, 'cultured' or artificial pearls can be made by deliberately inserting a grain of sand in an oyster shell. Pearls are also formed inside mussels and clams.

PEAT consists of dead and decomposed plants. It is found in marshes, bogs and on the slopes of mountains. In Ireland it is cut from bogs and used instead of coal for heating. The word may come from the Latin *petium,* meaning a fragment or piece of land.

PECCARY This animal is a small wild hog, found in North and South America; the northern or collared peccary is about 3 feet long, while

A pelican has a pouch slung below its bill

complete swing is determined by the length of the string, and is independent of the size of the weight. An interesting type is the Foucault pendulum which is used to show the rotation of the earth on its axis; there is one in the Science Museum, London.

PENICILLIN To understand what penicillin is, we should first understand the meaning of the word antibiotics. These are drugs which act directly on the germ or bacteria which is the cause of an illness; they do this by interfering with the growth of the germ that is doing the harm and so stop it gaining ground. Many drugs are used against bacteria but the drugs called antibiotics do least harm to the patient's own body tissues, and one of the most effective antibiotic drugs is penicillin, discovered by Sir Alexander Fleming, the famous bacteriologist, in 1928. The word penicillin comes from the Latin *penicillium,* meaning a mould, and Fleming discovered that a certain fungus, mould or mildew, similar to that which grows on cheese or jam, had the power to kill and dissolve germs. This was one of the great medical discoveries of the 20th century, and penicillin was responsible for saving many thousands of lives in the Second World War; it has also saved millions of lives in peace-time and shortened many serious illnesses.

the southern, white-lipped peccary is a few inches longer.

PELICAN is a large water-bird which has a huge yellowish or pink bill with a pouch which it uses for catching the fish on which it feeds. It has a fairly long neck, a thick body, and short legs with large feet. The feathers are usually white, greyish or brown, with black markings. It often catches its main diet of fish by diving upon its prey from the air. Pelicans nest in colonies, and the eggs, two or three in number, are whitish. A fairly close relative of the pelican is the gannet.

PENDULUM is a weight or bob suspended from a fixed point by a string or rod, and caused to swing to and fro. The time required for a

PERSIA See **IRAN**

PERU is a republic in South America bordering the South Pacific Ocean. It is 531,000

The peccary is found in North and South America, and is a smallish pig. It can be very dangerous if cornered or disturbed

square miles and has a population of about 13½ millions, the majority of whom are descended from the INCAS or are of mixed Indian and Spanish descent. The capital is Lima. The country produces petroleum, iron ore and lead. It has recently become the chief fishing country in the world.

PETROLEUM is a mineral oil found below the surface of the ground. It is obtained by boring through the earth –usually a very thick layer of hard rock– to the oil, which rushes up to the surface in 'gushers'. Crude petroleum from the earth is a thick, black oil. At oil refineries this crude oil is refined to petrol, paraffin, lubricating oil, grease, and many other products. Some of the richest oil fields in the world are in Iran (Persia), at Baku in the U.S.S.R., and in Texas in the U.S.A.

PHILATELY is stamp-collecting, a popular hobby in all lands and also an important trade. The word philately is rather hard to explain; it comes from Greek words and really means, 'love of something which has been exempted from payment'; that is, when postage stamps of the right value are bought and stuck on a letter or parcel, nothing further has to be paid when the letter or parcel is posted. The hobby of stamp-collecting really began when the penny postage was introduced into England on 10 January 1840. A new and special stamp had to be printed; it became known as the 'Penny Black'

and people rushed to buy specimens of the very first issue. A Penny Black stamp is now very valuable. The stamp collector can learn a lot about both history and geography from his hobby, also about animals, birds and fishes, because all these appear on different stamps; there are, in fact, stamp pictures of almost every imaginable person, place, or thing. Just to show how valuable a stamp collection can be, in 1873 a schoolboy sold a single stamp for six shillings; it was a one-cent, black-on-magenta stamp issued in British Guiana (now called Guyana); in 1940 it changed hands again for £12,774.

PHILIPPINES consists of a large group of islands in the Pacific Ocean. There are just over 39 millions inhabitants. Most of them are Malays but are known as Filipinos, nearly all of whom are Christians. The capital is Manila on the island of Luzon, the largest island. The country produces rice, coconuts and timber.

PHOTO-ELECTRIC CELL is a form of valve or tube which becomes a conductor of electricity when exposed to ordinary light. Photo-electric cells are used in such devices as burglar alarms, exposure-meters for cameras, etc.

PHOTOGRAPHY is the science and art of using a camera. It is based on the fact that when light falls on a plate or film, an image is formed; this is the result of the action of the

Left, the main parts of a simple camera. *Right,* a diagram showing how light from an image passes through a lens and is focused on a film.

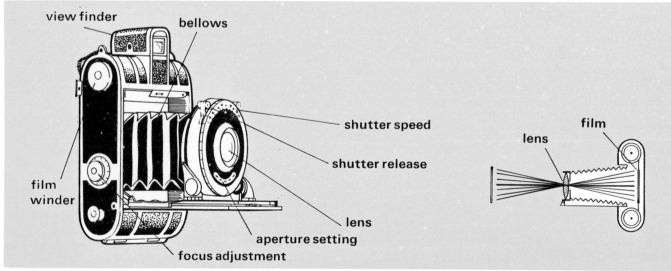

South America

PACIFIC OCEAN

ATLANTIC OCEAN

RIO BRANCO
AMAPA
Branco
Negro
Japura
Amazon
Manaus
Amazon
Belem
PARA
Maranon
Fortaleza
Jurua
ACRE
AMAZONAS
Madeira
Tapajos
Xingu
Araguaia
Tocantins
S. Francisco
Huascaran 22,211
MONTANA
ANDES
Lima
Madre de Dios
BRAZIL
BAHIA
Cuzco
MATO GROSSO
Campo
Salvador
Lake Titicaca
Illampu 21,490
La Paz
Plateau of Mato Grosso
Santa Cruz
BOLIVIA
Brasilia
Brazil Plateau
MINAS GERAIS
Paraguay
PARAGUAY
Pilcomayo
Parana
Belo Horizonte
SAO PAULO
CHILE
Llullaillaco 22,150
CHACO
Asuncion
Sao Paulo
Rio de Janeiro
Tucuman
Uruguay
RIO GRANDE DO SUL
Porto Alegre
Cordoba
Santa Fe
Aconagua 23,080
Rosario
URUGUAY
Valparaiso
Mendoza
Santiago
Buenos Aires
Montevideo
ANDES
Bahia Blanca
Negro
ARGENTINA
CHONOS ARCHIPELAGO
PATAGONIA
Port Stanley FALKLAND ISLANDS
TIERRA DEL FUEGO

light on the silver atoms contained in the film or plate. When either is soaked in a fluid, called a developer, the image is fixed, and becomes what is known as a 'negative'. What we call a photograph is really a copy of the negative on special paper, and this is called a 'positive'. In its simplest form, a camera is a box fitted with a lens which focuses what is intended to be photographed on to the film or plate. The first men to make permanent photographs were two Frenchmen, Nicophore de Niepce and Louis Jacques Daguerre; the latter became the more famous of the two, and the plates that he produced are still known as daguerreotypes. The biggest step forward in the development of photography was in 1888 when George Eastman produced both the roll film and the first roll-film camera, called Kodak.

PHYSICS is the branch of science which studies HEAT, LIGHT, SOUND, ELECTRICITY, MAGNETISM, etc. It is sometimes called 'natural philosophy'. People who study physics are called 'physicists'. Amongst the great physicists of all time are Galileo, Sir I. Newton, Michael Faraday, Albert Einstein, Madam Curie and Lord Rutherford. See TABLE 4.

PIANOFORTE or **PIANO,** as it is generally called, is a musical instrument which was invented in the eighteenth century. When a black or white key on a piano is depressed it operates levers which actuate a hammer to strike a wire string. The sound of the piano can be controlled by two pedals; the left one (soft) makes it possible to play very softly; the right pedal (damper) allows notes to sound on after the fingers have been lifted from the keyboard. There are two main types of piano: 1, the upright in which the strings are upright or vertical; 2, the grand, in which the strings are horizontal; the grand piano is the type usually played upon by professional pianists at concerts for both piano recitals or piano concertos.

PIG The domesticated pig is believed to be descended from the European wild boar which once roamed freely and which still survives in remote parts of the continent. There are many kinds of wild pig: the crested wild boar of India, the pygmy wild boar of Borneo and Sumatra, the pygmy wild hog of Nepal and Bhutan, the barbiroussa of Indonesia, and the various wild pigs of Africa including the common bushpig, river-hog, forest-hog, and warthog; there are also the American wild pigs or 'peccaries'. They all live usually in forest or bush areas, and feed mainly on roots, tubers and other vegetables.

PILGRIM FATHERS were a band of people, called PURITANS, who sailed to the New World in a ship called the *Mayflower* on 6 September 1620. They left England because they wanted to be allowed to worship in their own way; King James I severely punished anyone who differed from himself in religious views, and the Puritans received especially harsh treatment because they did not adhere to all the teachings of the Church of England. So 78 men and 24 women set out on the trip which was to make the name of the 'Pilgrim Fathers' immortal. They crossed the stormy Atlantic Ocean and landed over three months later at a place which they called Plymouth, after the town of the same name in Devon from which they had started their voyage. They founded a colony, and this was the beginning of the mighty American Republic. 'Thanksgiving Day' in the United States is held in commemoration of the thanks given to God by the Pilgrim Fathers for their first harvest in 1621.

PLANETARIUM is a dome-shaped building in which one can see the stars and planets in their courses. This is done by means of a special optical device, see drawing.

A domesticated pig and one of the many breeds which have been developed from the wild boar

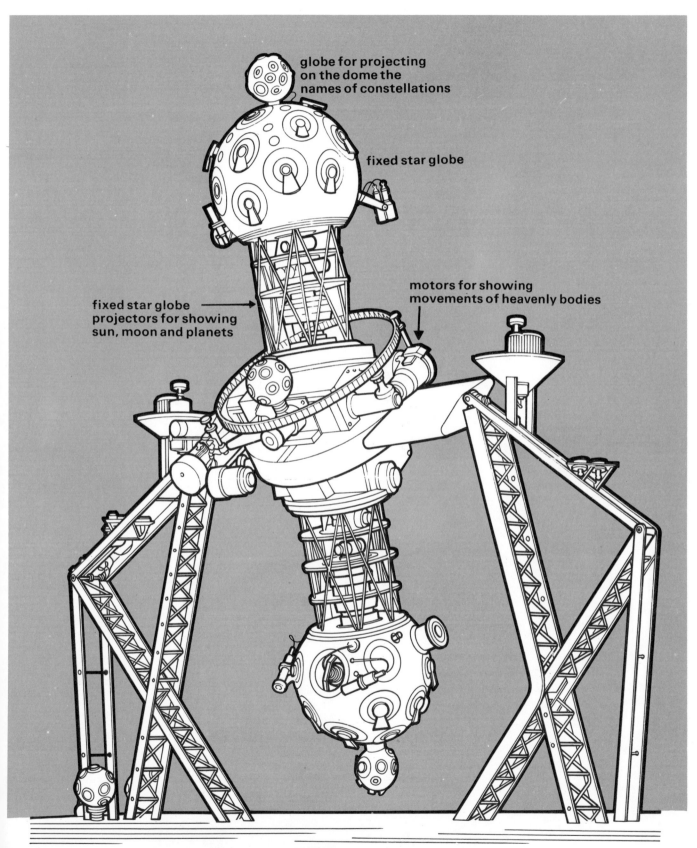

globe for projecting
on the dome the
names of constellations

fixed star globe

motors for showing
movements of heavenly bodies

fixed star globe
projectors for showing
sun, moon and planets

The main parts and structure of a planetarium. With this it is possible to show the movements of the planets in the solar system and the movements of the stars.

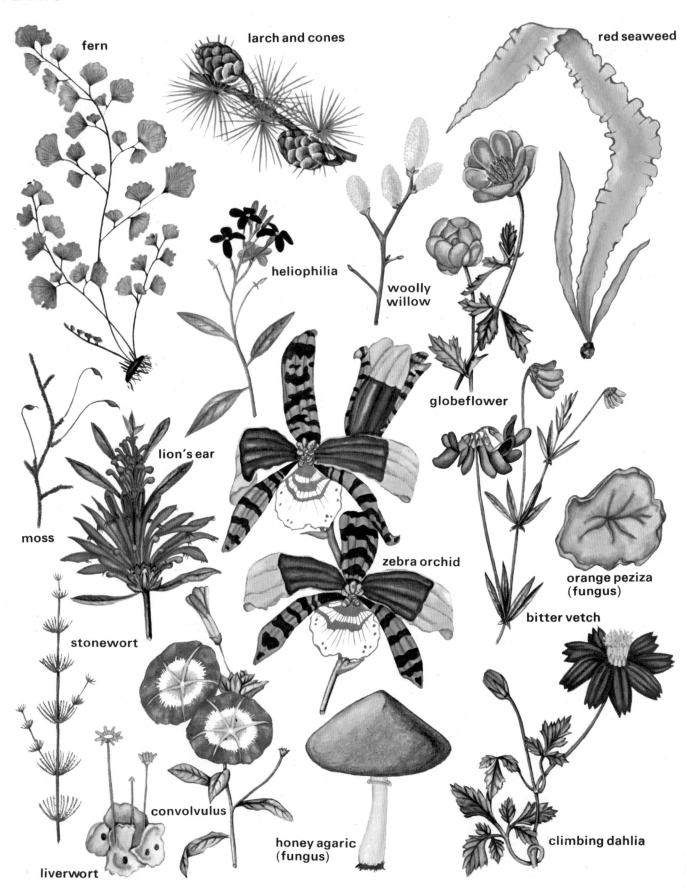

fern

larch and cones

red seaweed

heliophilia

woolly willow

globeflower

moss

lion's ear

zebra orchid

orange peziza (fungus)

bitter vetch

stonewort

convolvulus

honey agaric (fungus)

climbing dahlia

liverwort

PLANETS See **SOLAR SYSTEM**

PLANKTON consists of minute water plants and animals. It is the food of many kinds of fish, and of certain whales. Experiments have been made to see if it cannot be used as food for human beings.

PLANTS The simplest mushroom and the redwood giants of California both belong to the plant family of living things. There are so many plants and their products that we use everyday, almost without thinking about it. They provide us with food and wood, with clothing and medicines and with hundreds of industrial materials. Some plants live only for one year —they are called 'annuals' and when they have shed their seeds for next year they die. Others spend one year in growing and another to produce their seeds. These are called 'biennials'. Many grow for several years and produce seeds each year; these are called 'perennials'. Trees live longest of all the plants —some redwoods have been growing for over 2,000 years.

PLATYPUS This animal is also called a 'duckbill' and it lives in Australia and Tasmania. It makes its home in long burrows in the banks of rivers and streams. It spends most of its time in the water, where it feeds on small shell-fish and snails, storing them up in pouches in its cheeks to eat later. It is a strange little creature, and has jaws that are shaped like a duck's beak, a broad tail, short legs, webbed toes and strong claws, and is covered with beaver-like fur. It lays eggs which are hatched out by the heat from the mother's body, and the young are fed on her milk.

PLIMSOLL LINE is the mark on the side of a ship showing the depth to which she can safely be loaded. It came into use as the result of a Bill passed in 1876, the idea originating from Samuel Plimsoll. Before this, ships were often loaded beyond their safe capacity, and as a result many ships and lives were lost.

POLAND is a republic in the communist block of Eastern Europe. Its frontiers date from 1945. It has an area of 121,000 square miles and a population of over 32 millions.

The platypus of Australasia and one of the strangest creatures on earth with its duck-like bill and webbed feet and the fact that it lays eggs.

The Plimsoll line marked on the side of ships

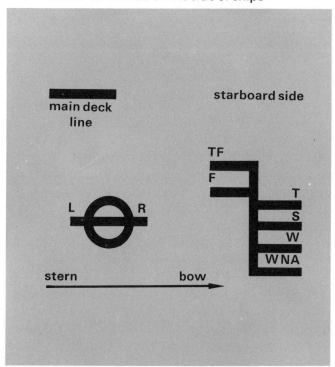

The capital is Warsaw on the River Vistula and the main port is Gdansk or Danzig on the Baltic. Poland is an industrialised country.

PORCUPINE is a member of the rodent family. It is well protected from its enemies by the sharp, erect black and white spines with which it is covered. The quills on its tail form a kind of rattle which shakes as it goes along. A porcupine can emit a very unpleasant smell. It spends the day in a burrow or sheltered place, and comes out at night to feed. Porcupines are found in Africa, southern Asia and a few parts of Europe. The tree-porcupine inhabits many areas of North and South America.

PORPOISE is a sea mammal which belongs to the whale family. It is black and white in colour and measures between 5 and 6 feet in length. It has a blunt-looking head and many teeth and is a very playful animal. It feeds on fish.

PORTUGAL is a republic in southern Europe on the western part of what is called the Iberian peninsula. It is about 24,500 square miles. Included in Portugal are the islands of Madeira and the Azores. The population is a little over 9½ millions. Portuguese is one of the Latin languages. The capital is Lisbon. Portugal is famous for port, which takes its name from the port of Oporto from which it is exported. Portugal also has important sardine fisheries.

POST The first 'Master of the Posts' was Brian Tuke who was appointed by England's King Henry VIII in 1510 to organize postal services along the main roads. Relays of horses were kept at the ready at points along the main highways to carry letters and other messages 'post haste'. Oliver Cromwell was the first to appoint a member of parliament as postmaster-general with an office known as the General Post Office. The custom of putting a date on letters was started by the Post Office in 1660. In 1839 the government introduced the penny post and in 1840 adhesive stamps were invented by Sir Rowland Hill. Since 1874 the nations of the world have joined together in the Universal Postal Union which has as its aim the maintenance and improvement of postal services; the Union is now part of the United Nations organization. The country with the largest volume of postal traffic in the world is the United States, whose people post an average of 75,000 million letters and packages a year compared with the United Kingdom where about 11,000 millions were posted in a record year. Because of the increasing number of letters new mechanical and electronic machines have been introduced to speed up sorting.

POTTERY is one of the oldest crafts in the world and was much practised by primitive peoples. Fragments of pottery found by archaeologists help them to know more about the people who have inhabited a particular place. Outstanding potters of long ago were the Egyptians, Greeks, Chinese, Japanese and the Indians of South America. In modern times some of the finest pottery has been made at Dresden (Germany), Sèvres (France), Delft (Holland), Tournay (Belgium), and in Britain at Chelsea, Worcester, Derby and Coalport.

POULTRY is the name given to fowls which have been domesticated, and are kept for food or their eggs. All domesticated breeds of fowl originated from the red jungle fowl which inhabits the forests and jungles of India, Indo-China, Malaya, the Philippines and Timor. Well-known varieties of fowl are Wyandotte, Rhode Island Red, Plymouth Rock, Leghorn, Sussex Red and Orpingtons.

PRAYER BOOK The Book of Common Prayer was originally compiled to teach all church going people to pray together. Its main author was Thomas Cranmer (1489-1156), Archbishop of Canterbury. The main contents are Matins and Evensong, with Psalms for both, the Holy Communion service, Epistle and Gospel for each Sunday of the Calendar and for Saints Days and Feasts. The Book also contains the English Litany, and services for baptism, burial, confirmation, marriage, and the consecration of new clergymen.

PRESIDENT is the head of a republic, and carries out the duties of a king or queen in a monarchy. In the U.S.A. the President is elected every 4 years.

NAME	INAUG-URATED	BORN, DIED
George Washington	1789	1732-1799
John Adams	1797	1735-1826
Thomas Jefferson	1801	1743-1826
James Madison	1809	1751-1836
James Monroe	1817	1758-1831
John Quincy Adams	1825	1767-1848
Andrew Jackson	1829	1767-1845
Martin Van Buren	1837	1782-1862
William Henry Harrison	1841	1773-1841
John Tyler	1841	1790-1862
James Knox Polk	1845	1795-1849
Zachary Taylor	1849	1784-1850
Millard Fillmore	1850	1800-1874
Franklin Pierce	1853	1804-1869
James Buchanan	1857	1791-1868
Abraham Lincoln	1861	1809-1865
Andrew Johnson	1865	1808-1875
Ulysses Simpson Grant	1869	1822-1885
Rutherford Birchard Hayes	1877	1822-1993
James Abram Garfield	1881	1831-1881
Chester Alan Arthur	1881	1830-1886
Grover Cleveland	1885	1837-1908
Benjamin Harrison	1889	1833-1901
Grover Cleveland	1893	1837-1908
William McKinley	1897	1843-1901
Theodore Roosevelt	1901	1858-1919
William Howard Taft	1909	1857-1930
Woodrow Wilson	1913	1856-1924
Warren Gamaliel Harding	1921	1865-1923
Calvin Coolidge	1923	1872-1933
Herbert C. Hoover	1929	1874-1964
Franklin Delano Roosevelt	1933	1882-1945
Harry S. Truman	1945	1884
Dwight D. Eisenhower	1953	1890-1969
John F. Kennedy	1961	1917-1963
Lyndon B. Johnson	1963	1908
Richard M. Nixon	1969	1913

PRINTING Two of the first printers in Europe were L.J. Coster of Haarlem (Holland) and J. Gutenberg of Mainz (Germany) who both worked about the middle of the 15th century. William Caxton, an Englishman, learned the art of printing in Europe, and on his return to England set up a printing press of his own at Westminster in 1476. In fifteen years he published about one hundred volumes. The early printing presses were rude wooden affairs in which a moist sheet of paper was pressed down upon an inked 'forme' of type. Later, hand-presses were invented, which were operated by a lever and the inking was done by rollers. Nowadays we have great rotary presses which print, fold and collate whole newspapers and magazines from continuous rolls of paper at the rate of about 60,000 or more copies an hour. After the types have been set up, proofed and corrected, a papier-mâché mould is taken; this mould is placed in a casting box, where melted metal is poured upon it and then rapidly chilled, producing a plate about one-eighth of an inch thick.

Many books are printed by what is called the letterpress method; that is, the faces of the type characters are raised so that they can be coated with ink from a roller and leave an impression when pressed on to paper. Pictures can also be printed by letterpress, but there is also the gravure method, by which the letters are in the form of small holes in a copper sheet; the holes are filled with ink, extra ink is wiped off, and then the paper is pressed against the holes. Or the type may be in the form of greasy surfaces on a metal plate, the greasy surfaces holding the ink while the rest of the damped metal plate is not affected; this is called lithography.

More and more publications are now being printed by what is called the offset litho method: the image is placed upon the zinc or aluminium sheet; in the rotary printing machine the plate is first damped with water and then immediately inked; the inked plate then comes into contact with a rubber blanket which receives the printing image, and it is from this blanket that the paper takes the impression, being pressed against it by a rotating cylinder. Some books are set photographically—they are printed from film instead of from metal typefaces. An electrically driven printing press can print more than 300,000 pages in one hour. See TABLES 2, 3, 6, pages 184, 185, 190.

PROPHET is a name which may be applied to people who claim to know what is going to happen in the future. This is the very general meaning of the word. In its biblical sense the word prophet meant 'Man of God', a teacher and a guide. The great Hebrew prophets were Elijah, Amos, Hosea, Isaiah, Micah, Jeremiah and Ezekiel.

PSALMS The word 'psalm' comes from the Greek word *psalmos*, meaning 'the sound of stringed instruments'. In the Bible the Book of Psalms contains 150 pieces which were originally Hebrew hymns. King David is always associated with the psalms, and in fact he may well have composed a number of them.

PURITANS were a group of religious people who desired strict simplicity in their services of worship and followed an equally strict code of behaviour. Two celebrated English Puritans were John Bunyan (1628-88) who wrote *Pilgrim's Progress*, one of the most famous books

A pyramid tomb built by the ancient Egyptians

A pyramid temple built by the ancient Aztecs

ever written, and John Milton (1608-74), England's greatest epic poet and the author of *Paradise Lost*.

PYGMIES are members of a race of small people. The word pygmy may also be applied to a very small animal or plant. In ancient Greek writings, mention is made of a race of very small people who lived in parts of equatorial Africa; in fact the word pygmy comes from a Greek word meaning the combined length of the human forearm and clenched fist—about $13\frac{1}{2}$ inches. Of course, human pygmies are bigger than this, but nevertheless they seldom grow as high as four feet six inches, and many are only three feet high. Some scientists think that the existing pygmy races are most nearly like our primitive ancestors. The greatest number and variety of pygmy peoples live in the forests of Central Africa. Pygmies are usually very clever hunters, and often use poisoned arrows to kill their prey; they also eat wild fruits and vegetables.

PYRAMIDS A pyramid is a geometrical figure—a solid with a triangular or square or polygonal base and sloping sides meeting at an apex. So any object with this shape is spoken of as a pyramid, but when we speak of 'the Pyramids' (with a capital P) we mean the name given to the royal tombs of the ancient Egyptians in the Nile Valley; these tombs were made of solid stone, and built on a square base with the four sides sloping at an angle of about 50 degrees. The most famous Pyramids are those at Gizeh, the largest being 480 feet high and 756 feet along the base. Pyramid-like buildings called ziggurats, with steps up the sides, were also built by the ancient Assyrians, Babylonians and Aztecs.

QUAGGA This animal, which became extinct about the year 1873, was a kind of zebra, related to the horse family, but differed from other zebras in that it did not have stripes on its hind quarters. It was found in several parts of Africa and got its name because the noise it made sounded like 'qua-ha-ha'.

QUARTZ is pronounced *kwawrts* and is the commonest rock-forming mineral; it is composed of silica and is found as crystals. Another name for it is 'rock crystals'. It is colourless and is one of the principal ingredients of the rock called granite.

RABBITS and **HARES** A rabbit can be a delightful pet; it can also, in some parts of the world, be a dreadful pest. The domestic rabbit has been produced from the wild rabbit which annoys farmers because it is a hungry eater of crops. The wild rabbit came to Britain from southern Europe. Both hares and rabbits are double-toothed rodents. They have two pairs of incisor teeth in the front of the upper jaw. Hares do not live together but rabbits live in colonies in burrows. Hares are not only larger than rabbits but also have longer ears and hind legs. In North America hares are sometimes called 'jack rabbits'.

RACCOON is found in North and South America. It is about the size of a large cat, is covered with long thick fur and has rather short legs. It spends most of the day in trees, where it also makes a rough nest for its young, and goes hunting at night for small birds and animals, fish, insects, fruits and berries. It has an amusing habit of dipping its food in water before eating it. Its fur is used for clothing.

RADAR was originally known as 'radiolocation', and developed just before the Second World War by a team of scientists led by Sir Robert Watson-Watt. It is an electronic method of detecting the position of objects at rest or in motion by means of radio waves. What happens in principle is that short pulses of radio waves are transmitted, and when they strike an object are reflected back. The distance the object is away is found by taking the time between the transmission on the pulse and receiving the reflected pulse. An advanced form of radar gives a 'light' map of the area being swept by the radio beam. This system is used by both ships and aircraft, and is a valuable aid to the safety of passengers and crews.

RADIO Although radio waves were discovered by H. Hertz as early as 1887, it was not until after the First World War that broadcasting actually started. The first radio station was KOKA Pittsburg, U.S.A. The following scientists made notable contributions to radio science: H. Hertz (1857-94), Lee De Forest (1873-1961), T.A. Edison (1847-1931), G.M. Marconi (1874-1937), Sir A. Fleming (1849-1945) and Sir O. Lodge (1851-1940).

The raccoon of North and South America

Aircraft and ships are fitted with radar to ensure safe navigation. It shows a radar map (top right) of the area to be navigated

radar picture of harbour

The type of radio telescope used at Jodrell Bank

RADIOACTIVE SUBSTANCES are a group of very heavy elements which emit rays and atomic particles. The best-known is radium, and discovered in 1902 by the French scientists, Marie and Pierre Curie. One of the important things about a radioactive element is that as it throws out rays and particles it changes into another element; for example, radium eventually breaks down to become the non-radioactive element lead. Today the most important radioactive substance is uranium, for it is this element which is used as a fuel in atomic power-stations, see NUCLEAR POWER.

Since the discovery that atoms can be split to release energy to do useful work, many new radioactive substances have been created. These man-made elements are made in powerful atom-smashing machines, and include Americium, Berkelium, Californium, Einsteinium, Fermium, Mendelvium and Plutonium. Radioactive substances can be detected by an instrument called a GEIGER COUNTER.

RADIO ASTRONOMY is one of the very latest branches of astronomy, and is a development of

RADAR. It was discovered that stars send out not only visible light, but radio waves. Also, and perhaps more important, some stars send out only radio waves, and are therefore invisible to the ordinary eye and telescope. These dark stars are thought to be nearly as numerous as visible stars, and to form an important part of the universe. The instrument used to detect radio stars is called a 'radio telescope'. The biggest in the world is at Jodrell Bank, Cheshire. In addition to studying radio stars, a radio telescope is used for tracking such things as space vehicles and other man-made satellites.

RADIO TELEPHONY is ordinary telephony (speech transmitted by means of a telephone) but relayed in the form of radio waves. The radio telephone is used for communications between places where it is not possible to run a submarine cable for reasons of expense or difficult sea and coastal conditions; for example the islands off the coast of Scotland. It is also used on the long trans-oceanic and ship-to-shore telephone service, and on trains and aeroplanes. Radio telegraphy is similar to radio telephony but instead of relaying speech it transmits messages in dots and dashes.

RAFFIA is made from the split leaves of the raffia palm. It can be plaited or woven to make floor mats, fruit baskets, napkin rings, sandals, etc. Raffia-work is a handicraft which even the youngest child can do, and it is not expensive.

RAILWAYS were made possible by the invention of the steam engine. The earliest railways were, however, used only for carrying coal and stone. The first public railway was the Stockton and Darlington Railway, and was opened on September 27, 1825. Its first engine, *Locomotion*, is now kept on a pedestal at Darlington station. Another pioneer railway was the Liverpool and Manchester Railway, opened in 1830. In the United States railways of the horse-or mule-operated type were built in 1826-27. One of the first railways to use steam locomotives was the Delaware and Hudson, which bought the *Stourbridge Lion* in 1827. The Baltimore and Ohio Railway quickly followed with American-built locomotives. The Mohawk and Hudson Railway was opened in 1831, and used the famous engine *De Witt Clinton*. France followed closely behind Britain, and in 1828 the St. Etienne Railway was opened. The following are the dates when public railways were started in various countries: Austria, 1827; France, 1828; Belgium, 1835; Germany, 1835; Russia, 1838; Italy, 1839; Switzerland, 1844; Spain, 1848; Sweden, 1851; Portugal, 1854; Turkey, 1860; Canada, 1836; South Africa, 1860; Australia, 1855; India, 1853; Japan, 1872; Mexico, 1873; China, 1875.

From these early—and often crude—beginnings the railway systems have risen to be the most important of all forms of transport, whether of goods or passengers. This was made possible by engineers who designed and made locomotives of greater and greater power. Also, the equally important advances in permanent ways, carriages, signalling system, bridges, etc. In many countries the steam locomotive has been replaced by diesel-electric locomotives, and, where electric power is plentiful, electric locomotives. It seems unlikely that atomic energy will be used for driving locomotives for many years to come. Experiments are being carried out on hovertrains for city-to-city high-speed travel.

RAINBOW is caused by light from the sun being bent as it passes through raindrops. When light passes through a triangular prism it forms a band of colours called a SPECTRUM. Rainbows are best seen when the sun is shining behind you and rain is falling in front at a distance.

RED CROSS is the name given to societies who care for the sick and wounded, particularly in time of war or disaster. It was a Swiss, Henri Dunant, who thought that nations at war should agree to observe rules for the care of the wounded and prisoners, and he secured international agreement for his idea in 1864. The symbol of the Red Cross was chosen because it was a Swiss who made the plan; the Swiss flag is a white cross on a red background, but this could not be adopted because the Society's aim is to give its special kind of help to anyone, Swiss or otherwise; so the symbol was merely reversed, and is thus a red cross on a white ground. All countries have their own Red Cross societies, though in Moslem countries they are called Red Crescent societies. The headquarters of the world Red Cross organization is at Geneva.

REFORMATION is the name given to the period during the 16th century when certain countries in Europe broke away from the Roman Catholic Church. But even before this, in the 14th and 15th centuries, opposition had been growing to many of the practices of the Church of Rome, and the movement's most prominent leaders included such men as John Wycliffe (died in 1384), often called 'the morning star of the Reformation', and John Huss (died in 1415). The leader of the Reformation in Germany was Martin Luther (1483-1546), a miner's son who became a priest. It was in Germany that the word 'Protestant' was first used to describe

An artist's impression of the opening of the Liverpool and Manchester Railway in 1830

Nicolas Cugnot's steam carriage 1769

Steam locomotive (4-2-2) of the
Great Northern Railway (Britain) 1870

George Stephenson's
'Locomotion' 1825

Diesel-electric locomotive of
British Railways S.R.

American steam locomotive about 1860

Garratt steam locomotive for hauling heavy trains

The General Motors streamlined 'Aerotrain'

Diesel-electric
locomotive of So
Australian Railw

'Gresley' Pacific steam locomotive (4-6-2)
hauled express trains up to 1930

Pacific steam locomotive used in
America for hauling heavy trains

sel loco hauling
ods train
w Zealand Railways)

Modern Japanese
electric express train

those who protested against the decrees issued by the Roman Church. In England, the Reformation began in earnest when Henry VIII (1509-47) defied and threw off the authority of the Pope and declared himself head of the Church (in England) and 'Defender of the Faith'. Henry's son (Edward VI) upheld the new religion but Mary (1553-58) restored the old faith, and it was not until the reign of Elizabeth (1558-1603) that the new Church of England became firmly established.

REFRIGERATOR is an apparatus or a container for producing and maintaining a low temperature. Nowadays such an apparatus is a familiar part of the modern kitchen, and it is usually referred to as a 'fridge'. (The Latin word for 'cold' is *frigus*.) A refrigerator works on the principle that a substance that absorbs heat at a temperature slightly below freezing point can give it out again at room temperature, and these requirements are met by certain gases. Domestic refrigerators are used to keep household foods fresh. In big cold-storage plants, refrigerators are called 'deep freezers' and the perishable foods stored in them will keep fresh for months and even years.

REINDEER This is the only member of the deer family in which both the males and females have antlers. The reindeer is equipped for living in cold climates. It is found in North America (where it is called caribou), and in northern districts of Asia and Europe. In Lapland the reindeer is a familiar sight because it has been domesticated by the people, who use it as a beast of burden and also for supplying them with milk, hides and meat.

RENAISSANCE was the period in the 14th and 15th centuries when Europe emerged from the Dark Ages. The period is marked by a revival in learning, the arts and the sciences. It began in Italy and spread to France, Germany, England and the Low Countries, reaching its full flowering in art in the 16th century. Great names associated with the Renaissance include Raphael, Leonardo da Vinci, Michelangelo, Corregio, Titian, Tintoretto, Benvenuto Cellini, Erasmus, Rabelais and Sir Thomas More.

REPTILES Unlike mammals, reptiles are cold-blooded creatures; this means that the temperature of their blood rises and falls according to the temperature of their surroundings instead of staying the same as it does with human beings. The skin of reptiles is usually covered with hard, protective scales, and they breathe with lungs. Most reptiles lay either hard-or softshelled eggs. In all cases the young, when hatched or born, are perfect representations of their parents, and do not undergo any form of change as do frogs or butterflies, for instance. The best-known reptiles are turtles, terrapins, tortoises, crocodiles, alligators, lizards, chameleons and snakes.

RESTORATION was the restoring to power of Charles II on 29 May 1660. This event used to be celebrated with special church services and the day was known as 'Oak Apple Day' because on the same day nine years earlier Charles had escaped capture by his enemies, the Roundheads, by hiding in an oak tree after the Battle of Worcester. Charles II reigned until 1685.

RHEA This is an ostrich-like bird found in South America. It is a fast-running bird of the grassy plains, and though it is smaller than the ostrich its habits are much the same. In recent years it has been widely hunted.

RHINOCEROS This animal is found in tropical parts of the world ranging from India to Borneo and in South and East Africa. It feeds entirely on vegetable foods such as grasses and foliage. It is a huge, ungainly animal and is covered with a tough skin; the legs are short and the head large, and although its senses of smell and hearing are very good it has poor eyesight. Most rhinoceroses have a single large horn on the muzzle, but some kinds, such as the 'black rhinoceros', have two, one behind the other. The horn is not true horn but formed of compressed hair.

RHODESIA is a self-proclaimed republic in Southern Africa with an area of 150,000 square miles. It has a population of about 4 millions. The capital is Salisbury and the chief industrial town Bulawayo. The Zambezi runs through the country. In 1965 the government of Rhodesia proclaimed a unilateral declaration of indepen-

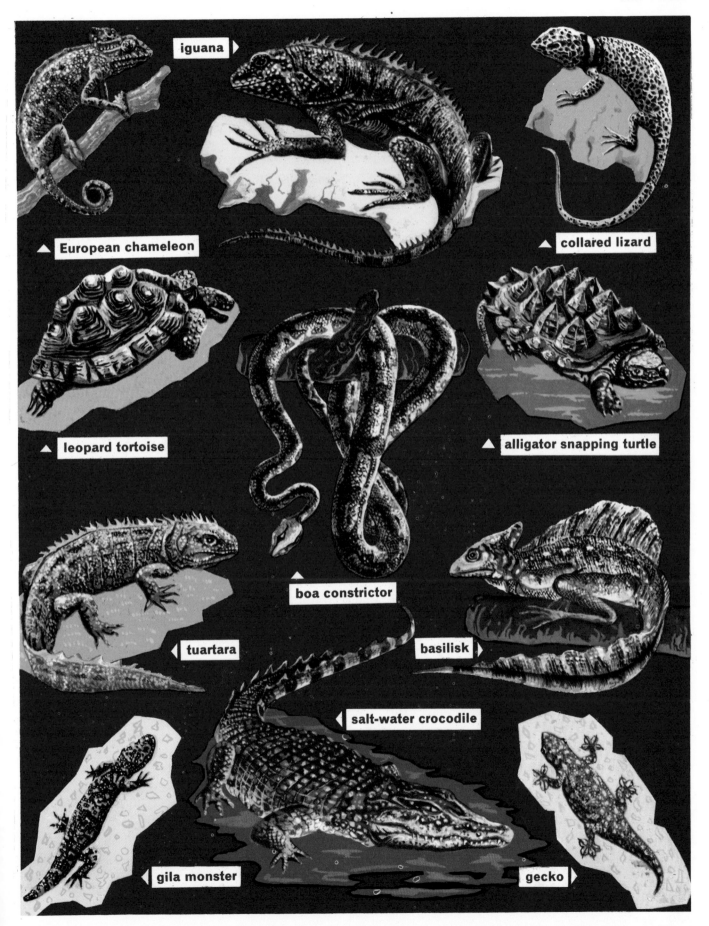

iguana

▲ European chameleon

▲ collared lizard

▲ leopard tortoise

▲ alligator snapping turtle

▲ boa constrictor

◄ tuartara

basilisk ►

◄ salt-water crocodile

◄ gila monster

gecko ►

made by the priests of Egypt about 200 years dence (or U.D.I.). It is mainly agricultural, its chief crop being tobacco.

RIVERS are streams of fresh, running water that flow to the sea or a lake. They are fed by rain or melting snow/ice running off mountains and hills. The following table shows the length of many of the best-known rivers of the world, in order of greatest length.

MAIN RIVERS OF THE WORLD

(Arranged in order of greatest length)

NAME	COUNTRY	LENGTH IN MILES
Nile	Egypt	4,150
Amazon	Brazil	4,000
Yangtse	China	3,400
Yenisey	U.S.S.R.	3,360
Congo	Africa	2,900
Yellow	China	2,900
Missouri	U.S.A.	2,700
Lena	U.S.S.R.	2,650
Niger	Africa	2,600
Mekong	China	2,600
Mackenzie	Canada	2,500
Mississippi	U.S.A.	2,350
Volga	U.S.S.R.	2,290
Yukon	Canada	2,000
Indus	Pakistan	1,900
Río Grande	U.S.A.	1,800
Brahmaputra	India	1,800
Amur	U.S.S.R.	1,760
Salween	Burma	1,750
Danube	Europe	1,725
Darling	Australia	1,700
Orinoco	Venezuela	1,700
Euphrates	Syria	1,670
Zambezi	Africa	1,600
Ganges	India	1,560
Dnieper	U.S.S.R.	1,420
Murray	Australia	1,200
Rhine	Europe	820
Elbe	Germany	700
Loire	France	625
Tagus	Spain and Portugal	570
Ebro	Spain	570
Seine	France	470
Po	Italy	400
Severn	Britain	220
Thames	Britain	210

ROBOTS are machines which can do things in much the same way as a human being; they can be made to walk, play games, and even smoke cigarettes and play cards. The name 'robot' was coined by the Czech playwright Karel Capek for a character in his play *R.U.R.* which was about mechanical men (the Czech word *robota* means work). The nearest science has got to creating a machine like Capek's robot is the 'electronic brain' or computer; this can work out complicated problems (if properly 'programmed') that might otherwise take years to work out.

ROCKET is a flying body or missile propelled by gases escaping from its rear. It is important to realize that the body moves forward because of its reaction, and not as a result of the gases pushing on the surrounding air—a mistake often made. As long ago as the thirteenth century the Chinese used gunpowder rockets as weapons of war. In the 18th and 19th centuries the British used rocket weapons, but when the gun developed to the stage that it could fire shells farther than rockets, then rocket weapons were discontinued. Between the First and Second World Wars many experiments were made with rockets, especially in Germany; in fact, it was this work which led the Germans to make their terrible flying bombs and V-2s. Until about 1939 rockets were powered by what is called solid fuel, which was either gunpowder or cordite. Most modern rockets are powered by liquid fuel, and work in the way shown in the diagram. A large three-stage rocket of the type used for launching satellites is shown in the illustration.

RODENTS are small animals with teeth specially adapted for gnawing. They are found in most countries of the world. There are two main groups: the double-toothed rodents, which include hares and rabbits; and the single-toothed rodents, which include squirrels, beavers, dormice, rats, mice, voles, jerboas, flying squirrels, porcupines, cavies, agoutis, and capybaras.

ROSETTA STONE is a part of a monument bearing an inscription in Greek, demotic script (the popular form of writing used in ancient Egypt), and ancient Egyptian hieroglyphics. It is now in the British Museum, London, but was discovered in Egypt (at Rosetta, an old city on the Nile) by one of Napoleon's officers in 1799. The Rosetta Stone is one of the most important documents in the world, because before it was found no one had been able to read the ancient Egyptian writing on that country's temples and tombs. It was realized that the three kinds of writing on the Stone were different versions of the same message, which proved to be an order

before Christ. Scholars already knew Greek and had a fair knowledge of the demotic, so by comparing these with the third form of writing they discovered what the hieroglyphics meant. Hieroglyphics were symbols representing objects which stood for words and sounds.

RUBBER is a gummy substance which is tapped from certain trees that grow in South America and the Malay Archipelago. A rubbery substance is also obtained from certain kinds of dandelion plant. When a rubber tree is tapped, a milk-like juice, called latex, dribbles out. This contains other substances besides rubber, and must be heated and treated to remove them. The rubber so obtained is called 'crude'. Latex is also used for making 'foam rubber' articles such as cushions, dolls, footwear, etc. Crude rubber is further treated to improve its strength and usefulness. The process is known as 'vulcanizing'. In recent years great strides have been made in producing synthetic rubbers (artificially made but of a similar nature), and some of these have better properties than natural rubbers.

RUMANIA is a communist republic in Eastern Europe with an area of about 91,600 square miles and a population of about 20 millions. The capital is Bucharest at the mouth of the River Danube. The main products are wheat, petroleum and other minerals.

SAFETY LAMP One of the most famous of English scientists was Sir Humphry Davy (1778-1829) who invented the miners' safety lamp. He did not, however, show much interest in science during his schooldays but preferred reading poetry and literature. Then his interest turned to medicine and he began to study various branches of science, in particular chemistry. He discovered that nitrous oxide or 'laughing gas' could be used safely as an anesthetic and published numerous papers setting out his observations on such subjects as the chemistry of agriculture and the tanning industry. But his name will always be remembered for one invention especially. This was the invention of the safety lamp. In his day, many miners lost their lives because of explosions caused when underground gases were ignited by the naked flames from the oil lamps or candles by whose light the miners worked. Davy devised a lamp with sides of metal gauze which protected the flame and screened its heat, and although his idea was subsequently much improved upon, the principle remains the same. Davy was knighted and later created a baronet for his services to science.

SAINTS are men and women whom the Roman Catholic Church recognizes as holy and

A simplified diagram of a liquid-fuel rocket. Although this is only a single-stage rocket the three-stage giants used on moon flights work on the same principle

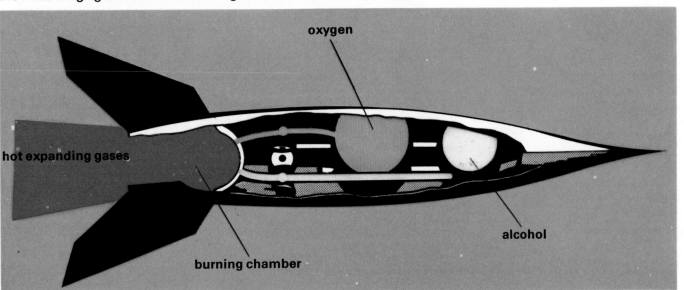

possessed of special virtues. Leading angels are usually looked on as saints, like St Gabriel, St Michael, and so on. The Church laid down the rule in about 1170 that only on its authority could a person become a saint. The ceremony is known as 'canonization'. Numerous countries have their own patron saint: for instance, St George for England, St Andrew for Scotland, St David for Wales, St Patrick for Ireland, St Denys for France, etc.

ST ELMO'S FIRE Sometimes electricity in the atmosphere takes the form of brush-like discharges which flash and glow as they play around pointed objects during stormy weather. They are seen particularly round the mastheads of sailing ships, and in olden days the sailors used to think that the lights were the souls of the dead who had come to protect them. Later, the flashes were thought to be signals of goodwill from St Erasmus, the patron saint of Mediterranean sailors; 'St Erasmus Fire' became corrupted into St Ermo's Fire and then into St Elmo's Fire. The real name of this Erasmus was Peter Gonzalez but his saintly name was bestowed on him by Pope Innocent IV about the year 1250.

SALAMANDER This little creature is a lizard-like amphibian (able to live both on land and in water) which belongs to the same family as newts. In ancient days the salamander was thought to be a magical creature which was able to live in fire and to be able to put fire out because its body was icy cold. On the contrary, the salamander dislikes heat and is found only in damp places. The European species live on land, but the tigrine salamander of the U.S.A. and Mexico lives in water. It is white, about seven inches long, has a tadpole-like tail, and four legs. See AXOLOTL.

SALT Common salt, which the chemist calls sodium chloride, is found in sea-water, salt flats and lakes, or mined from rock. It is an important raw material in many industries, as well as being an essential ingredient in food.

SAMOA, WESTERN is a state in the Pacific made up of several islands. It is a member of the British Commonwealth with the capital at Apia. It has a total area of 1,100 square miles and a population of about 141,000. It exports

St. Paul, one of the Saints of early Christendom

An artist's impression of St. Elmo's fire playing around the yards of an old sailing ship

The salamander is an amphibian and belongs to the same family as the newts

Scandinavia is rich in timber. It is transported down rivers to sawmills in floating log islands, as shown here

mostly copra, cocoa, beans, and bananas.

SAN MARINO is a tiny republic on the Adriatic coast of Italy. It has an area of 23 square miles and a population of about 19,000. The capital has the same name and the republic is best known for its colourful postage stamps.

SARGASSO SEA During the 16th century, mariners brought back tales which seemed to confirm a report first made by Columbus about a vast collection of seaweed in the western Atlantic Ocean. It was supposed to be a reedy waste through which no ship could sail, and legends grew that Spanish galleons, laden with treasure, had become trapped there. What happens is that bits of a plant called 'sargussum', or gulf-weed, are torn away from the Caribbean coast and swept by the Gulf Stream northwards and eastwards into an area where there is a circular system of currents revolving round a calm area of sea. Here the weed collects; it floats on the water, is able to reproduce itself, and under its leaves flying fish lay their eggs. The nearest land to the Sargasso Sea is the island of Bermuda. The isolation of the Sargasso Sea (it is well off the main shipping routes) has helped to preserve its sinister reputation, but it is by no means impenetrable.

SAUDI ARABIA is a kingdom which contains most of the Arabian peninsula. It has an area of about 927,000 square miles and a population of about 7 millions. The capital is Riyadh. Mecca, which is the birthplace of the Prophet Mohammed, and Medina, his burial place, are in Saudi Arabia. Both these cities are sacred to the Moslems. The country is very rich in oil deposits.

SAXONS Saxony was formerly a state of Germany, and before 1918 there was a 'kingdom' of Saxony and also a province of that name; it is now part of Russian-occupied East Germany. In olden days the people of Saxony (Saxons) were a tall, fair haired, blue-eyed race, and they were famous as soldiers and pirates. They raided the coasts of France and Britain and in the 6th century had settled in parts of south-eastern England: Sussex was so named because it was the home of the 'South Saxons' and Essex because it was the home of the 'East Saxons'. Together with the Angles, another wave of invaders, they made up the Anglo-Saxon race which became the English.

SCANDINAVIA is the name given to the group of countries which usually includes Sweden, Denmark, Norway, Finland and Iceland. The Scandinavian peninsula consists of Norway and Sweden.

SCILLY ISLES lie 25 miles west-south-west of England's county of Cornwall, and consist of five inhabited islands named St Mary's, Tresco, St Martin's, St Agnes, and Bryher; there are also about 32 other islands and an additional 100 or so islets and rocks. The climate of the Scilly Isles is mild, and the people are employed chiefly in growing flowers and vegetables.

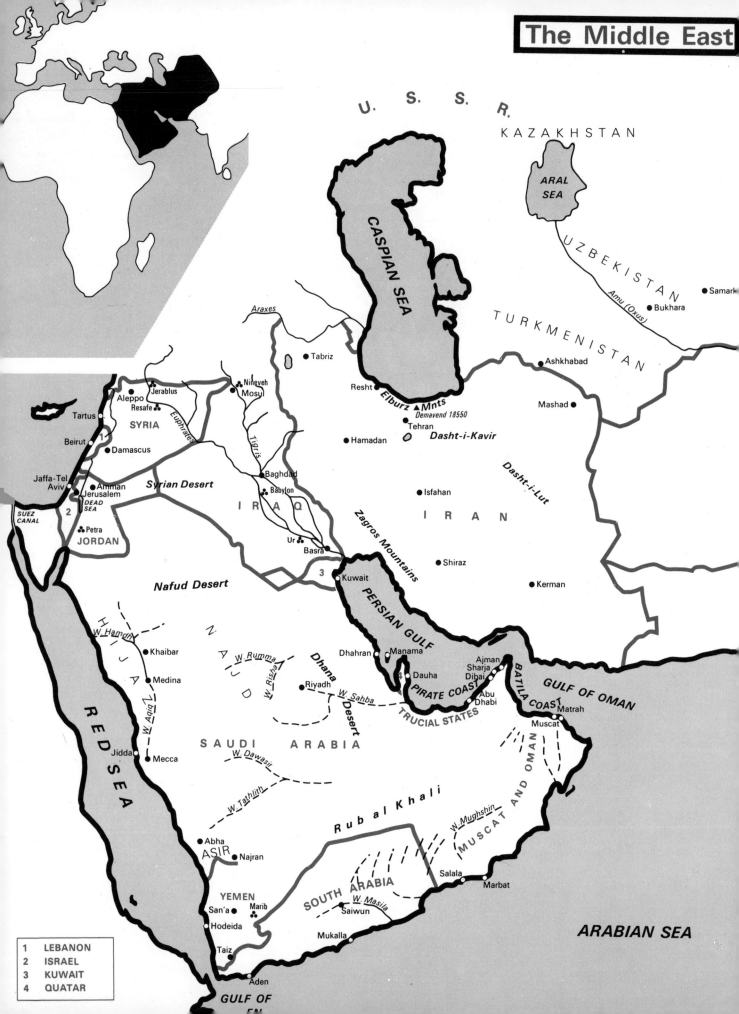

The Middle East

U. S. S. R.

KAZAKHSTAN

ARAL SEA

UZBEKISTAN

● Samark

● Bukhara

Amu (Oxus)

TURKMENISTAN

CASPIAN SEA

● Ashkhabad

Araxes

● Tabriz

Mashad ●

Resht ●

Elburz ▲ Mnts

Demavend 18550

● Nineveh

Mosul

Jerablus ●

● Aleppo
Resafe ●

Tartus ○

SYRIA

Tehran ●

Dasht-i-Kavir

● Hamadan

Beirut ○ 1

● Damascus

Euphrates

Tigris

Dasht-i-Lut

Jaffa-Tel
Aviv ●

● Amman
Jerusalem ●

Syrian Desert

Baghdad ●

Babylon ●

I R A Q

● Isfahan

I R A N

DEAD
SEA

2

SUEZ
CANAL

♣ Petra
JORDAN

Zagros Mountains

Ur ●

Basra ●

● Shiraz

● Kerman

Nafud Desert

3 ● Kuwait

PERSIAN GULF

W. Hamdh

Z

Khaibar ●

A J D

W. Rumma

Dhana

Dhahran ●

○ Manama

Ajman
Sharja ○
Dibai ○

BATILA COAST

GULF OF OMAN

R E D   S E A

H I J A Z

W. Aqiq

● Medina

W. Risha

● Riyadh

W. Sahba

Dauha

4

Abu
Dhabi

Matrah ●

○ Muscat

Desert

PIRATE COAST

TRUCIAL STATES

● Jidda

● Mecca

W. Dawasir

S A U D I   A R A B I A

W. Tathlith

Rub al Khali

W. Mughshin

M U S C A T   A N D   O M A N

● Abha

ASIR

● Najran

SOUTH ARABIA

Salala ●

○ Marbat

W. Masila

W. Masila

YEMEN

Marib

San'a ●

● Saiwun

Marbat

Hodeida ●

Mukalla ●

Taiz ●

ARABIAN SEA

○ Aden

GULF OF
EN

1	LEBANON
2	ISRAEL
3	KUWAIT
4	QUATAR

SCOTLAND is the part of the United Kingdom that lies north of England, and includes many groups of islands, the most important of which are the Orkneys, Shetlands and Hebrides. The population of Scotland is over 5 millions. Its capital is Edinburgh, and the largest city is Glasgow. The country can be divided into three regions: the Highlands which, as their name tells us, are very mountainous, the Central Lowlands where most of the large towns and industries are found, and the Southern Uplands where there are mostly farms. Scotland's greatest length is 274 miles and the greatest width is 154 miles. At one time Gaelic, a Celtic language, was the only language spoken in Scotland, but now comparatively few people are able to speak it.

SEAL is an animal which is specially adapted for life in the water; it can be found in nearly all seas except in the tropics. Its body is tapered from the shoulders down to the tail, and the limbs are in the form of fin-like paddles which are webbed. Besides the true seal there is the sea-lion, and this animal's fur is used for making clothes. It differs from the true seal in having small external ears and close, woolly fur under long hair, and spends more time on land than does the true seal. Seals and sea-lions are flesh-eating, their diet being fish of various kinds. Another member of the seal family is the sea-elephant or elephant-seal.

SEAS See **OCEANS AND SEAS**

SEA-SNAKES are snakes which, as their name indicates, live in the sea, mostly in tropical waters bordering Asia and Africa. They usually have the tail flattened at the sides; this makes them powerful swimmers but awkward on land. All sea-snakes are poisonous.

SEASONS A year is divided into four seasons: spring, summer, autumn and winter. The earth moves in three ways: it revolves on its own axis; it moves in orbit round the sun; and as it revolves and as it orbits it also 'wobbles' a bit, that is, it tilts towards and away from the sun as it travels round it. This results in the sun's rays being warmer at some times than at others, and this is the reason for the differing season. For instance, in Britain in winter, that part of the earth is tilted away from the sun, so that the sun's rays have farther to travel and do not warm so much; while this is happening, of course, the people in Australia, on the other side of the world, enjoy their summer, because their part of the earth is tilted towards the sun. Places on or near the equator—the imaginary line drawn round the earth's circumference—do not have sharply contrasted seasons because that part of the earth is always about the same distance away from the sun.

SEAWEEDS are plants that grow and float in the sea. There are over 400 different kinds of seaweeds, which vary greatly in size and colour. They are divided into three main groups: green, red and brown. The green sea-

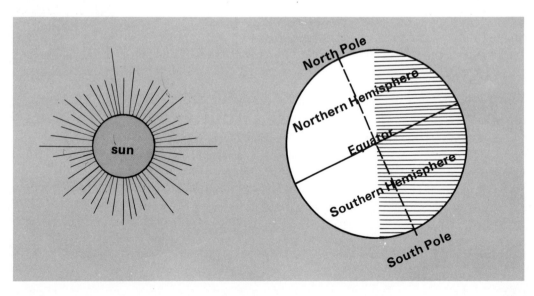

Because the earth revolves round the sun on a tilted axis the sun's rays are warmer at some times and less so at others. This is the basic reason for different seasons

weeds are found nearest to the surface, the red seaweeds are usually lower, while the brown varieties can be found at all depths. Seaweeds can be used in the manufacture of fertilizer, soap, jelly and paper varnish, and in some parts of the world the red seaweeds are used as a food.

SEISMOGRAPH is an instrument used for recording earthquakes. It is chiefly made up of a heavy weight balanced on a lever which moves when a region of the earth trembles and shakes. The other end of the lever is fitted with a special pen which records the earth's movements and rumblings on a roll of paper. An instrument like a seismograph and working on the same principle is used in prospecting for oil.

SENATE was the governing body in ancient Rome; nowadays it is the name for a legislative or deliberative body, especially the upper house of a national or state legislature. Certain British universities also have a governing body called a senate. Federal government in Australia is by a Senate of sixty members and a House of Representatives consisting of twice the number of senators. The Senate is also the Upper House in the U.S.A. Congress. See HOUSE OF REPRESENTATIVES.

SEVEN WONDERS OF THE WORLD were: the Pyramids of ancient Egypt, the Colossus (an enormous statue) of Rhodes, the Hanging Gardens of Babylon, the Temple of Diana at Ephesus, the Tomb of Mausolus at Halicarnassus, the statue of Jupiter or Zeus at Olympia, and the Pharos lighthouse at Alexandria. Of all these, only the Egyptian Pyramids can still be seen in anything like their original state; only fragments remain of the Temple of Diana, and nothing at all of the other five 'wonders'.

SEXTANT is an instrument used for guiding ships or surveying land. It measures the angular distance between two points; that is, between the sun and the horizon, and is worked with the aid of two mirrors and a telescope. By using a sextant, sailors can find out their latitude, and so work out their exact position at sea.

SHARK is a very large fish which is found in most seas. It belongs to the same family as

A selection of green, red and brown seaweeds

The pyramids of ancient Egypt were one of the seven wonders of the ancient world.

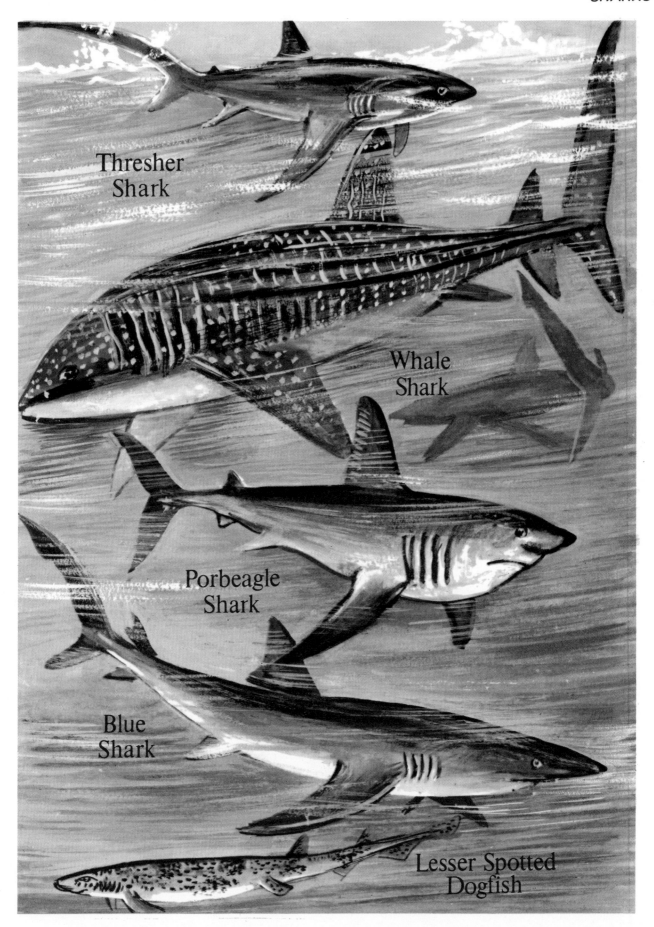

Thresher
Shark

Whale
Shark

Porbeagle
Shark

Blue
Shark

Lesser Spotted
Dogfish

the dog-fishes and rays. It is usually a bluish colour, has a pointed snout, and many teeth. Some of the largest sharks grow to a length of 50 to 70 feet.

SHEEP Wild sheep, of which there are many kinds, are found mostly in Europe, Asia and North America. The domesticated sheep has a softer coat or fleece, which is used for making wool, while its flesh provides much of the world's meat supply. Among the best-known breeds of sheep are: Cotswold, Welsh, Devon, Ryeland, Exmoor, Shropshire, Dorset, Suffolk, Wensleydale, Blackfaced, Hampshire and Cheviot.

SHERIFF In Anglo-Saxon times each shire or county had its steward or bailiff; he was called the 'shire reeve', so you can see how the word sheriff came about. Today the sheriff of an English county is the chief officer of the Crown in that shire; in Scotland he is the chief judge of a county; in the United States he is the chief executive officer in a county, with a duty to maintain law and order, attend courts, guard prisoners, serve processes, and execute judgements. There are various classes of sheriff in some instances, such as honorary sheriffs, high sheriffs and sheriffs-substitute.

SHIPS Man's first attempt to travel over water was probably made on a log, using his hands to paddle it along. It is also quite possible that he lashed several logs together to make a raft. Later, when he had mastered the art of making and using tools, he hollowed out a tree trunk and made crude but effective oars to pull the craft along. Although specimens have never been found, there is little doubt that they were very like the dug-out canoes still made by the primitive peoples of Africa and the Amazon. The ancient Egyptians made sailing boats with flat hulls and long flat bows to sail the Nile. The Phoenicians, a race of born seamen, constructed fine ships which voyaged as far south as the Cape of Good Hope, and all over the Mediterranean. The Greeks and Romans used galleys, often with several decks, and propelled by slaves chained to the oars. The Ancient Britons built basket boats, called 'coracles'. In northern Europe the finest and most daring seamen were the Vikings from Scandinavia, who sailed finely-built longboats.

During the Crusades ships were like floating castles. When gunpowder was introduced towards the end of the fourteenth century, two types of ship came into being, the man-of-war and the merchant ships. The seventeenth and

A one-man submarine. This type of craft has been developed in recent years for underwater exploration

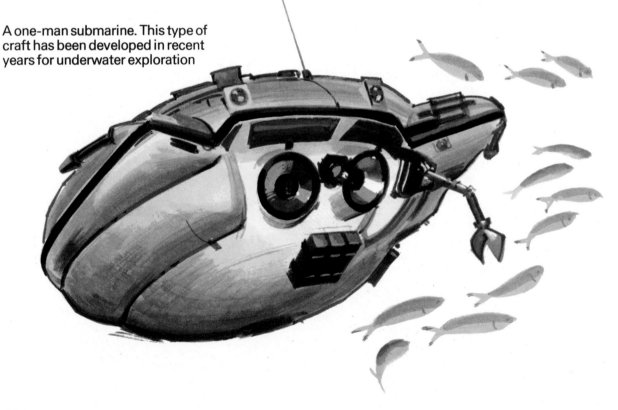

Egyptian trading vessel 1500BC

Roman merchantman 300 AD

American clipper 1850s

H.M.S. 'Victory' 1759

The 'Great Eastern' 1859

rbinia' the first steam-
bine craft 1897

aircraft carrier

cruiser-racer with spinnaker

high speed motorboat

New Guinea 'lakatoi'

eighteenth centuries saw great competition in trade, and as trade meant travel, great strides were made in shipbuilding. It was in this period that fully-rigged ships reached their highest development; that is, the barques, brigs, schooners and sloops, and later clippers. Early in the eighteenth century experiments were made with steam engines. The first successful steam crossing of the Atlantic was made from America to Ireland in the American ship *Susannah*. The *Great Western* was the first British steamship to cross the Atlantic. Sir Samuel Cunard (1787-1865), founder of the famous shipping company, had four small wooden-paddle steamships built. One, the *Britannia,* left Liverpool on July 4, 1840 and reached Boston 14 days later. The first really successful iron steamer was the *Himalaya,* built about 1853. Modern ocean liners are driven by steam turbines or diesel-engines. However, it may not be long before atomic power is being used to propel ships the size of the *Queen Elizabeth* and *United States*. Already the United States have atomic powered submarines, and the Soviet Union an atomic powered icebreaker.

SHREW resembles a mouse or rat but has a very long pointed snout and rounded ears. It feeds mainly on insects, snails and worms, while the water-shrew also feeds on fish. There are many different kinds of shrews, and they are found in many different parts of Europe, Asia, North America and the northern parts of South America. Most of them live on land, but some are adapted for life in water, while others yet again spend most of their time in trees. Typical shrews are: the common British shrew, pygmy shrew, water shrew, tree shrew and jumping shrew.

SIAM   See **THAILAND**

SIERRE LEONE is a republic in West Africa and a member of the British Commonwealth. It has an area of about 27,930 square miles and a population of over 2 millions. The capital is Freetown. Main exports are diamonds and iron ore.

SILK is a fine fibre produced by mulberry silkworms in making their cocoons. The making of silk is a very ancient Chinese craft, and China's rich silks have been much sought after all over the western world. Silk is obtained by unwinding a cocoon on to a reel; one cocoon can yield up to 3,000 feet. Artificial silk is made from a chemical compound called nitrocellulose.

SILVER is a white precious metal, found not only in a free state but also mixed with other ores. The chief silver-producing regions of the world are Canada, U.S.A., Mexico, South America, Australia and Spain. The metal has been known and used by man since prehistoric times. It is one of the metals which were once called the 'noble metals' and is, next to gold, the most 'workable' of metals and has the best ductility or stretching power next to platinum. Among

The shrew, a rodent, has a long pointed snout

The slow moving three-toed sloth

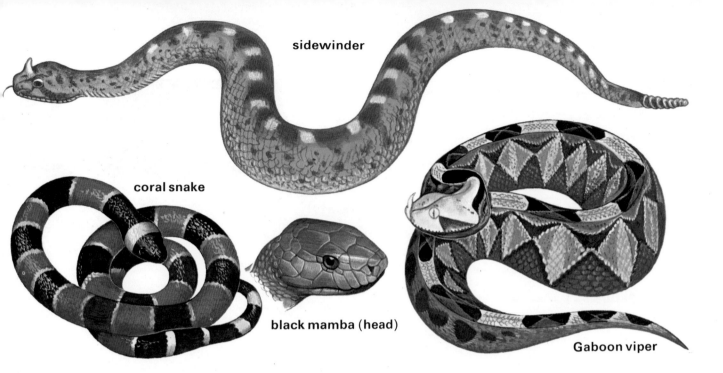

sidewinder

coral snake

black mamba (head)

Gaboon viper

metals it is the best conductor of electricity. The best art of the silversmith exhibits silver in its most beautiful forms. In the United Kingdom, all silver articles made in that country must have a 'hall mark' stamped on them as a guarantee of silver content.

SIMOON is a hot, dry wind carrying sand and dust. It blows in the Sahara and Arabian deserts but seldom lasts more than twenty minutes; however, during its duration it can almost suffocate the traveller and the word simoon does in fact come from an Arabian word meaning 'to poison'.

SINGAPORE is a republic on the island of Singapore and surrounding islands with an area of 225 square miles. It is a member of the British Commonwealth with a population of over 2 millions. Singapore separated from Malaysia in August 1965; it is an important port and there is some heavy industry.

SIPHON is a device used to transfer a liquid from one vessel to another by means of air pressure. It consists of a tube bent so that one end can be lowered into a vessel containing a liquid, while the other end is placed at a lower level outside the vessel. As soon as the tube becomes filled with water, the vessel is automatically emptied, see diagram.

SIROCCO is a dry, hot wind which blows north from the Sahara across Libya and the Mediterranean. By the time it reaches Italy it has become warm and moist.

SKUNKS are found in many parts of North and South America. They are rather like a small badger with a bushy tail which is always black or dark brown with white stripes. The skunk feeds mainly at night on birds, frogs and insects. It is well known for its method of getting rid of enemies, which it does by emitting a liquid with a nauseating smell in the direction of the attacker. Any animal or human being, having once experienced this, will never get too close to a skunk again! There are many different kinds of skunk, including the hog-nosed skunk, Humboldt's skunk and the little skunk.

SLOTH lives almost entirely in trees and even sleeps hanging from a branch. It has a coarse, shaggy coat, is clumsy in its movements, and feeds on leaves which it pulls within reach of its mouth with its long, hooked claws. The sloth is found in South America, the two main types being the 'two-toed' and the 'three-toed' sloths.

SNAIL has a spirally coiled shell and slug-like body. Most snails are vegetable eaters but some, such as the common British Testacella (snail-slug), live mainly on earthworms. Some kinds of snail live entirely in the water.

SNAKES are reptiles and are most numerous in the tropics, but they are also found in smaller

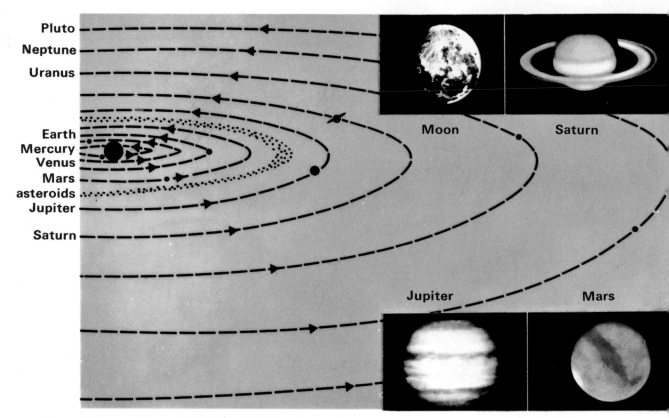

Diagram of the relative positions of the planets in the solar system

numbers in many other parts of the world. They are related to lizards and have an extremely long body which is covered with scales, and no real limbs. Snakes do not have any ear openings or movable eyelids, and the tongue, which is cleft or forked, is long. When feeding, a snake will swallow its food whole and digest it later. Some kinds of snakes are poisonous; that is, they have a gland which contains poison which they inject into any animal they wish to kill; they do this through a special grooved or hollow tooth, sometimes more than one tooth being used for this purpose. Other snakes, such as the huge python or boa, rely on their strength to crush their victims after winding themselves around them.

SNOW is the light white flakes in which frozen vapour falls to earth. It is made up of ice crystals which are produced when the temperature at cloud level is below freezing-point; this causes the water vapour in the air to form around dust particles. A remarkable fact about snow crystals is that they all have six sides or angles.

SOCIETY ISLANDS lie in the south Pacific Ocean and are under French protection. The islands are named after the Royal Society of London, members of which went with Captain Cook when he explored that part of the Pacific in 1769. There are about 13 islands in the archipelago, the largest island being named TAHITI, on which is Papeete, the capital and chief port. Phosphate and copper are produced, also copra (which is obtained from coconuts) and mother-of-pearl.

SOLAR SYSTEM consists of the sun and all the bodies that revolve about it. It includes planets, moons, comets and meteors.

Name of Planet	Distance from Sun in miles	Diameter in miles	Number of Moons
Mercury	36,000,000	3,100	—
Venus	67,000,000	7,700	—
Earth	93,000,000	7,900	1
Mars	142,000,000	4,200	2
Jupiter	483,000,000	89,000	12
Saturn	886,000,000	75,000	Ring of moons plus 9
Uranus	1,783,000,000	32,000	5
Neptune	2,793,000,000	31,000	2
Pluto	3,670,000,000	7,700	—

SOLENOID consists of a coil of wire which

produces a magnetic field when an electric current passes through it. A solenoid coil is used in such things as motor-car starters, magnetic brakes, switches, etc.

SOLOMON ISLANDS are a British protectorate in the south Pacific Ocean. The islands have an approximate area of 11,500 square miles and an estimated population of 140,000. The capital is Honiara on the island of Bougainville. The soil is volcanic. Copra, timber and nickel are produced.

SOUND is caused by molecules in the air moving to and fro, and is detected by the EAR. Sound has a speed of approximately 1,100 feet per second, and travels through air, gases and solid objects, but *not* through a vacuum. Some substances, like glass wool, are poor conductors of sound, and it is for this reason that it is used for sound-proofing rooms. The science of sound is called 'acoustics'.

SOUTH AFRICA, Republic of, is a large independent state in the southern tip of Africa. It has an area of 472,360 square miles and a population of about 21 millions. There are two capitals—Pretoria in the north for the administration and Cape Town where Parliament meets. The country produces more than half of the world's gold and much of its diamonds.

SPACE FLIGHT It was on April 12th, 1961, that Major Yuri Alexevich Gagarin, a Russian, was launched into orbit around the Earth to become the first man ever to make a space flight. This flight and all those following it were made by rockets, usually built in four stages, three of which were used to escape the Earth's atmosphere and the fourth being the capsule in which the astronauts (or cosmonauts as the Russians call them) travel. This is a very wasteful way of doing it but the only one we have available. Man has successfully landed on the Moon, but until a much more efficient motor is produced, voyages to even the planets closest to us, like Venus and Mars, are almost impossible. There are many other problems to be overcome before we start moving out into our solar system. Lack of gravity is one in particular; the effect of weightlessness on the human body is not fully known as yet. Another is the peril of meteorites which can puncture the walls of the capsule and allow the supply of air to escape, or damage the motors and other essential parts of the capsule. Since the original landing on the Moon in July 1969, much fascinating information has been brought back by the various space missions. Scientists have learnt a great deal about the Moon itself and also about the Earth. Both the Americans and the Russians sent unmanned probes to the Moon before the actual manned landing and they have done the same to both Mars and Venus. The last probe that the Americans sent to Mars, the Mariner Project, sent back several hours of film of the surface of the planet, and the probes to Venus have also established much about this planet that is wrapped in cloud. However, the day when a man steps out on to either of these planets is far in the future, and the day when man leaves our solar system to head towards another star is much, much farther still. There are so many problems still to overcome, but it can be done. Fifty years ago, the idea of man on the Moon was considered impossible.

SPAIN is a republic in Southern Europe in what is known as the Iberian peninsula. It has an area of 196,700 square miles and more than 31 million people. The capital is Madrid, other important cities being Seville and Barcelona. Main products are sherry, oranges and cork. Spain also rules the Balearic Islands in the Mediterranean and the Canary Islands.

SPECTRUM is the name given to the band of colours which compose white light. These are

A spectrum can be formed by passing white light through a glass prism

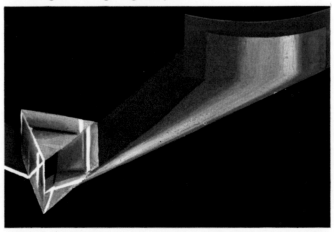

red, orange, yellow, green, blue, indigo and violet, and can be seen in a rainbow. When sunlight falls on a glass prism or piece of cut-glass, it is broken up or refracted into these seven colours which form the spectrum. That white light is made up of these colours was discovered by Sir Isaac Newton.

SPIDERS are found in most parts of the world. Most of them live on land, but some are adapted for life in the water. Their main food is insects, but some of the larger spiders feed on lizards and mice. Many of them spin a web which acts as a trap for other insects.

SPONGES are found in most seas and can be all shapes and sizes. Although a sponge does not look like an animal, that is what it really is. The most simple kind is made up of a short tube with an opening at the top, but others are quite complicated and have many branches, some being very beautiful. The sponge lives on minute particles of food which are taken in through numerous pores in the walls of the body. Some of the sponges form a horny kind of skeleton around themselves, and it is this skeleton which is used to make the kind of sponge you use in the bath.

SPRINGBOK is a species of antelope, that numerous family which belongs to a group between cattle and goats, and which includes the common antelope, the pygmy antelope, as well as roan, sable, wildebeeste and hartebeeste. The springbok or springbuck lives in Africa and its nearest relative is the gazelle; it gets its name because of its ability to jump; it can make a leap of 10 or 12 yards reaching a height of 10 or 12 feet.

SQUIRREL There are many kinds of squirrel, some living mostly in trees and a few on the ground. Two of the most common are the red squirrel and the American grey squirrel. These have furry bodies and long, bushy tails, and feed on nuts and fruits and seeds; sometimes they eat mice, small birds and eggs. Other squirrels live in various parts of Europe, Asia and North America, among them being the ground squirrels and flying squirrels.

STALACTITES and **STALAGMITES** are words that sound very similar and they could be described loosely as examples of the reverse actions of the same thing. Both are shapes of carbonate of lime but the difference is this: in some limestone caves, water evaporates as it percolates through, and drips from the roof; tiny particles of calcium carbonate are left behind and the result is a hanging cone that looks like a large icicle. This is a stalactite. The drops that fall on the floor of the cave, either straight from the roof or from a stalactite, leave particles of limestone that build up into a conical formation. This is a stalagmite. Both words come from Greek words meaning, drop, drip and dripping. The longest known free-hanging stalactite in the world is one of 38 feet in a cave in County Clare, Ireland; the tallest known stalagmite in the world rises 90 feet from the floor of a cave in the Aven Armand, France.

STARFISH As its name suggests, the starfish has a flattened, star-shaped body and lives in the sea. It feeds mainly on molluscs, the shells of which it pulls open. The common starfish has three arms but there are others with as many as 20 arms. Some starfish living in the Pacific grow to two or more feet across.

STEAM ENGINE The first practical steam engine was invented by Thomas Savery and Thomas Newcomen about 1698, and employed to work pumps in coalmines, which were often flooded. The steam engine as we know it today was developed by James Watt (1736-1819). The basic working principles are shown in the diagram. It should be realized that Watt's improvements and new ideas made possible the great strides in industry of the nineteenth century—the INDUSTRIAL REVOLUTION.

STEEL See **IRON AND STEEL**

STETHOSCOPE may seem a rather difficult word but its meaning becomes quite clear when we look at three other separate words: the first one is a Latin word, *auscultare*, to listen; the other two are Greek, *stethos* meaning chest and *skopeein* meaning to examine. When, therefore, medical men wanted a word to describe a new instrument specially designed for 'listening in' (auscultation) to the human body, in this case the chest, so as to be able to examine it, they hit

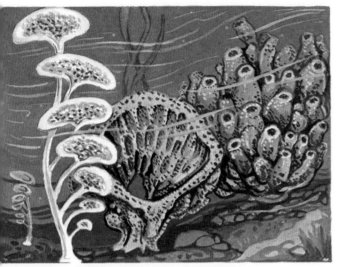

A selection of different forms of sponges

A stalactite hangs from the roof of a cave and a stalagmite grows up from a cave floor

The many-armed feather star

on the word *stethoscope.* A stethoscope is a Y-shaped instrument; the doctor places the ends of the 'branches' or listening-pieces in his ears and places the end of the 'stem' on the chest of his patient. In this way his trained ears will tell him of any irregularities in his patient's lungs or heart.

STOAT is an animal related to the WEASEL but is larger. Its head and body measure about 11 inches and the tail 5 inches. It feeds on poultry, game birds and hares. It is distributed widely over Europe, Asia and North America. In countries other than Britain the stoat is more frequently called the ermine. It is a very active and bloodthirsty little creature. In winter, in cold countries, the brown summer coat of the stoat turns white, with the exception of the tip of its tail which is black. This white fur is the ermine once much used to trim ceremonial robes.

STONE OF SCONE, now in Westminster Abbey, is generally known as the Coronation Stone. It was once kept at Scone, in Perth, Scotland, the place of residence and coronation of the early Scottish kings (see Shakespeare's *Macbeth* Act 2 scene 4 where Macduff says that Macbeth has 'gone to Scone to be invested'). Scone, by the way, is pronounced Scoon. There is a tradition that the Stone was actually the one on which Jacob rested his head for a pillow when he had the dream in which he saw a ladder stretching from earth to heaven and heard God speak to him. The Stone was taken from Scotland by England's King Edward I (1272-1307).

STONEHENGE, on Salisbury Plain in Wiltshire, is said by many historians to be the most important remaining monument of antiquity anywhere in the British Isles. It consists of four groups of big stones arranged as outer and inner rings. Many stones are now missing from the outer circle but sixteen of them still stand, the top of the highest being about thirteen feet above the ground. In the next ring are a number of stones about six feet high; and inside this again are two horseshoe groups of stones with two stones twenty-two feet high with a huge 'cap-stone' on top. In the centre of Stonehenge are the so-called 'altar stone', 'slaughter stone' and 'hele stone'; the last-named (from the Greek *helios,* sun) casts its shadow on to the altar stone

The stork often builds its nest in chimney-tops

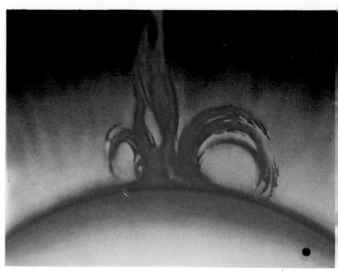

A solar flare shooting from the sun's surface

at sunrise on 21 June. No one can say for what purpose Stonehenge was built in the early Bronze Age, about 4,000 years ago; it may have been a burial ground, a place of worship or even some kind of observatory.

STORK is a large wading bird, found in many parts of the world. It feeds mainly on frogs and insects which it collects from marshes and fields. It has a large, red bill, red legs, and feathers which are usually black and white. A stork will often build its nest on the top of a building where

it will lay three to six eggs. It is a familiar sight in European countries, particularly in Germany and the Netherlands where people sometimes place a large box or improvise some kind of platform on the roof of a house to encourage the stork to nest there.

STRATOSPHERE is a region seven to eleven miles above the earth and far above the zone of winds. The region below the stratosphere is called the 'tropospere', and the imaginary region separating these is called the 'tropopause'.

A nuclear submarine: 1, nuclear reactor; 2, reactor control room; 3, escape hatch; 4, diesel generator; 5, main turbine; 6, rudders; 7, control rooms and crew's quarters; 8, torpedo rooms; 9, periscope, radar and radio aerials.

Many passenger airliners fly in the lower part of the stratosphere.

SUBMARINES are vessels which are able to travel long distances below water. This is made possible by special tanks which are flooded with water, the extra weight causing the vessel to sink. The submarine is then controlled by horizontal and vertical rudders which allow it to be steered up and down and sideways. The men inside the submarine can see what is going on above them by means of a long tube called a periscope, which can be raised above the water level. Most submarines are driven by electric or diesel motors but there are also atomic-powered submarines. The U.S. submarine *Nautilus*, launched in 1955, was the first atomic-powered marine craft in the world. Atomic – powered submarines now usually carry long-range rocket missiles.

SUDAN is a republic in eastern Africa to the south of EGYPT. It has an area of about 976,800 square miles and a population of over 15 millions, of whom half are Arabs and half Negroes. The capital is Khartoum on the River Nile and the White Nile and Blue Nile also flow through it. The Sudan mostly produces cotton.

SUEZ CANAL was built by Ferdinand de Lesseps, a French engineer, and was opened in 1869. It enables ships to sail from the Mediterranean into the Red Sea without having to go right round Africa; it can thus save a ship about 10,000 miles on a trip to the Far East. The Canal is more than 100 miles long and took ten years to build. Britain became one of the largest shareholders of the canal company, but this company was nationalized by the Egyptian Government on 28 July 1959.

SUGAR is the name for a substance which has a sweet taste. Sugar used for sweetening cakes and puddings is made mainly from sugar cane but some is obtained from beet sugar. The sugar cane is really a grass which grows to a height of fifteen to twenty feet. After it is cut the cane is crushed, and the juice that is squeezed out is boiled to obtain the sugar contained in the juice. There are man-made substitutes for natural sugar, one of which is 'saccharin'; it is nearly 300 times sweeter than ordinary sugar made from cane or beet.

SUN is a star about 330,000 times more massive than the earth. The temperature at its surface is about 6,000 deg. Centigrade. The great heat generated by the sun is thought to be caused by hydrogen atoms fusing together to form helium atoms—the same process as that used in a H-bomb. See SOLAR SYSTEM.

SUNDIAL Everyone knows what the sun is, and the word 'dial' comes from the Latin *dies*, day. So a sundial is something designed to tell what time of day it is by means of the sun's shadow. The sundial may thus be said to be the ancestor of the dials on all clocks and watches. It was invented by the Babylonians about 3,000 years ago, and was probably the very first method devised for marking the passing of time. The Babylonians were clever enough to notice that the position of a shadow changed during the hours of daylight, so they fixed a pole in the ground and saw that its shadow moved round; the shortest shadow was of course when the sun was right over the pole, so that was called noon or twelve o'clock midday. The hours were later engraved on a metal plate which was fixed on a wall or on top of a short pillar; the short rod or pin which casts the shadow is called the gnomon. Many highly decorative sundials adorn gardens of old houses.

SWEDEN is a kingdom in SCANDINAVIA in northern Europe. It has an area of about 173,000 square miles and a population of about 8 millions. The capital is Stockholm and the chief port is Gothenburg. The main products are timber, paper and iron-ore.

SWITZERLAND is a republic in central Europe in the Alps. It has an area of 16,000 square miles and a population of over 6 millions. The capital is Berne but better known cities are Geneva, Zurich and Basle. The country is made up of 22 cantons and it is traditionally neutral. Switzerland is famous for its watchmaking industry and also for its banking skills.

SYRIA is a republic on the eastern shore of the Mediterranean. It has an area of about 70,800 square miles and a population of about 6 millions. The capital is Damascus, the oldest city in the world. It exports cotton and grain.

TABERNACLE, THE There is a Latin word *taberna,* which means a hut, and the small version is *tabernaculum.* So the word tabernacle really means a little hut (or tent) used for a special purpose. It was originally the tent which the Jews carried with them and used as a temple when they were wandering in the desert. The word was later applied to the famous Temple of the Jews in Jerusalem and later still to other houses of worship.

TADPOLE is a frog, toad or newt at the stage of its life between the egg and the fully grown adult. The tadpole lives entirely in the water and breathes by means of gills. The body is very small and rounded, and the tadpole swims by means of a long, thin tail. See AMPHIBIA.

TAHITI is an island in the Pacific, part of the Society Islands belonging to France. Its capital is Papeete and it has a population of 77,000. It is a well-known tourist attraction.

TAJ MAHAL is considered to be one of the most beautiful buildings in the world. It was erected at Agra, India, by the Mogul emperor Shah Jehan who ruled from 1614 to 1666. He built it as a tomb for his favourite wife whose name was Mumtaz Mahal, so the building signi-fied 'the resting place of Mahal'. It is constructed of white marble in the Persian style of architecture (it was the Moguls who introduced Persian civilization into India in the early 16th century) and is surmounted by a huge dome; the whole of the outside is ornamented with precious stones and stands on a marble terrace above the river Jumna. It has been said that the best time to see this fairy-like building is by moonlight.

TALMUD is the book containing the religious law of the Jewish people. In the same way as the Bible teaches the Christian religion by means of legends, parables, and so on, the Talmud sets out the way in which all good Jews should live. The word Talmud in Hebrew means teaching or learning. The book is in two parts; the Mishnah, written in Hebrew, and the Gemara, written in Aramaic, the language which Christ spoke..

TANKS used in warfare are very heavily armoured vehicles. They were invented and built by the British in the First World War (1914-18) and came into general use in the Second World War (1939-45). They usually run on caterpillar or crawler tracks and carry powerful guns. The construction of a military tank en-ables it to travel over very rough and uneven country, and to demolish trees and walls. Am-

An artist's impression of the Tabernacle of the Old Testament. 1, the Golden Lampstand; 2, the Ark of the Covenant; 3, the Table of Shrewbread; 4, the the Altar of Incense

phibious tanks are those which can travel not only over land but also through water.

TANZANIA is a republic in East Africa and a member of the British Commonwealth. It is made up of two ex-colonies, Tanganyika and Zanzibar. It has an area of 362,800 square miles and a population of about 12 millions. The capital is Dar-es-Salaam and the chief city of Zanzibar is Zanzibar Town. The country produces diamonds, cloves (from Zanzibar), sisal, cotton and coffee. Mount Kilimanjaro, Africa's highest mountain, lies within the borders.

TAPIR is related to the rhinoceros and is found in Central and South America and Indonesia. The legs and tail are very short, and the snout is in the form of a thick, short trunk which is used for hooking leaves into the mouth. The tapir feeds mostly at night, and is a very timid animal. The young differs greatly from the adult in colour, being a deep brown, patterned with white stripes and spots which disappear after about six months.

TASMANIA is an island in the south Pacific about 180 miles south of AUSTRALIA. It is part of the Commonwealth of Australia. It has an area of 26,380 square miles and population of 392,500. The capital is Hobart and the main occupations are mining, farming and forestry.

TEETH Most living creatures have some sort of teeth to help them to chew or grind up the food that they eat, and so make it easy for their digestive system to deal with. The teeth are firmly fixed in sockets in the jaws, and in human beings the front ones have sharp edges for cutting, while the back ones are used for chewing or grinding the food. Humans have two sets of teeth, the first one appearing between the ages of one and two years, when there are twenty teeth; and a second set at about six years, which consists of thirty-two teeth.

TELEPHONE is an electrical instrument which is used for transmitting sounds from one place to another. When a person speaks into a telephone, the sound waves that are made by the voice are changed into electrical signals. These are carried over conductors or wireless links to wherever they are required, and changed

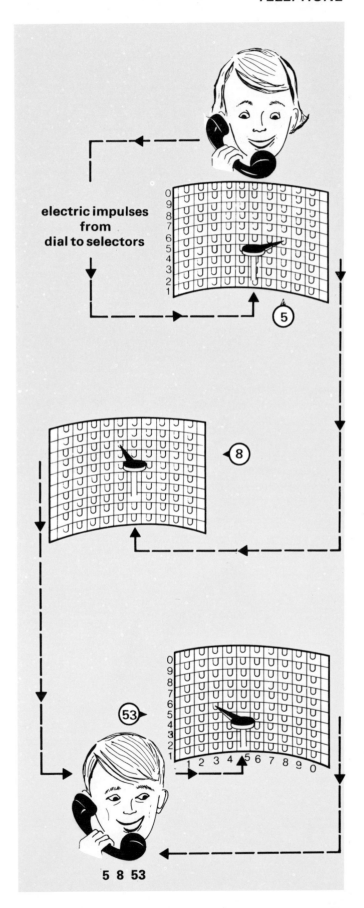

electric impulses from dial to selectors

5 8 53

Above, side view of a spiral nebula and, *below,* front view of a spiral nebula. Such photographs are taken by giant reflecting telescopes, see right

Section of a termite's nest. Inset is the female

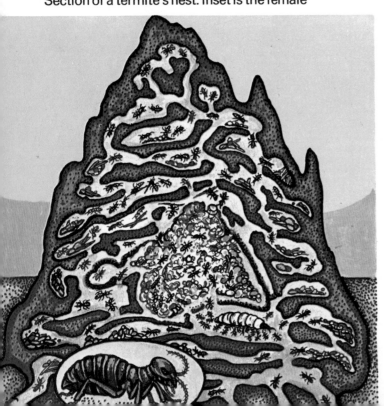

back into sound waves again so that the person at the other end of the telephone can hear exactly what has been said by the person speaking into the instrument, see diagram.

TELESCOPE is an optical instrument for magnifying or enlarging distant objects. About 1610 the great Italian scientist, Galileo, made a telescope to observe the heavens. His observations entirely changed man's ideas about the shape and form of the sun, moon and planets as, amongst other things, it was found that, instead of the moon being smooth, it was covered with craters, and the sun's surface contained dark spots. There are two kinds of telescopes used today, the 'refractive' and 'reflecting' telescopes. The refractive telescope is based on the bending of light, and was the type used by Galileo and Newton. An example of a reflecting telescope is the giant 200-inch telescope now used on Mount Palomar in America. An entirely new type of telescope is the radio telescope now used for probing deep space. See RADIO ASTRONOMY.

TELEVISION is the means by which a picture can be transmitted by radio waves from one place to another without wires. It is done by changing the picture which is picked up by the television camera into a series of radio signals. These are sent out from a television mast and received by the aerial of a televisión receiving set. As soon as the signals reach the set, they are changed back again into a picture by means of an electronic device called a cathode-ray tube. A pioneer of television was John Logie Baird (1886-1946), who broadcast television pictures as early as 1929.

TERMITES are insects, often called 'white ants'. They are found only in warm countries and live in colonies in trees, underground, or in mounds which they build of earth held together with saliva. These mounds are very strong and may reach a height of 20 feet. Termites organize their lives in much the same way as bees and ants, one female laying the eggs while the 'worker' termites build the nest, keep it clean and prepare the food. 'Soldier' termites protect the rest of the colony from enemies.

TERRAPIN belongs to the group of water-tortoises and is a member of the TURTLE fam-

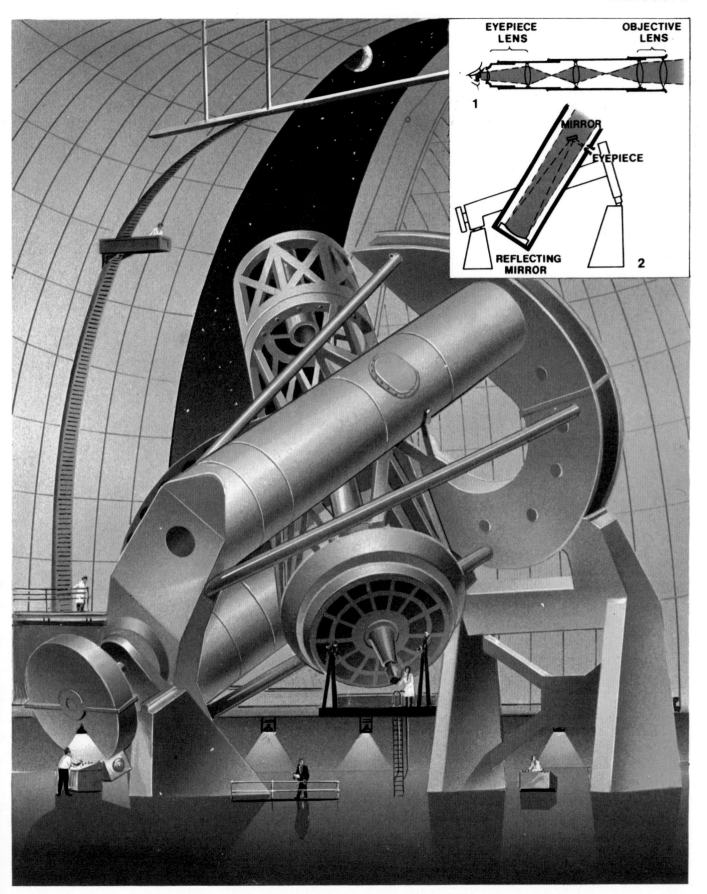

ily. It is found in the United States and the name *terrapin* is actually an American-Indian word.

THAILAND or Siam as it used to be known, is a kingdom in south-east Asia. It has an area of 198,245 square miles and a population of about 35 millions. The capital is Bangkok and the main exports are rice and rubber. Siamese cats originally came from there, where they were kept as royal pets. Thailand is the only country in that area that has never been ruled by a European country.

THEODOLITE is an instrument used for measuring distances on the surface of the earth, and a surveyor's most important tool. It consists of a small telescope mounted on a stand which can be moved up and down and from side to side. The theodolite is fitted with marked circles from which the measurements can then be read off and distances calculated.

THERMOMETER is a device used for measuring the degree of temperature of a body; that is, its hotness or coldness. Mercury is generally used for measuring ordinary temperatures, and alcohol for low temperatures. Two main types of thermometer scale are in use: 1, the Centigrade scale, which reads from the melting point (O deg.) of ice to the boiling point (100 deg.) of water, and 2, the Fahrenheit scale, which reads from the melting point (32 deg.) of ice, to the boiling point (212 deg.) of water. A 'clinical' thermometer is the type used for measuring the temperature of the human body, which ranges between 97.8 deg. F. to 98.6 deg. F.

THERMOSTAT is a device used for automatically controlling the temperature of such things as refrigerators, gas-cookers, electric irons, furnaces, water heaters, etc. A typical thermostat consists of a piece of metal which expands or contracts on having heat or cold applied to it, and so turns on or cuts off the supply of electricity, gas, air, hot or cold water, etc.

THUNDERSTORMS are caused when the tension between the positive and negative electric charges in certain kinds of cloud becomes so strong that a discharge takes place, which is marked by a flash of lightning. A discharge

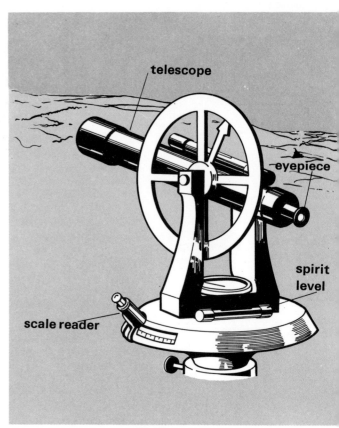

Main parts of a theodolite for surveying

may also take place between a cloud and the earth. The thunder which is heard after a flash of lightning is caused by the sudden expansion of the heated air and its equally rapid contraction. Sheet lightning is the reflection of a flash of lightning a long way off. See LIGHTNING

TIBET is a large country in Central Asia, and consists mainly of a wide expanse of tableland, most of which is 10,000 feet above sea level. It is bordered on the south by the Himalayas. It has a population of about $1\frac{1}{4}$ millions, and the capital is Lhasa. The country is a self-governing province of the Chinese Republic. Sheep, yak and buffalo are bred, and woollen cloth is the chief article of manufacture. The Tibetan people follow the religion of Lamaism, which is very like Buddhism. The monks are called 'lamas' which means 'the spiritual or holy ones'.

TIDES are caused by the pull of the moon on the earth. Whenever the moon rises over the sea, it heaps up the water beneath it into a peak pointing directly from the earth's centre to the centre of the moon; with the movement of the earth the 'peak' passes away from the moon's

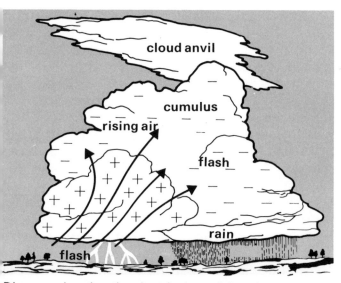

Diagram showing the electrical conditions in a thunder cloud and lightning flashes

influence and the waters go down again. Tides occur twice each day. The sun, when the moon comes into line with it as well as the earth, helps the moon to pull the waters of the earth, thus causing very high tides which are called 'spring' tides; these occur twice a month. When the sun and moon are not in line with the earth, but at right angles to each other, the tides are low and are called 'neap' tides.

TIERRA DEL FUEGO consists of a group of bleak, windswept islands off the tip of South America, from which they are separated by the Strait of Magellan. The two principal towns

Diagram showing how tides are caused on earth

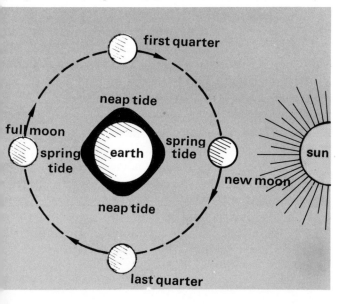

are Ushuaia and Magellanes, and the inhabitants are mostly wandering Indians. The islands are divided politically between Chile and Argentina.

TIGER is a member of the cat family and found only in Asia. The tiger lives in forests and jungles where its striped coat makes it almost invisible. It feeds mainly on deer, cattle, goats and wild pigs, but when hungry will eat frogs, lizards, fish and insects. Some tigers, called man-eaters, will atack human beings for food. It has been found, however, that most, if not all, man-eating tigers attack human beings only because they have suffered some kind of injury which makes it difficult for them to hunt their natural prey.

TOBACCO The use of tobacco was unknown in Europe before the discovery of the New World. When Europeans went there in the 15th century they found the native Indians smoking pipes (their word for these pieces of wood being *tobago)* in which they burned the dried leaves of the plant which came to be called Nicotiana after a Frenchman, Jean Nicot (1530-1600), who helped to make tobacco-smoking popular. The tobacco plant is sown as a seed, and when in full leaf the point of the centre shoot is cut off to prevent flowering. When the leaves begin to turn yellow, they are collected, dried and fermented. The greatest tobacco-growing countries are America, Russia, Mexico, Turkey and Rhodesia. Most governments put a tax on imported tobacco, and sometimes it is very high, making for an important source of revenue. In recent years it has been found that tobacco smoking is the cause of many chest complaints and young people are now being discouraged from taking up the habit.

TORNADO is a whirlwind which occurs over a small area, or a storm which is usually accompanied by a spiral or funnel-shaped cloud. When a tornado occurs over the sea, a waterspout is often formed. Tornadoes occur very often in the central plains of the Mississippi. A tornado travels across country at about twenty-five to forty miles an hour, and makes a deafening roar. The low-pressure core of the tornado has tremendous suction power, with the result that great destruction can be caused as it passes over inhabited areas.

TORPEDO is a steel, cigar-shaped weapon used mainly in submarines and destroyers to attack enemy ships. A torpedo is launched through a special tube, above the water in destroyers and below in submarines, and is propelled through the water by its own small engine. A steering device inside it keeps it steady on the course on which it has been fired until it strikes the target, when the high explosive inside it is set off. The force of this explosion is able to tear a hole even in the thickest armour plate. The torpedo was invented in 1866 by Robert Whitehead.

TORTOISE is the name commonly given to the types of TURTLE which live on land. The main difference between a tortoise and a turtle is that the legs of a tortoise are clubbed instead of being webbed or paddle-like. The tortoise often has a higher or more dome-shaped shell, and usually lives on vegetable food.

The toucan with its long curved beak

TOUCAN is a tropical bird with a large curved beak which is often very brightly coloured. It feeds mainly on fruits, seeds and sometimes insects and small birds. Two white eggs are usually laid in a hollow tree. It is found in Central and South America.

TOWER OF BABEL You may often have heard the expression 'a babel of voices'. The word babel can be traced back to the ancient legend of the Tower of Babel, mentioned in the Book of Genesis. The story goes that the descendants of Noah wanted to build a tower that would reach as high as Heaven, and they began to do so, but God was very angry and caused all the workmen suddenly to speak in different languages, so that one could not tell what another was saying. This meant that the building of the tower could not be carried on; it was left to crumble into ruins, and the people who had been building it dispersed to different parts of the world. It is a fanciful story but it was the way in which the early Hebrews cleverly tried to explain why different tribes spoke different languages. Babel was a settlement in the plain of Shinar in Babylonia, a region in the country now called Iraq. The capital of Babylonia was Babylon, and not far from the site are ruins of a tower (on a mound called Birs Nimrud) which scholars say may have been the original Tower of Babel.

TOWER OF LONDON is situated on the north bank of the river Thames at the south-east angle of the city wall. It is not, however, included within the City boundary. A legend attributes the building of the Tower to Julius Caesar (Shakespeare mentions this) and certainly Roman remains have been found in the neighbourhood, but it was William the Conqueror who really began it in 1078. He built what is now called the White Tower to overawe the citizens of London and to guard the river approaches, his architect being a bishop—Gundulf of Rochester. Additions to the Tower were made by Richard I, Henry III, Edward I and other monarchs. The Tower has been at various times a royal residence, a fortress and a prison. The CROWN JEWELS are kept in the Wakefield Tower or Jewel House. Familiar figures at the Tower are the Yeomen Warders in their picturesque Tudor uniforms; they should not be confused with the YEOMEN OF THE GUARD ('Beefeaters').

TRACTOR is a machine used for hauling and driving ploughs, rakes, threshing machines, harvesters, etc. It is fitted either with wheels or caterpillar tracks. If wheels are used, the rear ones are generally fitted with large rubber tyres and if the tractor is used on soft muddy ground the wheels are usually spiked for gripping; the front wheels, which are smaller, are used for steering. Most tractors are powered by diesel engines.

TRADE WINDS are winds which blow almost continuously in tropical seas. They are caused by the hot air which is continually rising from the Equator being replaced by cool air. Owing to the rotation of the earth, the winds blow from the north-east in the northern hemisphere and from the south-east in the southern hemisphere.

TRANSFORMER is an electrical machine which changes the pressure of electrical energy to either a higher or lower pressure. It has no moving parts and works only with alternating currents.

TRANSISTOR is an electronic device for amplifying electric currents, and is based on the amplifying properties of the elements silicon and germanium. It is very simple in construction, and in time will, no doubt, replace the radio valve. It is used in a very wide variety of electronic equipment, especially transistor radios.

TREATY is a signed contract or agreement between two states. A word which is often used instead of 'treaty' is 'convention' which applies to an agreement which may be signed by any nation. Other words which may be used to mean much the same thing are 'covenant' and 'pact'. Two famous treaties were the Treaty of Versailles in 1919 (peace with Germany following the First World War) and the Treaty of Paris in 1947 to mark the end of the Second World War.

TREE is a woody plant, usually with a single trunk or bole and many forking branches. Most trees are deciduous, which means that they shed their leaves in the autumn. The evergreen trees, which are green all the year round, also shed their leaves, but not all at once. In tropical countries many trees, because of the climate, do not lose their leaves. A shrub differs from a tree in that it is smaller, and the branches fork out from the roots or a small trunk just above the ground.

TRIGONOMETRY is the branch of mathematics based on the relationships that exist between the angles and sides of a triangle. It is essential in surveying, navigation, engineering—in fact, in any subject where it is necessary to calculate distances and angles.

The Tower of London was really begun by William the Conqueror in 1078

TRISTAN DA CUNHA is the largest of a group of small islands in the south Atlantic Ocean. It is only about 30 square miles in area, is a dependency of St Helena (where Napoleon died in exile), and belongs to Britain. The small population of some 300 live mostly by growing fruit and vegetables, fishing and rearing poultry. The main importance of this little island lies in the radio and weather stations built there. The 'capital' of the island is named Edinburgh.

TSETSE FLY is a blood-sucking fly not unlike the ordinary house-fly. It is found in the tropical regions of Africa where it lives and breeds in ponds and other similar places. It carries the germ of sleeping sickness which it injects into the bloodstream of the human beings it bites, and it also carries a disease that is fatal to cattle.

TUNISIA is an Arab republic on the southern shores of the Mediterranean with an area of about 45,000 square miles. There is a population of about 5 millions and the capital is Tunis. It exports dates, oil, gas and phosphates. The ruins of ancient Carthage lie close to Tunis.

TURBINE is a type of engine driven by steam, water, gas or air. The simplest form of turbine is the water-wheel. The steam turbine is widely used for the generation of electric power. It consists of two main parts, the rotor or moving part, and the stator or stationary part. There are two main types, the impulse turbine and the reaction turbine. In the impulse turbine a number of wheels, each carrying a row of blades, are attached to a shaft. In front of each wheel is a stationary plate provided with openings which form nozzles through which steam is directed on to the blades. After the steam has passed through the first wheel it is directed by a second set of nozzles on to the next wheel, and so on through successive stages, until all the useful energy of the steam has been used up. In the reaction type turbine the nozzles are replaced by rings of stationary blades between the rows of moving blades, and power is obtained from the reaction of the steam as it passes between the fixed and moving blades. Since the steam loses some of its energy after passing from one set of blades to the next, the blades are made larger and larger from the first to the last wheel to enable the steam to give up most of its energy. The exhaust steam is reduced to water in a device called a condenser, and returned to the boiler to be again changed into steam. A water turbine is really a specially designed water-wheel, and used where there is plenty of natural water available. In many parts of the world water turbines are used to generate power. A gas turbine is better known as a 'JET ENGINE'. However, it works on the same principle as steam and water turbines.

TURKEY is a republic in Asia Minor with a small foothold on the European side of the Bosphorus. It has an area of 294,500 square miles and a population of over 35½ millions. The capital is Ankara but far better known is Istanbul which lies across the Bosphorus (the narrow channel that connects the Black Sea to the Mediterranean. The original name of Istanbul was Byzantium; it was re-named Constantinople in A.D. 330, and the present name was adopted after 1923. Turkey's chief exports are cotton, fruits, tobacco, minerals, and cereals.

TURTLE is a REPTILE, and lives in water.

A tortoise is a turtle that lives on land. The body of the true turtle is short and rounded, and is nearly always protected by a bony shell, the upper part of which is called the 'carapace', and the lower part the 'plastron'. The legs are either webbed or paddle-shaped to enable it to swim easily, and it has beaklike jaws. The eggs are laid on land, and are usually buried in loose earth or sand. There are many different kinds of turtle but the largest known is the 'leathery' or 'leather-back' turtle, which is covered with soft skin instead of a shell, and often grows as long as 8 feet, weighing anything up to a ton. Turtles live to a great age; one is known to have lived for over 150 years.

TYPEWRITER is a machine for writing. It has a keyboard with all the letters of the alphabet as well as punctuation marks, figures, and various signs. The first machine designed to reproduce characters similar to those in printing was a rather crude affair invented by an English engineer named Mills in the early 18th century. Then came other machines, each of which represented some improvement, but the first really practical typewriter was put on the market in 1874 by the American firm of Remington, which had previously been famous for making guns; it was based on the idea of an American journalist named Sholes. The latest typewriters are electrically operated.

TYPHOON is a hurricane or tropical cyclone which occurs in the western Pacific, usually between July and October. It is most commonly experienced in the China Sea between Korea and the Philippines, and in fact the word typhoon is a Chinese word, meaning 'great wind'.

UGANDA is a republic in Central Africa and a member of the British Commonwealth. It has an area of 91,100 square miles and a population of nearly 10 millions. The capital is Kampala. The chief exports are coffee, cotton and timber.

About 13,000 square miles of Uganda's territory is water in the form of various lakes and the Nile rises within its borders.

ULTRAVIOLET LIGHT is a part of the sun's light which cannot be seen by the eye. It is, in fact, beyond the violet end of the SPECTRUM. Ultraviolet light can also be produced in special kinds of lamps, and used medically for treating the skin. It is also used for destroying germs. Ultraviolet light will not pass through ordinary glass.

UNESCO is the abbreviation for the 'United Nations Educational Scientific and Cultural Organization', which is a part of the United Nations. Its headquarters are in Paris, where it was formed in 1946. Among its many tasks has been to teach people to read and write, for even today many millions still cannot do this. UNESCO also helps scientists, scholars, etc., to share their knowledge with other nations. It publishes many books and pamphlets.

UNICORN is a legendary animal which was supposed to have the head and body of a horse, the hind legs of an antelope, the tail of a lion, and a single, sharp, twisted horn in the middle of its forehead. The royal arms of Scotland include the unicorn, which is said to be an equal opponent of the English lion (a well-known nursery rhyme tells of a fight between the lion and the unicorn).

UNITED KINGDOM is the kingdom which unites England, Wales, Scotland, Northern Ireland and the many islands around the British Isles. Usually it is abbreviated to U.K.

UNITED NATIONS (U.N.) was set up after the Second World War to preserve peace in the world. The Charter of the U.N. was signed at San Francisco in 1945. The headquarters are in New York. Although the U.N.'s main work is to settle quarrels between nations without war, it has many other jobs to do and which affect the welfare of all nations. It includes the following organizations: World Health Organization, UNESCO, Universal Postal Union, International Labour Organization, World Bank, Court of International Justice, Food and Agricultural Organization, International Civil Aviation Organization, International Telecommunications Union, International Children's Emergency Fund, and the World Meteorological Organization.

UNITED STATES is a republic in North America and a union of fifty states: Alabama, Alaska, Arizona, Arkansas, California, Colorado, Connecticut, Delaware, District of Columbia, Florida, Georgia, Idaho, Illinois, Indiana, Iowa, Kansas, Kentucky, Louisiana, Maine, Maryland,

An artist's impression of the Manhattan skyline, a world-famous view of New York.

North America

ARCTIC OCEAN

BERING STRAIT

Brooks Range

BEAUFORT SEA

ELLESMERE ISLAND

A L A S K A

Yukon

Mt McKinley
20300

Alaska Range

BAFFIN
BAY

Alaska
Peninsula

YUKON

VICTORIA
ISLAND

DISTRICT OF FRANKLIN

Whitehorse

Mackenzie

Juneau

Liard

DISTRICT OF MACKENZIE

Great Bear Lake

BAFFIN ISLAND

PACIFIC

Coast Mountains

Peace

DISTRICT OF
KEEWATIN

Great Slave Lake

HUDSON

BAY

LABRADOR

BRITISH COLUMBIA

R o c k y

Fraser

ALBERTA

C

A

N

Churchill

OCEAN

VANCOUVER
ISLAND

Vancouver

Mt Robson 12972
Edmonton

SASKATCHEWAN

MANITOBA

QUEBEC

A

D

St John

Victoria

Seattle

Columbia

Snake

WASHINGTON

M o u n t a i n s

Saskatchewan

Lake
Winnipeg

Regina

O N T A R I O

A

Laurentian Highlands

NEWFOUNDLA
Gre
Ba

Cascade Range

OREGON

IDAHO

MONTANA

Winnipeg

N.DAKOTA

MINNESOTA

Lake Superior

Quebec

Montreal

PRINCE EDWARD IS
NEW
BRUNSWICK
Charlottetown
NOVA SCOTIA

San Francisco

Sierra Nevada

CALIFORNIA

NEVADA

Great Salt
Lake

UTAH

WYOMING

U N I T E D

Missouri

S.DAKOTA

NEBRASKA

Platte

IOWA

WISCONSIN

Minneapolis

Milwaukee

L Michigan

Chicago

L Huron

MICHIGAN

Detroit

Ottawa

Toronto

Buffalo
Niagara Falls

St Lawrence

NEW YORK

MAINE

Mountains

2

Fredericton

Halifax

3

NEW YORK

Boston

5

Los Angeles

Mt Whitney
14495

Death
Valley

Grand
Canyon

Colorado

Plateau

S T A T E S

Colorado

Denver
COLORADO

KANSAS

Kansas City

MISSOURI

ILLINOIS

St Louis

INDIANA

Indianapolis

Cleveland

OHIO

Cincinatti

Ohio

PENNSYLVANIA
Pittsburgh

9

Philadelphia

Baltimore

8

Washington

6

LONG ISLAND

New York

San Diego

ARIZONA

NEW MEXICO

OKLAHOMA

Arkansas

KENTUCKY

TENNESSEE

Tennessee

VIRGINIA

N.CAROLINA

Appalachian

ATLANTIC

Rio Grande

TEXAS

Dallas

Memphis

ARKANSAS

MISSISSIPPI

ALABAMA

Atlanta

GEORGIA

S.
CAROLINA

LOWER CALIFORNIA

San Antonio

Houston

LOUISIANA

Red

Mississippi

New
Orleans

FLORIDA

CAPE KENNEDY

OCEAN

GULF OF

MEXICO

Miami

1 : VERMONT
2 : NEW HAMPSHIRE
3 : MASSACHUSETTS
4 : RHODE ISLAND
5 : CONNECTICUT
6 : NEW JERSEY
7 : DELAWARE
8 : MARYLAND
9 : WEST VIRGINIA

Massachusetts, Michigan, Minnesota, Mississippi, Missouri, Montana, Nebraska, Nevada, New Hampshire, New Jersey, New Mexico, New York, North Carolina, North Dakota, Ohio, Oklahoma, Oregon, Pennsylvania, Rhode Island, South Carolina, South Dakota, Tennessee, Texas, Utah, Vermont, Virginia, Washington, West Virginia, Wisconsin and Wyoming. Hawaii, the 50th state, was admitted as recently as 1959. The total area is 3,531,900 square miles with a population of over 204 millions. The capital is Washington D.C. (District of Columbia) but the largest city is New York, the second largest city in the world. The U.S.A. is a heavily industrialised country producing all its own needs and exporting many of its products.

UNIVERSE is all the countless stars, planets, moons and other matter scattered throughout space. It includes the many millions of nebulae that exist in the depths of space far beyond the Milky Way. From certain observations of the light received from nebulae, most astronomers believe that the universe is expanding, and that the nebulae are rushing away from each other at enormous speeds. It has been found by calculation that the farther away a nebula is, the greater is the speed at which it recedes. Astronomers have calculated that there are at least a hundred million of them, and that each contains anything from a hundred to ten-thousand million stars!

URANIUM is a heavy, radioactive element. Since the discovery in 1939 that uranium atoms can be split to release energy, it has become one of the most important substances in the world. Natural uranium consists of U238 and U235, and it is the latter that is used in atomic bombs. See NUCLEAR POWER.

URUGUAY is a republic in South America on the mouth of the Rio de la Plata. It is the smallest republic in South America with a population of nearly 3 millions and a land area of 72,175 square miles. The capital is Montevideo. It is a mostly agricultural country exporting wool and meat.

U.S.S.R. stands for Union of Soviet Socialist Republics of Russia. It is the largest country in the world with an area of 8,599,800 square miles and a population of 241 millions. The 15 states that make up the U.S.S.R. are the Russian Federal Republic, Ukraine, Belonissia, Uzbekistan, Kazakstan, Latvia, Kirghizia, Georgia, Azerbaidjan, Lithuania, Moldavia, Tadjikstan, Turkmenistan, Estonia and Armenia. The capital is Moscow and the country is fully industrialised with large collective farms.

VACCINATION The Latin word for cow is *vacca;* cows sometimes contract a mild disease called cowpox; so vaccination means giving a person a very mild form of a mild disease to prevent his becoming a much more serious one, in this case smallpox. Vaccination is also a form of INOCULATION against other diseases, such as typhoid fever and cholera. If a person has to be vaccinated against smallpox, the doctor will first scratch the patient's skin; then he will introduce through the scratch a preparation, called lymph, obtained from a calf; the calf had itself been inoculated with cowpox. The practice of vaccination or inoculation has saved millions of lives.

VACUUM or **THERMOS FLASK** is a container in which tea, coffee, or other similar drinks can be kept hot (if such drinks are preferred taken hot, as they usually are) or kept cold (in the case of drinks which are required this way). Hot drinks are kept hot because the silvered walls and vacuum prevent heat radiating away. They also prevent any heat from getting into the flask, and so anything that is already cold when put into the flask will remain cold. The flask really insulates its contents against the outside temperature which thus cannot affect it.

VANDALS were warlike people from Germany who in the 5th and 6th centuries invaded many countries in Europe and sacked Rome in A.D. 455. They had no respect for anybody or anything, and behaved barbarously as they swept through Europe, looting temples and chur-

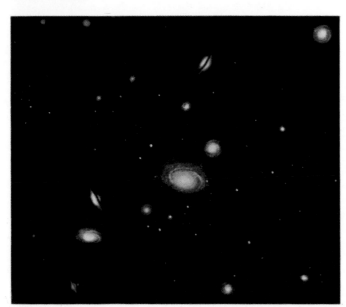

Spiral nebulae scattered in space
like stars in the night sky

The 'Horsehead' nebula in Orion

The 'Great Nebula' in Orion

A nebula cluster

A small section of stars in the Milky Way

The core of a giant spiral nebula

ches, shattering statuary, destroying priceless art treasures and libraries, and plundering rich people's mansions and poor people's homes. The word vandal was simply the name of the principal tribe among these robbers and murderers, but nowadays anyone who behaves in a senseless and destructive way is called a vandal and his reckless acts of destruction 'vandalism'.

VATICAN CITY is the capital of the Vatican State. Its official name is Stato della Citia del Vaticano (State of the Vatican City) or Holy See, and the city has an area of about 108 acres and a population of just under 1,000. Various papal states covered mid-Italy until incorporated in Italy on 13 May 1871, but the Vatican's independence was established by a treaty on 11 February 1929, with the Pope exercising complete sovereignty over this area. The Vatican is the official residence of the Pope, who is the Holy Father of the Roman Catholic Church. The Pope sends his own ambassadors to foreign countries; these priests are called 'papal nuncios' (from the Latin *nuncius*, envoy). The Vatican palace has about 7,000 rooms and stands on a hill called Mons Vaticanus, hence the name. The Holy See has its own flag of yellow and white vertical stripes with a crest of crossed keys (the keys of St Peter, who guards the gate of Heaven) surmounted by the triple crown of the Pope.

VENEZUELA is a republic in the north of South America. It has an area of about 352,000 square miles and a population of over 10 millions. The capital is Caracas and the river Orinoco runs through the country. Main exports are petroleum, iron ore, coffee and cocoa. Diamonds and gold are also mined there.

VERTEBRATES are animals having a backbone made up of separate bones called 'vertebrae'. Vertebrates are sometimes called the 'higher animals', not only because they have larger and more complicated bodies, but because they have true brains. They include all the four-footed animals, birds and fish. The backbone in a human being consists of thirty-three individual vertebrae.

VESUVIUS is a still active VOLCANO overlooking the Bay of Naples, Italy. Its present height is about 3890 feet and it is about 30 miles in circumference at its base. Some of its eruptions have been particularly damaging, as in 1906 and 1631, but the worst destruction caused by an eruption of the volcano occurred in A.D. 79 when the mountain's top blew off and the Roman towns of Pompeii and Herculaneum were buried beneath a mass of lava and ash.

VIETNAM was divided into two republics in 1954, when France relinquished it as a colony. The northern republic has a communist government ruling from Hanoi over an area of 63,000 square miles and a population of about 21 millions. The southern republic is ruled from Saigon over an area of 66,280 square miles and a population of about 18 millions. There has been war between the two republics for the last 10 years with America supporting the south.

VIKINGS were seafaring people from Scandinavia. They were fearless warriors and raided the coasts of Britain and northern Europe, where people came to dread the sudden onslaughts of the Norsemen or Northmen as they called them. It is thought that the Vikings may have crossed the Atlantic in their open longboats and discovered the New World centuries before Columbus. The Vikings were great story-tellers and loved to record their adventurous voyages in verses which were recited or sung by ministrels or skalds.

VIOLIN This musical instrument has the greatest range of expression of any, and can sound the most 'sympathetic'. The violin is the chief among what are called the 'violin family' of instruments, the other members being the viola, the cello and the double bass. The instrument dates from the early 16th century and, like other members of its family, is played by a bow drawn across strings. As the bow is drawn across the four strings on the violin (or the five strings sometimes possessed by the double bass), four fingers of the left hand press the tops of the strings in a technique called 'stopping'. In some pieces of music the composer has called for a special effect called 'pizzicato' and to achieve this the violinist plucks the strings with the forefinger of his right hand, instead of using the bow. A violin that can be proved to have been made by one of the great violin-making families of Italy in the 16th, 17th and 18th centuries—the Amati, Guarneri, and Stradivari—is worth a great deal of money, and may change hands for tens of thousands of pounds.

VIPER, or **ADDER,** is the only poisonous snake found in the British Isles. It is common over many parts of Europe, Asia and Africa. It can be recognized by the dark zig-zag band which runs down its back and the V-shaped marking on the back of its head.

VIRUS is the name given to the smallest form of germ or bacteria. It is so small, in fact, that it cannot be seen with an ordinary microscope but only by an ELECTRON MICROSCOPE. Among the diseases caused by viruses are influenza, infantile paralysis (polio), measles and the common cold.

VITAMINS (from Latin words meaning 'appertaining to, or of the nature of, life') are substances which the body cannot make for itself but which it cannot do without. They are thus very important to life. Minute quantities of them are contained in the food we eat and are essential to health. If a person doesn't eat sufficient vitamins he or she becomes ill; and there is a lot of truth in the half-humorous remark made by a famous medical man and dietician who said, 'Vitamins are things which will kill you if you don't eat them'. More than forty different vitamins have been identified but only six may actually be so lacking in human diet as to cause illness. These six have been graded under main heads as follows: Vitamin A, found in animal but not vegetable fats, and in milk,

Diagram showing how a volcano erupts and the formation of a volcanic mountain

butter and halibut-liver oil; guards against xerophthalmia, a disease which can affect the tearducts of the eye. Vitamin B, the anti-beriberi vitamin, is really a mixture of several vitamins; it occurs mostly in yeast, lean meat, tomato juice and eggs; vegetables and fruits contain very little, and there is no Vitamin B in oils or fats. Vitamin C (anti-scurvy) is abundant in cabbages, citrus fruits and certain root crops. Vitamin D is found in liver and fish and prevents rickets. Vitamin E is the anti-sterility vitamin; abundant in wheat germs and lettuce. Vitamin K is found in green-leaf foods, pig-liver fat and hemp seed; it helps blood capillaries to heal themselves and is believed to arrest tooth decay.

VOLCANO is a mountain built up from the lava, ashes and rocks thrown up when molten

A Viking longship which, it is thought, crossed the Atlantic long before Columbus

rock erupts from the inside of the earth; the formation of a volcano is shown in the diagram below. There are about 430 volcanoes in the world, but only a few are still active.

VOLCANOES OF THE WORLD

NAME	COUNTRY	HEIGHT IN FEET
Vesuvius	Italy	3,900
Etna	Sicily	10,700
Stromboli	Lipari Islands, near Sicily	3,000
Hekla	Iceland	4,800
Askja	Iceland	4,600
Kartala	Comoro Islands in Indian Ocean	8,500
Kilimanjaro	Africa	19,500
Fujiyama	Japan	12,400
Asosan	Japan	5,200
Father	New Britain in Pacific Ocean	7,500
Mauna Loa	Hawaii	13,700
Ngauruhoe	New Zealand	7,500
Wrangell	Alaska	14,000
Lassen Peak	U.S.A.	10,500
Popocatepetl	Mexico	17,900
Cotopaxi	Ecuador	19,300

VOLE belongs to the RODENT family. The water-vole is much the same colour as the common brown rat but is smaller in size. It lives in burrows in the banks of streams and rivers. The field-vole is about the size of a house mouse.

The bald-headed vulture is a bird of prey and lives mainly on the flesh of dead animals

It lives in fields and makes its nest in the grass. The LEMMING of Scandinavia is a vole, as is the musk-rat or musquash of North America. The musk-rat is bred in large numbers on special farms for its valuable fur, which is used for making coats.

VOLTMETER is an electrical instrument for measuring the voltage of a current. See ELECTRICITY.

VULTURE is a bird of prey. It usually has a bald head and neck, and a large hooked beak. Vultures feed on dead bodies and this is why the word 'vulture' always has a sinister sound. The best-known vulture is the 'griffon' vulture, found in remote parts of Spain. In America the most common are the 'turkey' vultures, and the CONDOR, which has a wing-span of up to 10 feet.

WALES is in the west of Britain, and is a part of the United Kingdom. It is a mountainous country; Mount Snowdon (3,560 feet), in North Wales, is one of the highest peaks in Britain. South Wales has many important coal mines and steel mills. Many people, especially in the central and northern parts, speak Welsh, which is a Celtic language. The capital is Cardiff, a large industrial centre and seaport. The Act joining England and Wales was passed in 1536. Ever since the reign of Edward I the eldest son of the sovereign has always been created Prince of Wales. The present Prince of Wales is Charles, the eldest son of Queen Elizabeth II.

WALLABY is a small kangaroo which lives in Australia. Like the kangaroo, it is a marsupial, which means that the mother carries her young in a pouch. There are many different kinds of wallaby including the rock-wallaby, the hare wallaby, and fawn and black-tailed wallabies.

WALRUS lives on the coast and ice-floes of the Arctic. It resembles the sea-lion but has a much heavier body and almost hairless skin. Two of the upper teeth form a pair of strong tusks which grow downwards, sometimes projecting as much as 18 inches below the mouth. It also has very long, thick whiskers. The walrus is a rather clumsy animal on land and quite a slow swimmer. It feeds mostly on the bottom of the sea, eating clams and other shell-fish which it tears off rocks or digs up from the mud with its tusks.

WAPATI belongs to the deer family, and is found in Central Asia and North America, where it is known as the 'elk'. It grows to a height of about 5 feet at the shoulder, and the antlers are long with the ends bent sharply backwards.

WARTHOG This animal, with its four huge curving tusks and long mane of coarse, bristly hair, belongs to the pig family and has been called one of Nature's freaks. There are two main species of this pig; the average height is about 30 inches at the shoulder, and the weight is up to 200 1bs. Its general colour is brownish-grey and the creature's skin is so cracked that it looks like dried mud. It can be a very savage animal, especially if its young are threatened.

WATER is a substance composed of the chemical elements oxygen and hydrogen. It occurs in three forms, solid (ice), fluid and gas (steam). Water is one of the most abundant substances on earth, and is essential to all forms of life. In countries where running water is plentiful, it is used to drive TURBINES to generate electric power.

WATERFALLS The following table gives some of the world's most famous waterfalls. They are arranged according to greatest height to the nearest 10 feet.

HEIGHT IN FEET	NAME	COUNTRY
3,300	Angel	Venezuela
1,900	Sutherland	New Zealand
1,800	Tugela	South Africa
1,600	Ribbon	U.S.A.
1,400	Gavarnie	France
980	Staubbach	Switzerland
850	Vettisfos	Norway
830	Gersoppa	India
650	Terni	Italy
500	Marina	Guyana
450	King George's	South Africa
400	Herval Cascades	Brazil
340	Victoria	Rhodesia
300	Grand	Labrador
160	Niagara	U.S.A.-Canada

WATERSPOUT is to the sea what the TORNADO is to the land. Waterspouts occur more frequently in tropical waters then elsewhere, and are caused by the action of a tornado over a lake, river or ocean. A waterspout is seen as a whirling column of water that rises from the surface of the sea to a height of 1,500 feet or so; it can be 300 feet in diameter, and travels at about 15 to 20 miles per hour.

WEASEL is a small flesh-eating mammal, found in most countries in the northern hemi-

The walrus lives partly on arctic ice-floes

When attacked a warthog can be very savage

sphere. About 10 inches long, it has reddish-brown and white fur; the body is remarkably slender, with very short legs, a long neck and a long tail. The weasel feeds on rats and mice and other small creatures, and sometimes will attack rabbits and poultry.

WEAVING is interlacing threads at right angles to each other so as to form a fabric or cloth. This art has been practised in the earliest stages of all the great civilizations. There is hand weaving and machine weaving. The former is carried out on a comparatively small frame called a LOOM, while the latter is done on electrically powered looms which can carry out the operation of weaving with great speed and cheapness.

WEEDS are uncultivated plants which grow among cultivated plants, as, for instance, dandelions and thistles grow among wheat. As well as preventing many crops from growing properly by choking them, weeds are often poisonous to animals, and may harbour unwanted insect pests.

WEEVILS belong to a family of various BEETLES, many of which are great pests to the farmer. They have a long beak or snout, and for this reason are sometimes called snout beetles. The female often lays her eggs in the bark of dead or dying trees, and uses her beak to make a hole in which to lay them. The weevils are vegetable feeders and often seriously damage such crops as wheat, barley and rice, as well as the blossom of apple trees, etc.

WEIGHTS AND MEASURES play an important part in our lives. They are essential to business, science, engineering—and almost everything else. There are two systems in use in the world, (1) the British, based on the foot and pound, and (2) the Metric, based on the metre and gramme. The table shows not only the details of each system, but how to convert British to Metric and *vice-versa.* It should be noted that the British system is to be replaced by the Metric system. The reasons for this are that the Metric system being decimal is simpler, and that most of the world, excepting Britain and America, use the Metric system for everything connected with measuring and weighing.

WEIGHTS AND MEASURES

Avoirdupois

7,000 grains	1 pound
16 drams	1 ounce (oz.)
16 ounces	1 pound (1b.)
14 pounds	1 stone (st.)
28 pounds	1 quarter (qr.)
4 quarters	1 hundredweight (cwt.)
20 hundredweights	1 ton (tn.)

Imperial Dry Measure

2 glasses	1 noggin (5 oz.)
4 noggins	1 pint (1 lb. 4 oz.)
2 pints	1 quart (2 lb. 8 oz.)
4 quarts	1 gallon (10 lb.)
2 gallons	1 peck (20 lb.)
4 pecks	1 bushel (80 lb.)
8 bushels	1 quarter (640 lb.)

Metric Weight

1 gramme	
1 decagramme	10 grammes
1 hectogramme	100 grammes
1 kilogramme	1,000 grammes
1 myriagramme	10,000 grammes
1 decigramme	$\frac{1}{10}$th of a gramme
1 centigramme	$\frac{1}{100}$th of a gramme
1 milligramme	$\frac{1}{1000}$th of a gramme

British Linear Measure

12 inches (in.)	1 foot (ft.)
3 feet	1 yard (yd.)
2 yards	1 fathom (f.)
5½ yards	1 pole (rod or perch)
40 poles	1 furlong (fur.)
8 furlongs	1 mile (m.) (1,760 yds.)

Metric Measure

1 metre	
1 decametre	10 metres
1 hectometre	100 metres
1 kilometre	1,000 metres
1 myriametre	10,000 metres
1 decimetre	$\frac{1}{10}$th of a metre
1 centimetre	$\frac{1}{100}$th of a metre
1 millimetre	$\frac{1}{1000}$th of a metre

Troy Weight

24 grains	1 pennyweight (dwt.)
20 pennyweights	1 ounce
12 ounces	1 pound

Square Measure

144 square inches	1 square foot
9 square feet	1 square yard
30¼ square yards	1 square pole
40 square poles	1 rood
4 roods	1 acre
4,840 square yards	1 acre
640 acres	1 sq. mile

Metric Square Measure

1 are	100 square metres
1 decare	10 ares
1 hectare	100 ares
1 deciare	$\frac{1}{10}$th of an are
1 centiare	$\frac{1}{100}$th of an are

Apothecaries' Weight

20 grains	1 scruple (scr.)
3 scruples	1 dram (dr.)
8 drams	1 ounce (oz.)
12 ounces	1 pound (1b.)

Cubic Measure

1,728 cubic inches	1 cubic foot
27 cubic feet	1 cubic yard
$24\frac{3}{4}$-25 cubic feet	1 solid perch (mason's measure)

Metric Cubic Measure

1 litre	
1 decalitre	10 litres
1 hectolitre	100 litres
1 decilitre	$\frac{1}{10}$th of a litre
1 centilitre	$\frac{1}{100}$th of a litre
1 millilitre	$\frac{1}{1000}$th of a litre

Conversion Table—Metric to British

1 millimetre	0.0394 inch
1 centimetre	0.3937 inch
1 decimetre	3.937 inches
1 metre	39.3701 inches
1 kilometre	0.6214 mile
1 centiare	1.196 square yards
1 are	3.954 square poles
1 hectare	2.471 acres
1 decigramme	1.543 grains
1 gramme	15.432 grains
1 hectogramme	3.527 ounces
1 kilogramme	2.2046 pounds
1 litre	1.76 pints

Conversion Table—British to Metric

1 inch	25.399 millimetres
1 foot	30.479 centimetres
1 yard	0.914 metre
1 chain	20.1164 metres
1 furlong	201.164 metres
1 mile	1.609 kilometres
1 square foot	9.29 sq. decimetres
1 acre	0.405 hectare
1 square mile	2.599 sq. kilometres
1 grain	0.0648 gramme
1 ounce	28.33 grammes
1 pound (avoird.)	454 grammes
1 pound (troy)	373 grammes
1 hundredweight	50.8 kilos
1 ton	1,016 kilos
1 pint	0.568 litre
1 gallon	4.546 litres
1 peck	.9.087 litres
1 quarter	2.908 hectolitres

WELDING means joining two pieces of metal by raising the temperature at the joint by means of external heat; or by a heavy electric current (resistance welding); or by an electric arc and pressure (arc welding); or by pressure alone (cold welding). A small welding job may be done by means of an oxy-acetylene hand torch, but a big welding job such as needed in ship building may have to be done by big machines which can weld together pieces weighing many tons.

WEST INDIES are a group of islands in the Atlantic which stretch between South and North America. They were discovered by Columbus in 1492, and named West Indies by him because he thought that he had discovered a western sea route to India.

WESTMINSTER ABBEY has an 'official' name which hardly anyone ever uses: the Collegiate Church of Saint Peter. It is sometimes referred to as the premier historical monument in England and it is certainly the finest example of Early English architecture. The abbey stands on low ground which was once a small island where thorn-bushes grew thickly, so it was called Thorny Isle. Here, so legend has it, the first Christian king of the East Saxons (Sebert) built a church which was consecrated by Melitus, first Bishop of London. This little church must have vanished when Edward the Confessor (1042-66) built on the same site a bigger church which grew into Westminster Abbey. Henry III, Edward III, Henry V, and Henry VII all added to it. When a famous person dies, it is considered a very great honour for them to be buried in Westminster Abbey.

WEST POINT (U.S.A.) Many countries with a long military history train their army officers at special schools or colleges. England's Sandhurst has become world famous. In France it is the military academy of Saint Cyr. And though the military history of the United States of America is short compared with that of England, France and other countries, it has an old-established training school where young men are trained for professional army careers. On the west bank of the Hudson River, just to the north of New York City, there was formerly a military post during the War of American Independence (1775-83) and this was the site chosen in 1802 for the new academy now known as West Point.

WHALE is a large sea-mammal of fish-like form. It swims by moving its tail up and down in the water, and usually rises to the surface every 5 or 10 minutes in order to breathe. Some of the larger whales, however, can remain under water for nearly an hour without coming up to breathe. On reaching the surface the whale lets out a stream of warm air which, on coming into contact with the cold atmosphere, forms a column of mist; this is called 'spouting' because the column of mist used to be mistaken for actual water which was thought to come out of the whale's nostrils. This action of the whale gave rise to the expression among seamen. 'There she blows'. There are many kinds of whales but they are all similar in appearance; some of the biggest reach a length of 100 feet.

WHITE HOUSE (U.S.A.) is the official residence of the President of the United States. It is in the city of Washington, the federal capital of the nation, and is a stately building surrounded by lawns and trees. Washington was the first city in the world to be built especially as the capital of a country. The plans for it were drawn up by Major Pierre Charles L'Enfant (1754-1825), who was a French engineer on the side of the American colonists during the war of inde-

pendence. It was decided to call the city Washington after George Washington, the first president. Since George Washington there have been thirty-six presidents of the United States and the majority of them have lived at the White House. See PRESIDENT.

WILD FLOWERS are those flowering plants which grow in fields, woods, on banks, in hedge rows and the like. They are quite distinct from garden flowers, which are usually larger and brighter in colour, although many garden flowers were developed from wild flowers. See PLANTS

WIND may be described simply as air in motion. It is the natural flow of air over the surface of the earth—natural because our planet is always revolving within its own atmosphere the pressure of which varies. In an area where the sun has been shining, the hot air rises and more air flows in to take its place. Such a flow of air is a wind. The TRADE WINDS and 'Roaring Forties' (strong winds experienced at the 40th degrees of latitude) are permanent winds while other winds, such as the monsoon, are seasonal.

WOLF is a flesh-eating member of the dog family. It used to roam many parts of the world, including Britain, but now it is rare to

A selection of five well-known whales. Remember, the whale is a mammal and not a fish

hear of wolves being seen in settled areas, most of the larger wolves being found only in the northern, colder parts of the world. The wolf is very much like a large dog in appearance but the teeth are bigger and the hair longer and coarser. Wolves hunt in packs and when hungry will not hesitate to attack bigger animals and sometimes even man.

WOLVERINE is an animal distinct from the wolf. The wolverine is also known as 'glutton' because it is a great eater; it is related to the marten (a member of the weasel family) and has the general appearance of a small bear. It inhabits the forested districts of the northern hemisphere and is mainly terrestial, that is, it does not live among the trees. It is one of the most cunning of animals, and is disliked by trappers whose traps a wolverine will rob for food.

WOMBAT is the name given by the aborigines of Australia to a marsupial (pouched) mammal of the same order as the opossums. The wombat is also found in Tasmania. It looks like a large, furry guinea-pig and has paws which are well adapted for digging. It usually lies in its burrow during the day, coming out at night to feed on grasses, roots and the bark of trees. There are two kinds of wombat; the 'ursine' (like a bear) wombat and the 'hairy-nosed' wombat.

WOOL is a soft, warm material obtained from the fleeces of sheep. Its chief use to man is in the making of cloth, and it has been used for this purpose in Europe since before the Roman invasions. Wool has been found to be the most comfortable kind of clothing in northern and some western countries, because it keeps in the heat of the body; cotton garments are more popular in warmer countries. Wool fibres and the clothing made from them act as an insulating material, and the fibres stretch easily. The finest wools are obtained from the fleece of the Spanish merino sheep. There are many stages in the production of woollen cloth. After the wool is sheared from the sheep it has to be scoured, washed, oiled, carded (separating the fibres), combed, spun into yarn, dyed, teaselled, pressed and drysteamed. These processes may be modified or varied according to individual methods of manufacture. Australia, New Zealand and the Argentine are the greatest wool-producing countries in the world; sheep and lambs' wool make up about 32 per cent of Australia's total exports.

WOOLSACK In the entry immediately preceding this you will have read how wool making was one of the earliest industries in Europe. England built up a most important woollen trade during the Middle Ages and wool was, in fact, the chief source of the nation's wealth for very many years. It was King Edward III (1327-77) who had the idea that his subjects should be constantly reminded of this fact, so he decided that the Lord High Chancellor of England (who is highest in rank in the kingdom after the royal family and the Archbishop of Canterbury) should sit in the House of Lords on a big bag of wool. This is the origin of the term 'woolsack' and of the Lord Chancellor being 'appointed to the Woolsack'. The large, square bag of wool is covered with red cloth and is without back or arms, and it faces the throne where the sovereign sits when he or she opens Parliament.

WORM is a legless, rod-like creature. The most common type is the earthworm. It spends most of the daytime in a burrow near the surface of the earth, and obtains its food from the earth which it passes through its body. It lays eggs which are covered with a hard cocoon and hatch out after a few weeks. There are many different kinds and varieties of worm, some living in water and mud. However, they are all similar in shape.

X-RAYS were discovered by the German scientist, Prof. W. G. Röntgen, in 1895. X-rays are produced when a stream of electrons strikes a metal target. Since their discovery X-rays have been used for medical purposes. More recently, however, they have been employed for examining metal parts for internal faults. X-rays belong to the same family as light, but they are of much shorter wavelength. The shorter the

1 Traveller's joy
2 Dog rose
3 Foxglove
4 Hemlock
5 Traveller's joy (seed)
6 Brome grass
7 Wild Teasel
8 Honeysuckle
9 Bryony
10 Wood anemone
11 Ladies smock
12 Ox-eyed daisy
13 Field poppy
14 Chicory
15 Ragged robin
16 Agrimony
17 Woody nightshade
18 Coltsfoot
19 Cuckoo-pint
20 Celandine
21 Bugle
22 Wild strawberry
23 Centaury
24 Harebell
25 Scarlet pimpernel
26 Bird's foot trefoil
27 Forget-me-not
28 Cuckoo-pint (fruit)

wavelength of X-rays the more penetrating they are.

XYLOPHONE is a musical instrument consisting of a series of wooden blocks of various sizes which are played with small mallets or hammers.

YAK is an ox-like animal of the Himalayas. It has a long, low body from which hangs thick hair. It is at home among mountains and can climb to a height of between 15,000 and 20,000 feet. The Tibetan people have domesticated the yak, and it provides them with meat and milk. It is also sometimes used as means of transport.

YEAST consists of minute fungi, plants which consist each of a simple, single cell. New cells are produced by budding and a chain of cells is thus produced which cling closely together. Yeast has the property of being able to extract oxygen (which the plants must have in order to live) from substances which contain sugar, and the result of this 'fermentation', as it is called, is alcohol and carbon dioxide gas. So yeast is used in brewing and wine-making and also to make bread. The gas produces little bubbles in the dough as it is baked; this results in little 'pockets' of air, and so the bread 'rises' and is made lighter and more appetising than it would be if yeast were not used.

YEOMEN OF THE GUARD are in attendance on England's sovereign and their prime duty is the protection of his or her person. They are sometimes called 'Beefeaters' because they used to taste the monarch's food to see if it were poisoned. They should not be confused with the Yeoman Warders of the Tower of London, who wear a similar uniform, dating from the time of England's first Tudor king, Henry VII, who founded both bodies.

YUGOSLAVIA is a communist federal republic in Eastern Europe with an area of 98,730 square miles and a population of about 21 mil-

lions. The capital is Belgrade. The country is basically agricultural although it is moving towards an industrial basis. It has large mineral resources. The six member states are Serbia, Croatia, Slovenia, Montenegro, Macedonia and Bosnia-Herzegovina.

ZAMBIA is a republic in Central Africa, with an area of 290,600 square miles. It is a member of the British Commonwealth and has a population of over 4 millions. The capital is Lusaka. The country produces much of the world's copper, also tobacco, maize and groundnuts.

ZEBRA This animal belongs to the horse family and is found only in Africa. The general colour is very dark brown with white or cream stripes. This peculiar colour pattern of the zebra renders it very conspicuous when seen, for instance, in a zoo among other animals, but in its homeland of Africa the colours really act as camouflage, and the zebra is very difficult to see when standing motionless in the light-flecked shade of a tree. The largest of the zebras is called Grevy's zebra; two other kinds are Hartmann's mountain zebra and Chapman's quagga.

ZEBU is the name of the Indian ox. It has a characteristic hump on the shoulders and a large dewlap. There are many breeds of zebu, just as there are different kinds of cattle.

ZODIAC is an imaginary zone in the heavens in which the sun, moon and planets follow their paths. It is divided into twelve sections according to what seem to be the positions of the sun during the twelve months of the year. Astrologists make use of the zodiac in certain calculations, on the basis of which they claim to be able to predict the future and cast 'horoscopes' (the influence the heavenly bodies are supposed to have on people's lives). The zodiac was the idea of the ancient Babylonians who thought wrongly that the stars and planets were fixed in their places, whereas they are always on the move. It is this that causes critics of astrology to say that the 'science' is valueless.

ZOOLOGY is the branch of biology devoted to the study of animal life. The first zoologist was the Greek thinker, Aristotle, who is generally known as the 'Father of Zoology', and whose writings were studied until about the sixteenth century. Zoology covers many subjects; for example, classification or the naming of animals and grouping them into families; study of how animals are constructed; how the internal organs work; how animals behave, etc.

ZULU is the name of a tribe of African people of Bantu stock. The Zulus live mainly in Natal, a province of the Republic of South Africa. They were very powerful in the early nineteenth century but the British subdued them and took over Zululand in 1887. The Zulus are a people of magnificent physique and great courage; in battle they fought with wooden 'knobkerries' or clubs and shields of ox hide.

TABLES

Table 1 Composers

Born	Died	Name	Nationality	Composition[s]
1526	1594	Palestrina	Italian	Religious music
1567	1643	Monteverdi	Italian	Operas and religious compositions
1658	1695	H. Purcell	British	Church music and operas also music to *The Fairy Queen*
1685	1750	J. S. Bach	German	Religious music; *Mass in B Minor*
1659	1725	D. Scarlatti	Italian	Music for harpsichord
1685	1759	G. F. Handel	German	Operas and choral music; *The Messiah*
1714	1787	C. W. Gluck	Bavarian	Operas
1732	1809	F. J. Haydn	Austrian	Symphonies, chamber and choral music
1756	1791	W. A. Mozart	Austrian	Chamber music and operas; *The Magic Flute*
1770	1827	L. Van Beethoven	German	Symphonies and chamber music
1786	1826	K. M. F. E. Weber	German	Operas; *Oberon*
1792	1868	G. Rossini	Italian	Operas; *The Barber of Seville*
1797	1828	F. Schubert	Austrian	Symphonies and songs
1803	1869	H. Berlioz	French	Symphonies and operas
1804	1857	M. Glinka	Russian	Operas; *Russlan and Ludmilla*
1809	1847	F. Mendelssohn	German	Symphonies and choral music; *Elijah* and music to *Midsummer Night's Dream*
1810	1849	F. F. Chopin	Polish	Piano music
1810	1856	R. Schumann	German	Piano music; *Carnival*
1811	1886	F. Liszt	Hungarian	Piano; *Hungarian Rhapsodies*
1813	1901	G. Verdi	Italian	Operas; *Aida* and *La Traviata*
1813	1883	R. Wagner	German	Operas; the opera cycle *The Ring of the Nibelung*
1818	1893	C. F. Gounod	French	Sacred music and operas; *Faust*
1819	1880	J. Offenbach	French	Light operas; *The Tales of Hoffman*
1825	1899	J. Strauss	Austrian	Light music; *The Blue Danube*
1833	1897	J. Brahms	German	Symphonies and chamber music
1835	1921	C. Saint-Saëns	French	Symphonies and music for opera
1838	1875	G. Bizet	French	Operas; *Carmen*
1840	1893	P. I. Tchaikovsky	Russian	Symphonies and ballet music; *The Sleeping Beauty*
1842	1900	Sir A. S. Sullivan	British	Light operas with Gilbert and known as *Gilbert and Sullivan* operas
1843	1907	E. H. Grieg	Norwegian	Orchestral music; music for *Peer Gynt*
1844	1908	N. Rimski Korsakov	Russian	Russian operas; *The Golden Cockerel*
1854	1932	J. P. Sousa	American	Military marches; *Stars and Stripes for Ever*
1857	1934	Sir E. Elgar	British	Religious music; *Dream of Gerontius*
1858	1919	R. Leoncavallo	Italian	Opera music; *I. Pagliacci*
1858	1924	G. Puccini	Italian	Operas; *La Boheme*; *Madam Butterfly*
1860	1911	G. Mahler	Austrian	Symphonies and choral works
1862	1918	C. Debussy	French	Orchestral music; *Clair de Lune*
1862	1934	F. Delius	British	Orchestral music; *On Hearing the First Cuckoo in Spring*
1862	1936	Sir E. German	British	Light operas; *Tom Jones*; *Merrie England*
1864	1949	R. Strauss	German	Operas and orchestral music; *Don Quixote*
1865	1957	J. Sibelius	Finnish	Symphonies
1872	1958	R. Vaughan Williams	British	Symphonies, opera, ballet, film music, songs, etc.; *Greensleeves*

Born	Died	Name	Nationality	Compositions
1873	1934	S. Rachmaninov	Russian	Piano music
1874	1934	G. Holst	British	Orchestral music; *The Planets*
1875	1937	M. Ravel	French	Orchestral music; *Bolero*
1877	1953	R. Quilter	British	Light music; *Children's Overture*
1882	1971	I. Stravinsky	Russian	Ballet music; *Firebird*
1882		Z. Kodaly	Hungarian	Orchestral music; *Harry Janos*
1883	1953	Sir A. Bax	British	Symphonies, chamber music, etc.; Master of King's Music 1942–1954
1891	1953	S. Prokofiev	Russian	Symphonies; *Peter and the Wolf*
1902		Sir W. Walton	British	Symphony, film and choral music; *Belzhazzar's Feast*
1904		A. Khachaturyan	Russian	Orchestral music; *Sabre Dance*
1906		D. Shostakovich	Russian	Symphonies
1913		B. Britten	British	Operas; children's opera *Let's make an Opera*

Table   2   Poets

Born	Died	Name	Nationality	Famous work[s]
700 B.C.		Homer	Greek	*Iliad* and *Odyssey*
65 B.C.	8 B.C.	Horace	Roman	Many Odes
c. 1070		Omar Khayyam	Persian	*The Rubaiyat*
1265	1321	A. Dante	Italian	*The Divine Comedy*
1340	1400	G. Chaucer	British	*Canterbury Tales*
1544	1595	Tasso	Italian	*Jerusalem Delivered*
1573	1631	J. Donne	British	*Songs and Sonnets*
1591	1674	R. Herrick	British	*Hesperides*
1608	1674	J. Milton	British	*Paradise Lost* and *Paradise Regained*
1688	1744	A. Pope	British	*Essay on Man*
1716	1771	T. Gray	British	*An Elegy Written in a Country Churchyard*
1731	1800	W. Cowper	British	*John Gilpin, The Task*
1757	1827	W. Blake	British	*Songs of Innocence* and *Songs of Experience*
1759	1796	R. Burns	Scot	Much poetry and songs; *Auld Lang Syne*
1770	1850	W. Wordsworth	British	*To Daffodils; The Prelude*
1772	1834	S. T. Coleridge	British	*Ancient Mariner; Kubla Khan; Christabel*
1779	1852	T. Moore	Irish	*Irish Melodies*
1788	1824	Lord Byron	British	*Childe Harold*
1792	1822	P. B. Shelley	British	*To a Skylark; Prometheus Unbound*
1795	1821	J. Keats	British	*Eve of St. Agnes* and *Ode to a Nightingale*
1797	1856	H. Heine	German	Gentle lyric poems
1799	1837	A. Pushkin	Russian	*Eugene Onegin*
1807	1882	H. W. Longfellow	American	*The Village Blacksmith; Paul Revere's Ride* and *Hiawatha*

Born	Died	Name	Nationality	Famous works
1809	1849	E. A. Poe	American	*The Raven; The Bells*
1809	1892	Lord Tennyson	British	*The Charge of the Light Brigade; Idylls of a King*
1812	1888	E. Lear	British	*The Owl and the Pussy Cat*
1812	1889	R. Browning	British	*The Ring and the Book; The Pied Piper of Hamelin*
1819	1892	W. Whitman	American	*Leaves of Grass*
1822	1888	M. Arnold	British	*Sohrab and Rustum*
1844	1930	R. Bridges	British	*The Testimony of Beauty*
1859	1936	A. E. Housman	British	*A Shropshire Lad*
1865	1939	W. B. Yeats	Irish	*Innisfree*
1878	1967	J. Masefield	British	*Saltwater Ballads; Reynard the Fox*
1884	1915	J. E. Flecker	British	*Hassan*
1886	1967	S. Sassoon	British	Poems on First World War
1887	1915	R. Brooke	British	Poems on First World War
1888	1965	T. S. Eliot	American, later British	*The Waste Land; Murder in the Cathedral*

Table 3 Playwrights

Born	Died	Author	Name of play[s]
1557	1595	T. Kyd	*The Spanish Tragedy*
1564	1593	C. Marlowe	*Doctor Faustus, Edward II, Tamburlaine the Great*
1564	1616	William Shakespeare	*All's Well That Ends Well, Antony and Cleopatra, As You Like It, Comedy of Errors, Coriolanus, Cymbeline, Hamlet, Henry V, Henry VIII, Julius Caesar, King John, King Lear, Love's Labour Lost, Macbeth, Measure for Measure, The Merchant of Venice, The Merry Wives of Windsor, A Midsummer Night's Dream, Much Ado About Nothing, Othello, Pericles, Richard II, Richard III, Romeo and Juliet, The Taming of the Shrew, The Tempest, Timon of Athens, Titus Andronicus, Troilus and Cressida, Twelfth Night, Two Gentlemen of Verona, A Winter's Tale*
1572	1632	T. Dekker	*The Shoemaker's Holiday*
1579	1625	J. Fletcher	*The Island Princess*
1580	1625	J. Webster	*Duchess of Malfi, The White Devil*
1583	1640	P. Massinger	*A New Way to Pay Old Debts*
1584	1616	F. Beaumont	*The Knight of the Burning Pestle*
1572	1637	Ben Jonson	*Bartholomew Fayre, Every Man in his Humour, The Alchemist, Volpone*
1640	1716	W. Wycherley	*Plain Dealer, The Country Wife*
1670	1729	W. Congreve	*Way of the World*
1685	1732	John Gay	*Beggar's Opera*
1749	1832	Goethe	*Faust*
1751	1816	R. B. Sheridan	*School for Scandal, The Critic The Rivals*
1854	1900	Oscar Wilde	*Lady Windermere's Fan*

Born	Died	Author	Name of play[s]
1856	1950	G. B. Shaw	*Androcles and the Lion, Caesar and Cleopatra, Man and Superman*
1860	1937	J. M. Barrie	*Peter Pan*
1871	1909	J. Synge	*Playboy of the Western World*

Table 4 Pioneers of Science

Born	Died	Name	Nationality	Most important work[s]
c. 582 B.C.		Pythagoras	Greek	Mathematics, especially geometry
384 B.C.	322 B.C.	Aristotle	Greek	Whole range of science—especially biology. Father of zoology
c. 330 B.C.	260 B.C.	Euclid	Greek	Geometry
287 B.C.	212 B.C.	Archimedes	Greek	Mathematics. Invented the water screw. Discovered theory of how bodies float and levers work
A.D. 131	A.D. 201	Galen	Greek	Wrote many works on medicine and human body
1214	1294	Roger Bacon	English	Wrote on importance of practical experiments in science
1452	1519	Leonardo da Vinci	Italian	Mechanical inventions: made drawing of aircraft for vertical flight
1473	1543	Copernicus	Polish	First to prove that earth and planets revolve round the sun
1540	1603	William Gilbert	English	Studied magnet and magnetism
1550	1617	John Napier	Scot	Discovered logarithms
1561	1626	Francis Bacon	English	Showed importance of experiments in science
1564	1642	Galileo	Italian	Made important discoveries in astronomy, physics and mechanics. One of the world's greatest scientists
1571	1630	Kepler	German	Discovered laws of how planets move in orbits round the sun
1578	1657	William Harvey	British	Circulation of blood
1596	1650	René Déscartes	French	Many branches of science and mathematics. Known as the *Father of modern thought*
1602	1686	Otto von Guericke	German	Invented air-pump
1627	1691	Robert Boyle	British	Father of modern chemistry
1642	1727	Sir Isaac Newton	British	Many branches of science, especially law of gravitation. One of the world's greatest scientists
1646	1716	G. W. Leibnitz	German	Mathematics
1656	1742	Edmund Halley	British	Astronomy—especially comets

Born	Died	Name	Nationality	Most important work[s]
1686	1736	G. D. Fahrenheit	German	Invented mercury thermometer
1706	1790	Benjamin Franklin	American	Electric charges—invented lightning conductor
1707	1778	K. Linnaeus	Swedish	Natural history. Invented modern way of naming animals and plants
1731	1810	H. Cavendish	British	Chemistry, especially nature of gases
1733	1804	J. Priestley	British	Chemistry and electricity
1737	1798	L. Galvani	Italian	Animal electricity
1738	1822	F. W. Herschel	British	Astronomy. Discovered planets Saturn and Uranus
1743	1794	A. L. Lavoisier	French	Chemistry. Showed importance of oxygen in process of burning
1745	1827	A. Volta	Italian	Devised first electric pile or cell
1753	1814	Count Rumford	American-British	Nature of heat and friction
1766	1844	John Dalton	British	Chemistry. Composition of the atmosphere. Scientific theory of atoms
1777	1851	H. C. Oersted	Danish	Showed connection between electricity and magnetism
1778	1850	J. L. Gay-Lussac	French	Laws of how gases combine
1778	1829	Sir H. Davy	British	Chemistry. Invented miner's lamp
1791	1867	Michael Faraday	British	One of the world's greatest experimental scientists. Made many advances in chemistry and electricity. Most important was electric motor
1796	1831	N. L. S. Carnot	French	Principles of heat engines
1797	1875	Charles Lyell	British	Modern science of geology
1809	1882	Charles Darwin	British	Theory of the evolution of plants and animals
1818	1889	J. P. Joule	British	Nature of heat
1819	1868	J. L. Foucault	French	Measured speed of light. Devised pendulum to test motion of earth on its axis
1822	1895	L. Pasteur	French	Modern theory of germs. Cure for anthrax and hydrophobia
1831	1879	J. Clerk-Maxwell	British	Mathematical theory of light
1832	1917	Sir E. Tylor	British	Scientific study of ancient and primitive man
1834	1907	D. Mendelejeff	Russian	Chemistry. Discovered "periodic table" of the elements
1847	1922	A. G. Bell	American	Many outstanding inventions, including telephone and phonograph (gramophone)
1849	1936	I. P. Pavlov	Russian	Nervous system
1852	1916	Sir W. Ramsay	British	Radioactive substances. Discovered rare gases helium, argon, neon, krypton and xenon
1856	1939	S. Freud	Austrian	Theory of the unconscious mind
1856	1940	Sir J. J. Thomson	British	Measured mass and electric charge of electron
1857	1894	H. R. Hertz	German	Showed the existence of radio waves by practical experiment

Born	Died	Name	Nationality	Most important work[s]
1857	1932	Sir R. Ross	British	Discovered that malaria was carried by mosquitos
1858	1947	Max Planck	German	One of the founders of modern science
1859	1906	Pierre Curie	French	Discovered radium
1867	1934	Marie Curie		
1861	1947	Sir F. G. Hopkins	British	Discovered vitamins
1871	1937	Lord Rutherford	New Zealander	Radioactive substances. Theory of structure of the atom. One of world's greatest scientists
1879	1955	Albert Einstein	German	One of the founders of modern science. Theory of Relativity
1881	1955	Sir A. Fleming	British	Discovered penicillin
1892		Sir R. Watson-Watt	British	Development of radar
1914		J. E. Salk	American	Vaccine against polio

Table 5 Artists

Born	Died	Name	Nationality	Most important work[s]
1255	1319	Duccio	Italian	Paintings in the Cathedral at Siena
1267	1337	Giotto	Italian	Frescoes in the Church of St. Francis at Assisi
1283	1344	S. Martini	Italian	Frescoes in many churches
1370	1426	H. Van Eyck	Flemish	*The Adoration of the Lamb* in Ghent Cathedral
1387	1455	Fra Angelico	Italian	Paintings in the Vatican and Cathedral at Orvieto
1375	1441	J. Van Eyck	Flemish	*The Adoration of the Lamb* in Ghent Cathedral
1401	1428	Masaccio	Italian	Frescoes in Carmine Church, Florence
1420	1492	Piero della Francesca	Italian	One of the pioneers in perspective
1431	1506	A. Mantegna	Italian	*The Triumph of Caesar* and *The Agony in the Garden*
1444	1510	Sandro Botticelli	Italian	*The Birth of Venus, Divine Comedy*
1452	1519	Leonardo da Vinci	Italian	*Madonna of the Rocks, The Last Supper* and *The Mona Lisa*
1471	1528	A. Durer	German	Engravings to illustrate the *Apocalypse* and *Life of the Virgin*
1475	1564	Michelangelo	Italian	Statues of *David, Moses* and *Bound Slave*
1487	1576	Titian	Italian	Portrait painter
1483	1520	S. Raphael	Italian	*Sistine Madonna* and *The Crucifixion*
1494	1534	Correggio	Italian	Paintings in the Cathedral at Parma
1497	1543	Holbein	German	Portraits of Henry VIII
1518	1594	Tintoretto	Italian	*Miracle of St. Mark*
1525	1569	Pieter Bruegel	Flemish	*Massacre of the Innocents*
1528	1588	P. Veronese	Italian	*Marriage of Cana*
1542	1614	El Greco	Greek	*Baptism, Crucifixion* and *Resurrection*
1569	1609	Caravaggio	Italian	*The Card Players* and *Gypsy Fortune Teller*
1577	1640	P. P. Rubens	Flemish	*Adoration of the Magi* and *The Blessing of Peace*

Born	Died	Name	Nationality	Most important work[s]
1580	1666	Franz Hals	Dutch	*The Laughing Cavalier*
1594	1665	N. Poussin	French	Scenes from Mythology
1599	1641	Sir A. Van Dyck	Flemish	Portraits of English notables
1599	1660	Velazquez	Spanish	*The Forge of Vulcan, Venus with a Mirror* and many Royal portraits
1600	1682	Claude-Lorraine	French	Landscapes
1606	1669	Rembrandt	Dutch	*The Night Watch* and *Lesson in Anatomy*
1617	1682	B. E. Murillo	Spanish	Street scenes and street urchins
1618	1680	Sir P. Lely	Dutch	Portraits of people in the reign of Charles I, Cromwell and Charles II
1684	1721	A. Watteau	French	Pastoral scenes
1697	1764	W. Hogarth	British	*Rake's Progress*
1723	1792	Sir J. Reynolds	British	*Mrs. Siddons* and large number of portraits
1727	1788	T. Gainsborough	British	*Perdita, The Blue Boy* and *The Morning Walk*
1732	1806	J. H. Fragonard	French	*The Swing* and pastoral scenes
1734	1802	G. Romney	British	Portraits of women and *Milton and his Daughters*
1746	1828	Goya	Spanish	Portraits and etchings (Disasters of war)
1748	1825	J. L. David	French	*Assassination of Marat* and *The Death of Socrates*
1757	1827	William Blake	British	Illustrations of religious subjects and poems
1776	1837	John Constable	British	*The Cornfield* and *The Hay Wain*
1780	1867	J. A. D. Ingres	French	*Vow of Louis XIII*
1796	1875	J. B. C. Corot	French	Landscapes
1798	1863	F. V. E. Delacroix	French	*Dante Crossing Acheron in Charon's Boat*
1814	1875	J. F. Millet	French	*The Gleaner* and *The Angelus*
1828	1882	D. G. Rossetti	British	Painter and poet
1829	1896	Sir J. E. Millais	British	*Christ in the Carpenter's Shop* and portraits
1832	1883	E. Manet	French	*Dejeuner sur L'Herbe* (Lunch on the Grass)
1834	1917	H. G. E. Degas	French	Studies of ballet dancers
1839	1906	Paul Cézanne	French	Landscapes
1840	1917	A. Rodin	French	*The Thinker* and *The Burghers of Calais*
1841	1919	P. A. Renoir	French	Pictures of women and children
1853	1890	V. Van Gogh	Dutch	*Sunflowers* and *The Starry Night*
1860	1942	W. R. Sickert	British	Scenes of everyday life
1878	1961	Augustus John	British	Portraits of famous people
1881		Pablo Picasso	Spanish	Great modern painter

Table 6 Novelists

Born	Died	Name	Nationality	Novel[s]
1547	1616	Cervantes	Spanish	*Don Quixote*
1660	1731	D. Defoe	British	*Robinson Crusoe*
1667	1745	Jonathan Swift	,,	*Gulliver's Travels*
1707	1754	Henry Fielding	,,	*Tom Jones*
1713	1768	L. Sterne	,,	*Tristram Shandy*
1721	1771	T. G. Smollett	,,	*Humphrey Clinker*
1730	1774	Oliver Goldsmith	,,	*Vicar of Wakefield*
1771	1832	Sir Walter Scott	Scottish	*Ivanhoe, Kenilworth, Rob Roy*
1783	1859	W. Irving	American	*Rip Van Winkle*
1785	1863	L. D. C. Grimm	German	Fairy stories
1786	1859	W. C. Grimm		
1789	1851	J. Fenimore Cooper	American	*Last of the Mohicans*
1792	1848	F. Marryat	British	*Mr. Midshipman Easy*
1797	1851	Mary Shelley	,,	*Frankenstein*
1803	1870	A. Dumas	French	*The Three Musketeers*
1803	1873	Bulwer Lytton	British	*Last Days of Pompeii*
1805	1875	Hans Andersen	Danish	Fairy stories
1811	1863	W. M. Thackeray	British	*Vanity Fair*
1811	1896	H. E. B. Stowe	American	*Uncle Tom's Cabin*
1812	1870	Charles Dickens	British	*Nicholas Nickleby, Pickwick Papers, Oliver Twist, A Tale of Two Cities, The Old Curiosity Shop, David Copperfield, A Christmas Carol*
1812	1870	C. Collodi	Italian	*Pinocchio*
1814	1884	Charles Reade	British	*The Cloister and the Hearth*
1815	1882	Anthony Trollope	,,	*Barchester Towers*
1818	1848	E. Brontë	,,	*Wuthering Heights*
1819	1875	Charles Kingsley	,,	*The Water Babies*
1819	1880	George Eliot	,,	*The Mill on the Floss*
1819	1891	Herman Melville	American	*Moby Dick*
1820	1878	Anna Sewell	British	*Black Beauty*
1822	1896	T. Hughes	,,	*Tom Brown's Schooldays*
1825	1900	R. D. Blackmore	,,	*Lorna Doone*
1827	1905	Lew Wallace	American	*Ben Hur*
1828	1905	Jules Verne	French	*Around the World in 80 Days, 20,000 Leagues Under the Sea*
1831	1903	F. W. Farrar	British	*Eric, or Little by Little*
1832	1888	L. M. Alcott	American	*Little Women*
1832	1898	Lewis Carroll	British	*Alice's Adventures in Wonderland*
1835	1910	Mark Twain	American	*Huckleberry Finn, Tom Sawyer*
1840	1928	Thomas Hardy	British	*Tess of the D'Urbervilles*
1846	1916	H. Sienkiewicz	Polish	*Quo Vadis*
1850	1894	R. L. Stevenson	Scottish	*Treasure Island, Kidnapped, Dr. Jekyll and Mr. Hyde*
1859	1930	Conan Doyle	British	*Adventures of Sherlock Holmes*
1859	1932	Kenneth Grahame	,,	*The Wind in the Willows*
1863	1933	Anthony Hope	,,	*The Prisoner of Zenda*
1865	1936	Rudyard Kipling	,,	*Stalky and Co., Kim*
1866	1946	H. G. Wells	,,	*The Invisible Man*
1867	1933	John Galsworthy	,,	*Forsyte Saga*
1875	1932	Edgar Wallace	,,	*Four Just Men*
1876	1916	Jack London	American	*The Call of the Wild*

Table 7 Inventors

Date	Inventor	Nationality	Invention
	Primitive man		Fire
	Primitive man		Wheel
250 B.C.	Archimedes	Greek	Water screw
1593 A.D.	Galileo	Italian	Thermometer
1643	Torricelli	Italian	Barometer
1650	Otto von Guericke	German	Air pump
1656	C. Huygens	Dutch	Pendulum clock
1752	Benjamin Franklin	American	Lightning conductor
1765	James Watt	British	Steam engine
1769	Sir R. Arkwright	British	Spinning frame (cotton)
1783	Montgolfier brothers	French	Hot air balloon
1785	E. Cartwright	British	Power loom (weaving)
1815	S. H. Davy	British	Miners' safety lamp
1831	M. Faraday	British	Electric dynamo
1835	Samuel Colt	American	Revolver
1837	Samuel Morse	American	Telegraph signalling
1839	G. Goodyear	American	Vulcanized rubber
1852	L. Foucault	French	Gyroscope
1861	R. J. Gatling	American	Machine gun
1866	A. B. Nobel	Swedish	Dynamite
1869	G. Westinghouse	American	Vacuum brake (trains)
1876	A. G. Bell	American	Telephone
1877	Thomas Edison	American	Gramophone (phonograph)
1893	Thomas Edison	American	Motion pictures
1895	G. Marconi	Italian	Wireless (radio)
1897	R. Diesel	German	Diesel engine
1903	Wright brothers	American	Heavier-than-air craft
1904	Sir J. A. Fleming	British	Radio valve
1914	Sir E. Swinton	British	Tank (army)
1931	E. O. Lawrence	American	Cyclotron